From Someplace Else

Ralph Osborne

MISFIT

ECW PRESS

Published by ECW PRESS
2120 Queen Street East, Suite 200, Toronto, Ontario, Canada M4E 1E2

NATIONAL LIBRARY OF CANADA CATALOGUING IN PUBLICATION DATA

Osborne, Ralph, 1943–
From someplace else: a memoir / by Ralph Osborne.
ISBN 1-55022-550-2

1. Osborne, Ralph, 1943– 2. Authors, Canadian (English) — 21st century — Biography.
3. Rochdale College — Biography. 1. Title

PS8579.S355Z53 2003   C813´.6   C2002-902172-3
PR9199.3.O79Z47 2002

A misFit book edited by Michael Holmes
Cover and Text Design: Darren Holmes
Production and Typesetting: Mary Bowness
Printing: Marc Veilleux Imprimeur

This book is set in Goudy

The publication of *From Someplace Else* has been generously supported by the Canada Council, the Ontario Arts Council, and the Government of Canada through the Book Publishing Industry Development Program. Canada

DISTRIBUTION
CANADA: Jaguar Book Group, 100 Armstrong Avenue, Georgetown, ON, L7G 5S4

UNITED STATES: Independent Publishers Group, 814 North Franklin Street, Chicago, Illinois 60610

PRINTED AND BOUND IN CANADA

ECW PRESS
ecwpress.com

For Tam

Acknowledgements

The author wishes to thank the Ontario Arts Council and the Toronto Arts Council for their generous support.

Thanks, again, to the brilliant Michael Holmes, and to Jack David.

Prologue

At the end of that ten-year portion of my life also known as the sixties, I spent almost two years at Rochdale College in Toronto, briefly becoming its general manager. Vilified, lampooned, and even faintly praised by the press of the day — usually described with words and phrases like "infamous," "hippie high-rise," "den of iniquity," "free university," "stoned-out, drug-addled, amoral cesspool of humanity's rejects," or, less frequently, "beacon of hope" — Rochdale was many things to many people. This book touches on what it meant to me.

Like the old joke about the sixties — *if you can remember them, you weren't really there* — when I finally sat down to write about the Rochdale I knew, I felt as if I had forgotten everything. So I started at the beginning of my deviation from "acceptable behaviour" and what led me to Rochdale in the first place. It was a path with precious little company at first, one that got delightfully jammed up for a while before inevitably thinning out.

In a matter of days, I went from the melancholy and gloom of being a night-shift janitor on the prairies, living in a one-room apartment, and brooding on the estrangement from my wife and son, to the riot and tumult of an eighteen-storey high-rise in downtown Toronto populated with a variety of misfits like me. I joined a commune on the top floor and, for the first time since childhood, experienced community from the perspective of a member in good standing. It was glorious.

There were lots of places to study astrophysics or economics, but only one Rochdale College — the only institution in the known universe, before or since, in which it was not only permissible to smoke dope but considered good form. You had to be prepared to share, of course, but the whiff of cannabis drew no more reproach than the smell of fresh-brewed coffee in the morning. We explored freely and no one came to harm, while the forces of righteousness howled and raged about the gates.

Miracles are normally of short duration, their importance being in the witnessing and telling. Rochdale went on perhaps two or three years too long. The way it ended as portrayed by the media, with people being dragged kicking and screaming from the garbage-infested rat hole it had become, had little to do with the time I was there. To me, it was a success, a refuge, and a delightfully amazing place. Who is to say it was not that for some of those at the end as well? I certainly can't.

I'm still sorting through the memories and uncovering gems from a twenty-two-month period that has proven to be one of the most significant and instructive times of my life. The sixties were so rich with experience I could have begun and ended at the same reference points and told two or three entirely different stories without once repeating myself. There are many people who are important to me who are not in this narrative, and others who make only cameo appearances in disproportion to their actual influence: in another version they might have featured prominently. For whatever reason, this is the story that elbowed its way to the fore.

Bighorn County

Bighorn County in southeastern Montana is, was, and ever shall be, Indian country — First Nations Territory, to be politically correct. But, when I first went there, Indian country was what it was called by the Indians/First Nations People that I knew. Most of the county, about 3,000 square miles, is taken up by the Crow Indian Reservation. The hub of this enormous reserve, and its administration centre, is called Crow Agency.

It's not a very big place — a couple of stores, a casino, and a string of modest bungalows that amble back from the highway. Even so, by the end of the nineties the town had grown to where I couldn't find the spot where we had camped almost thirty years earlier. Of course things change. You expect that. But, riding through the same spectacular western scenery of rolling foothill prairie and rock buttes, where the sky goes on forever and the ghosts of warriors and soldiers and herds of uncountable buffalo seem to lurk over every ridge, the land hadn't changed, and I suppose that lulled me.

My mistake was to look for the wide open field where, years before, bathed in the spotlight of the fullest of moons, I had lain high atop a stack of hay bales, stoned on mescaline, trying to get past the fate of a girl named Sylvia, whose death by overdose in Toronto I had only just heard about hours before. What had been an uncluttered view to the distant mountains was now a housing tract. And, judging by the condition of the peeling paint and the overgrown shrubs, the houses had been there awhile.

The second pass on a gravelled street revealed the small, white clapboard administration building we had camped beside. Like ants, the people in our group moved back and forth, night and day, using it like a clubhouse for cooking and washing up. It is now a daycare centre. And the circle of cottonwoods, grown larger, under which we had camped and had our fires, was now filled with playground equipment. It's a good spot for children, a hallowed place. A lot of powerful medicine had concentrated in that one small area, soaking into the landscape and taking root. Somewhere, in a trunk where I store my treasures, I still have a piece of magic bark from one of the trees.

The other side of the street was a grassy meadow where, in early August of 1970, the Crow tribe had hosted the first Indian Ecumenical Conference. Medicine men, wise men, elders, chiefs, and Indians came to this gathering from all over North, Central, and South America. Representatives of aboriginal First Nations from Abenaki to Zuni came together as a spiritual force to talk, share, and begin the task of collectively repossessing their cultural identity. Of the smattering of non-Indians present — excluding a small contingent of Lapps from Scandinavia — I was one of the few not with the clergy or some anthropology department, almost as rare as a herder of reindeer.

Also, just about a bow shot over two miles from the circle of trees where the children now play, is where Custer and his troops got wiped out at the Battle of the Little Bighorn on June 25, 1876, some ninety-four years before this particular conference. Some of the old men and women there had had fathers and grandfathers who were at that battle. They were walking history books.

One hundred and twenty-one years later, and twenty-seven years after my initial visit, I drove to the battlefield for the second time. It was morning, hot and sunny, as before, but capriciously windy in a noisy, irritating way that only the open plains can serve up. Again, the changes seemed superficial. There was a gatehouse now, and you paid admission to a park ranger. Where we once had parked at random in the dirt was now a paved lot with white lines, and the grass around it was manicured. The little interpretation hut containing a relief map of the area had been replaced by a much larger building. It housed facilities for the visiting tourists — mostly elderly — still numerous enough in late September to create quite a ripe aroma outside the toilets.

The battlefield is the same, of course, and the monument hasn't changed. Neatly painted signs on the dirt paths still urge you to beware of rattlesnakes. On the other side of the interpretation centre, away from the monument, are the rows of crosses as I had remembered, more than two hundred, to mark where the unfortunate members of the U.S. 7th Cavalry were buried. The way some Indians see it, since they regard the topsoil as being composed of the bones of their ancestors, they are at peace at last among their enemies.

Rounding the corner of the building I could see an open area under an overhang where people were sitting in rows to hear the lecture. So they have chairs now, plastic ones, I mused, thinking things don't get better, just tackier. I was going to take a quick gander at the audience; and the urge to stir up some shit was upon me, although I knew I likely wouldn't say anything. I'm still not as brave as Ernest was, nor am I ever liable to be, nor do I have the right, come to think of it. Not exactly, anyway. But I was feeling defiant; no doubt being prodded by the ghosts of old memories.

When I saw who was giving the lecture, my plan — to listen to a word or two then smirk my way knowingly up the hill — collapsed entirely. I stayed for the entire talk. There had been changes of a good kind. Off the field, other battles had been won — small but significant battles — and I felt that I had witnessed the beginning of those changes in a way. Somehow they seemed more direct and tangible than the quantum leaps taken in matters of science, gender equality, environmental awareness, mental and psychic health and so on — because there, telling the audience how the battle was fought and won, was a Sioux Indian.

He wore a ranger uniform, like the white guy at the gate, but there was no mistaking his long braids, his ancestry, or the way he told the story and how he felt. And it was different from the story-line of 1970 — wonderfully different. It was told from the Indian point of view, from the victors of the battle. Nor was it just a story of two sorts of soldiers. He spoke of life in the camp by the river, and how the people lived: horse trading, the kids at play, relatives having a visit, the young men posing in front of the maidens, and generally all the things that made up life as his people knew it before the troops rode into view, before Custer came to sort them out.

The whole thing also took me back to, of all places, just out-side Rochdale College, and the first time I saw Ernest Tootoosis. I will always think of him when hope springs from unlikely places.

Ernest, a Plains Cree, and Clifton, a Creek from Oklahoma, came walking down Bloor Street one dreamy afternoon wearing bones and feathers with a somewhat proud and superior air. It was the summer of 1969 and there was no better time in recent history to be attired in costume. The children of love also wore beads and feathers, flowers and headbands, and vests of all manner of mate-rials, including buckskin. But they were worn to declare: *My culture is lost; it has no connection to the earth or spirits anymore. Therefore I will adopt these symbols, and dress in this fashion. I'll borrow from others, live a simpler life, and hope that by turning my back on Mammon, I will find my way home.*

We weren't alone in appropriating symbols. The first sign of this pair was a brilliant white Stetson in the distance, bobbing above the post-lunch crowd like the bouncing ball in a sing-along. I have come to conclude that, having spent years of observation in the west, nobody wears a cowboy hat better than our First Nations brothers. In fact, were it not for Hollywood and certain loud-mouthed Texans, I'm convinced they'd be called Indian hats. It's tough to still believe in cowboys for one thing. But, looking up at Clifton, who stood six foot four or five at least, with the crown of his hat almost seven feet above the sidewalk, under which his broad, impassive face scanned us pale and lesser mortals, you sure as hell had to believe in Indians.

Ernest, the elder, crippled for some time, was no less impressive, walking beside his younger companion. He wore his hair top-knotted and braided with a pair of eagle feathers loosely attached and pointing down over his right ear. They both had bone chokers and moccasins, and Ernest wore a beaded moosehide vest. As they strode down the street, wearing tokens similar to what their grand-father's grandfather's great-grandfathers had worn, the crowd parted before them. We were humbled and in awe. There was depth, con-tinuity, meaning and belonging — most of all, belonging — and connection to the earth, the sky, and the four strong winds we were singing about. Both of them knew that as they walked, as they step-danced triumphantly down the sunny street. They were cultural heroes to the children of a people who had called them names, who had run them off the wooden sidewalks of Maple Creek into the mud, who had locked them up, shorn their hair, who had cheated and despised them.

The grandchildren and great-grandchildren of men who had given disease-laden blankets and skimpy, maggoty rations to the cold and hungry; of men who had herded people like cattle and for-bade them to speak in their own language and beat them when they did; of men who made it a crime to worship their own gods in their own country in their own way; and of men who would make golf courses over the graveyards of their ancestors, were forgiven by Ernest. He would say: "That's okay, it seems the white man can't help it for I see him do it even to his own people." It was a time when I was just beginning to see there was ample evidence of that.

Ernest, and Clifton too, had waited a long time for this. Without ever knowing it would happen they waited patiently. I have been told this is the Indian way. It is certainly the way of Zen. Meanwhile, the soft ching ching ching of the dancer's bells Clifton wore on his ankles, punctuated with the tapping of Ernest's cane, comprised the band for this tiny parade. The music along Bloor was more compelling than the chants of a thousand looming, insipid Hare Krishnas yet to come.

People, trying not to, stared. Mouths were agape. Yet oddly enough, for there was no shortage of yahoos, the attention was hushed and curiously respectful. A few of us had some pretty elaborate costumes of our own; outfits we could easily slip in and out of depending on need and circumstance. What passed before us, however, was the real thing, inasmuch as costumes could ever be termed real in the mystery-of-the-cosmos sense. And these guys were entitled to every bead and feather.

By the time of that first conference I'd had a couple of years of being reviled as a bearded hippie scum by the general populace. Several fights, catcalls, and a spitting incident had prepared me to be a visible minority — which was part of the intent. Suddenly, surrounded by over two thousand Indians, it was no longer a matter of shaving, slicking my hair back and putting on a suit to blend in. I couldn't step out of my skin any more than Ernest or Clifton could. For the first time ever I began to realize the implications of being a minority, of being dominated by a culture that was not my own.

Ernest Tootoosis has been gone for a long time, but not without remembrance.

Ernest's last stand took place at a bleak, mosquito-plagued, windswept, drowsy little intersection in a small town on the flattest part of the Saskatchewan prairie. He was on his way to a powwow when a drunken cowboy in a Pontiac drove through a stop sign and hit him right in the middle of the driver's side door of his campertopped half-ton. The two loudspeakers on the cab of his truck were strangely silent. Otherwise, had he been able, Ernest would surely have broadcast some insights into the opposing driver's ancestry, and driving habits, loud enough for the entire town to hear. It was the end of July and, at eighty, it was the end of Ernest. If only he had seen the cowboy coming, but that's how last stands go.

Larger than life, Ernest Tootoosis, Plains Cree medicine man, semi-cripple, defender of his people, ladies' man, raconteur, and lover of all mankind, became even bigger in death. Reports of hawks wheeling and circling above the wreck in a suddenly windless sky, followed by a hailstorm of biblical proportions that totally obliterated local crops, are not to be discounted. Ernest had power. Several years earlier, before I left Rochdale, I had seen him soundly defeat the U.S. cavalry and single-handedly win the rematch of the Battle of the Little Big Horn.

All that was returning to me, in a rush of joy.

Out of the Fog

One night, in a fit of five-finger discount consumerism, I ravaged a mall. We were poor. I had gotten around that stigma rather nicely in high school by assuming a Bohemian persona — the scruffy factory outlet desert boots, the same holey pants every day, were a statement. I was thankful for beatniks and their rant against materialism and that guy, Kerouac, whoever he was. Besides, I liked the idea of a beat generation. It stirred something within. Nevertheless, I looked around me at school and I hungered for things.

Before concepts like clinical depression became common place, I shared a small cold-water flat with my severely hearing-impaired mother and three brothers who were seven, nine, and eleven years younger. We lived in a neighbourhood where that was not an uncommon arrangement; in a rat's nest, according to one of my rugby team mates I had mistakenly invited in for water. I was depressed. My mother was depressed and so, probably, were my brothers. My father was depressed as well, I suppose, although he lived in a different city, drinking and gambling to take his mind off things. Now and again he'd appear and we ate well for a few days. I went to school less and less and took to sleeping until noon and staying up all night. My mother despaired, finally, of motivating me and adopted a similar pattern. I would get books for her from the library across town and we read, and read, and read. We were dreamers. She couldn't hear me, of course, when I sneaked out at night.

The first rock through the first window was the hardest. Then it got easier, and I got better. Working on skills more useful in times of war or extreme anarchy, I became good at certain things that didn't lead to Harvard — walking stairs softly on the outside of the tread, breaking glass without making a noise, or staying motionless in the shadows three feet from a patrol car. During these nocturnal sorties I was always alert and in the moment — exhilarated, in fact. As a fellow creature of the night I exchanged curt nods of recognition with prowling cats, noting, also, the faint scurry of rats. Just being out was enough to take me out of my head for a while. Mere Bohemian by day, I became, after dark . . . Night Guy.

It was a mercifully short career. After a brief apprenticeship served in schools and offices, and the neighbourhood grocers that had turned us down for credit, I felt I was ready to move up. The first mall, a little strip of a thing anchored by, although detached from, a department store, had been built over a playing field and woodlot a few blocks from my home. I hit the shoe store first and stumbled into what was then a huge amount of money, hundreds of dollars. It was a quantum leap from nickels, dimes, quarters, and the occasional single or packs of cigarettes. I felt a lot of things, looking at the wad of cash that had been hidden in a shoebox. Mostly, I was ashamed.

Two nights later, a better-dressed Night Guy was staggering down the street under the weight of a gigantic box full of clothing and sundry items from the department store. Upon returning to his hideout and reflecting upon the folly of firearms, not to mention how to explain it, he decided to return the rifle, a Marlin .30-30, and grab a camera and tape recorder instead. He was cool and detached. It went well. The following day he went to the department store early, seeking advice on how to work the camera which, as luck would have it, was not only a brand exclusive to the store but none had been sold. He left his address with the camera clerk. That night, coming home from a farewell party with a bus ticket out of town in his pocket — and too much beer in his system to wonder why two burly guys in bad suits were loitering outside his flat — Night Guy was invited to take a ride downtown.

It hadn't occurred to me to ask for a lawyer. Even if it had there was no hope of affording one in the days before legal aid. I made my confession to the "good" cop, not the guy who slapped me around whenever I was left alone with him. All he had to say was, "Son, sometimes you can trust a thief, but you can never trust a liar." And I caved. I didn't want to be a liar. Nevertheless, there was a significant discrepancy between their inventory of stolen goods and the items I had admitted taking. I would have needed a two-ton truck to carry all the stuff on that list. Of note was a half-dozen missing rifles. I visualized a fall hunting trip in which six department heads of a store which, in my case, could well be called Waterloo's, all arrived at the rendezvous with brand new .30-30s.

One could not walk more than a few yards before another steel door was unlocked and then slammed shut behind our procession to the cells. Down a grey corridor, open, slam. Up a set of stairs, open, slam. Another corridor, ditto. I had spent the previous night alone in the drunk tank. Its sulphur yellow brick walls, worn metal benches, smoke black initials burned into the low, arched ceiling, and the reeking porcelain cone shaped like a giant trumpet mouthpiece, waiting to accommodate whatever would be hurled its way, now seemed quaint, almost cozy, by comparison. On remand, I was being led deeper into the bowels of the justice system. Finally, after a dozen slams had impressed upon me that I might never, ever walk free again we ended up on the top floor of the old jail. The smell of creosote was overpowering.

Three days passed. I remember very little except a sense of despair so thick you could have sawed it into planks and made ebony coffins. There were three sets of double bunks arranged around the cell. I had the top bunk on the back wall beside a seat-less toilet; opposite, sat a table and two benches in front of a small window that overlooked a brick wall. The five guys I shared with were all older — from mid-twenties up to about sixty. They had various release dates, and seemed pretty much at peace with being there.

Meals came three times a day through a slot in the cell door and, for thirty minutes each morning and afternoon, all the doors were opened so you could walk around the corridor for exercise. This was the time when, one by one, inmates could drift back into the cell and have a bowel movement in relative privacy. There was little activity except waiting. We would sit and smoke, or pace the floor and smoke, each of us with our own papers and tobacco. After lights out we would lie on our bunks and smoke. During the day, two of the older guys spent time using a razor blade to slice paper matches in half so they'd last longer. Conversation was quiet, sporadic, and brief.

There was one available paperback, a dog-eared love story called *The Pink Hotel*. I read it through five or six times without remembering a thing. It might as well have been one of my high-school science texts. And, through the barred window at the end of the corridor, during exercise break, I could see, over the rooftops, the upper floors of the Admiral Beatty Hotel, then the city's finest. Oddly, I appreciated the irony. For the most part, however, I fretted in silence about what was to come. The youngest of my fellow inmates, a roly-poly, cheerful sort from a small town down the coast was halfway through a six-month sentence. I asked him what he had done to deserve that kind of time.

"I stole a shad." He said. Shad, a local delicacy, is not highly prized commercially, being a particularly bony member of the herring family.

"You got six months for stealing a fish?" I was horrified.

"Well, Jeezus, bye," he added, to provide the correct perspective, "it was a thirty-pounder!" When I told him what I had done, his mouth set and he just shook his head sadly.

"Well, it was my second offence," he offered finally to provide a glimmer of hope. But we both knew I was fucked. At least I had his respect.

I got probation — one year, with an eleven o'clock curfew. My probation officer had cautioned me to expect custodial time — on the prison farm if I were lucky. He was more surprised than I. The

Anglican bishop, under whose hands I had trembled while being confirmed, had spoken on my behalf. A few years earlier I had read the lesson in church on Sundays in my Boy Scout uniform and, for a short while, had been in the choir. Perhaps more significantly, the judge's son and I had been teammates on the high-school rugby squad. There was some sense that the break-ins were a group effort, owing to the large amount of missing goods, and that I was covering for the other guys, whoever they might be. Okay.

My mother, who had also come to the trial with diminished expectations, stood patiently beside me in King's Square while I broke down and cried. It was the end of June. We were across the street from the Admiral Beatty. A minute or so later she handed me a Kleenex and, after wiping up, I took my very good shoe off, reached deep into my sock and pulled out a sticky ten-dollar bill. She laughed. It was a trick I had learned from her — to always have a little something in reserve, no matter what, no matter how small. On the nights we had been most destitute, while my brothers slept, she would fish around in secret places, coming up with enough money to send me to the drugstore. I'd get a cardboard tub of maple walnut icecream for myself, and a banana split for her. She had her own special glass container, like the ones at the soda fountain, which she would send with me.

After grilled cheese sandwiches and a milkshake at Woolworth's, I bought us each a pack of tailor-mades, a *Family Journal* for her, and a *New Yorker* for me, after which I sprung for bus fare and gave her the change. I was sorry I hadn't given my tobacco to my ex-cellmates but they had been pleased enough by the gift of matches. Suddenly, I was in a hurry to get home. I had three days of beans, bologna, white bread, and oatmeal to get rid of.

My cover was blown. I was a convicted thief, not a Bohemian. It was a small enough town that it seemed everyone knew. Nor would I ever be able to live it down. I might as well have had a giant red T emblazoned on my forehead. Obviously, I had to get away, to go somewhere where nobody knew me. But first I had to serve a year of probation.

What saved me was a job as a lifeguard at a summer resort in St. Andrews, sixty miles down the coast. I was granted permission to go. It was the sweetest two months I could ever remember. I had met new people, gotten to sleep in a dormitory without bars, and fallen in love with a Dutch girl who had been babysitting for summer residents from Connecticut. It provided a buffer against the reality of returning to Saint John, and my shame, in the fall.

The memory of that summer kept me going. Still, the year dragged on and I longed to escape. Even the one place that accepted me without reservation, the pool hall, got old. Guys named Rocky, Killer, and Sluggo can only carry you so far. When I could no longer stand it, a few weeks before my probation was to expire, I took off for Montréal, where most of the students I had met at the resort went to school. I was later able to resolve my breach of probation with a phone call — my probation officer was a very nice guy and I continued to exchange letters with him for a while.

When I stuck my thumb out and got in that first ride, the pack of dogs that had been chasing me dropped off one by one. It would be okay as long as I kept moving.

Montréal

It was one of those overcast early October days, where the leafy reds and oranges and yellows glow like embers banked up against the leaden sky, and reflect quietly upon themselves in a fairy ring around the edges of the small, still Laurentian lake. The senator and I were walking a well-worn path about a hundred yards from the cottage we had come to shut down for the winter. Mrs. H., the senator's wife, was inside attending to all the details, checking item after item off a list in her typically brisk and efficient way. I was still grinning from the comment she had made as she straightened out some errant cushions, feigning disapproval of whomever the miscreant had been.

"There is a thin line," she said, in plummy tones, pausing for effect, "between simplicity and squalor." I erupted in laughter. I had been watching as she folded rich blankets of many colours, straightened deep and venerable chairs, and now the plump, oversized cushions. She was pleased, I think. So was I. That line proved a durable gift and, in the many times I have appropriated it over the years, I have never failed, silently at least, to give her credit. It was an expression the family often used, I was told, especially at the cottage. I knew a thing or too about squalor — as well as dry, Anglican humour — and it was oh so very true.

The senator, a diminutive chap, white-haired and cheerful, had a game leg for which he wielded a thick, black, wooden cane that also served nicely as a pointing device. He had been born in

England of a very good family, with a hyphenated surname and, in fact, was titled, or had been titled, until he passed on the right of succession that had fallen to him, and could be called "Sir" in more than one way. He had come to Canada as a young man, raised a family, pursued a career in law and, by gad, he was going to stay. He was a Liberal senator, not, as you might expect, a Conservative.

"How's the water, good for a swim, do you think?"

"Pretty cold," I said, withdrawing my hand from the shallows. It was like ice.

"Brisk, eh? Warm enough day, though. I believe I'll have a go."

The senator, having been fully attired in a sturdy pinstriped suit, proceeded to astonish me by undressing on the spot. In a trice, jacket, vest, school tie, wingtips, trousers, argyle socks, sock garters, shirt, undershirt, and striped boxers were festooned rakishly across some low bushes. He waded knee-high into the water, threw his cane farther out into the lake and dived in with a loud halloo, swimming to it in an elegant sidestroke, as befitting a seventy-odd-year-old gentleman of more than a little distinction. He floated and splashed around, squirting water into the air until I was shamed into following suit. After, we dressed and collected Bonnie, their woolly Bedlington terrier. I had been with them for a month, and they were still rearranging the way I thought about older people.

The cottage, which, to this day, would suit my needs as a principal residence, was properly closed and we headed home to Westmount. It had been a fine day. I washed the car, which was part of our arrangement. The other part was that I attend Westmount High and graduate, with a view toward entering university the following year. This was the catch, the tough part. I was already too old. In return, I lived in their home as a de facto distant relation, accorded all the privileges of family. The adolescent fantasy of thinking the babies had been switched at the hospital and that, really, one was secretly a member of a noble household, had come true. Eat your heart out, Goethe. I had to give it a try.

My room on the third floor was long, wide and deeply carpeted.

It had a real bed with thick wool blankets, bookshelves with tons of books, a radio, and, at the far end, an oak desk and chair beside a multi-paned, leaded glass window. It overlooked the grounds with the goldfish pond, whose inhabitants routinely spent the winters indoors at the Westmount library, less enamoured than I of the silky young things in the short, grey, pleated skirts ofThe Study, who gathered, bending close together, sharing secrets around the old, scarred tables. Heaven was just a whisper away.

"Think, now, what was the summer like?"

What indeed? That was the last line of a poem I had written in my grand new room to commemorate my twentieth birthday. Several weeks later it became even more germane when Kennedy was shot. The rest of the poem is lost, having since been destroyed with all the others.

The ten dollars I had borrowed to leave home with some two months prior had almost vanished that first time I landed in Montréal. Arriving broke was old hat to me. Through hitch-hiking I had seen Boston, New York, and the fabulous mecca of Baltimore, to which I had regularly tuned in to hear jazz on WBAL — "this is the Harley Show . . . Music out of Baltimore" — when the Maritime stations signed off at night. Montréal wasn't my first big city, just the only one I hadn't been passing through.

Early my first morning in La Belle Cité I was wandering around the park I had slept in — looking forlorn, I guess — when a quite attractive young woman approached and asked how I was. She invited me to her apartment for breakfast. She wasn't much older than I, a nurse, French, who had just come off shift. After we ate she said I was welcome to have a shower but she would go first. Great. I could understand this. I come from a long line of people where being polite to strangers was a way of life. Even today, if you have out-of-province plates and a bewildered look, any number of Saint Johnners will swarm you with offers of directions. I could see she was cut from similar cloth.

The running water sounded loud because she had left the bathroom door partially open. And then she was calling my name, which, at first, made me think I was hearing things. When I tentatively took a look around the door and saw her head peering out from behind the shower curtain, I was relieved to find that she had dropped the soap on the floor and would I please hand it to her — and, ha ha, no peeking. No problem. And, Mademoiselle, I would never. Modestly, I turned my head away as I handed her the soap.

When it was my turn in the shower *she* came into the bathroom. Man, the French are so easy-going — I could get used to this. She asked how I was and did I, ha ha, need any help washing my back. Well, she was a nurse. She was so trusting and friendly, if a bit odd, that I ha ha'd back that no, I was just fine thanks. I felt a little guilty that I had fantasized about her jumping in with me, especially since she had been so kind. But, coming from polite and chivalrous people as I did, there would be no suggestion of impropriety on my part. So I was somewhat puzzled by her change in demeanour when I got out of the shower. She appeared distant, not so friendly. Where was all the ha ha? I persisted in being cheery, which seemed to warm her up somewhat. But, after I had politely looked at a photo of her old dog that she kept in the bedroom, she suddenly and firmly had to go somewhere and I would have to leave. Oh well, I was cleaner and fed, but back on the street. Tony Davies later explained to me, when we were swapping stories about our first days in the city, how incredibly stupid I had been.

That night I slept in Windsor Station while pretending to wait for a train. I did it sitting up, so I was nodding off and waking with a start all night. In the morning I noticed that every time I opened my eyes an older man was staring at me. I was not naïve about this when he finally approached. However, I was still polite. He offered to meet me later and buy me lunch and, out of hunger, I went — telling myself I wouldn't. He fed me at a nearby tavern and was reasonably direct about his wants. I was even more direct in my refusal. But, as I got up to leave, having thanked him for the meal and maybe making him look good for some nearby friends, he handed me five dollars anyway, and a phone number in case I changed my mind. I told him that would never happen. It didn't really bother me, being young and marginalized on the streets. I just kind of accepted the fact that I would be prey, even before I had realized that I was.

I still had three dollars left when I selected an Anglican church on Ste-Catherine St. for my third night's sleep. There was a row of short bushes behind a set of spotlights with enough room to make a bed of newspapers between them and the stone wall of the church. I was getting discouraged and a little lonesome. I saw that the church, too, was a defense station, in what I was beginning to think was the most well protected city in the world. I know the Sun Life building a few blocks away had been built with a concrete foundation on every floor, and was considered impregnable enough to store the Dutch crown jewels during the Second World War. Anyway, these stations were all over the downtown area, indicated by signs in the wordier French: *Defense de Stationner*.

The weather, also a new experience, was hot and muggy, even at night. My quasi-sleeps weren't giving me much rest and in the morning I found a door open and went inside the church, hoping to lie down on a pew in the back for a few hours. Instead, I met the Reverend Bothwell, dean of Christ Church Cathedral. It was a shock to discover you could make confession in the Anglican Church. Before long I was kneeling and unburdening, with my woeful tale. It didn't make me feel any better except, in the narcissism of youth, it was always good to talk about oneself. But I did end up cleaning out the reverend's garage for a generous ten dollars that very afternoon. I also agreed to an extraordinary meeting that eventually resulted in my moving to the senator's house in September. That only left the rest of June plus July and August to get through.

Place Ville Marie had just been built and I took to hanging around the underground concourse that hooked up to Windsor Station. Beside the walkway was a bookstore, Classic's Books. It was the first real bookstore I had ever been in and I had been haunting it for days. With my garage-cleaning money I now had enough to treat myself. Knowing I was going to actually buy something empowered me to have a deep browse. At home I had bought paperbacks off the rack at the downtown magazine store that carried the *New Yorker*. They were mostly Bantams and Dells. Here, at Classic's, they had paperbacks from publishers I had never heard of, with fabulous covers. Ballantine, Viking, Grove Press, New American Library, Doubleday Anchor, and the fascinating black-and-white City Lights. I set about learning them at once. I loved being in a bookstore. I was happy, looking at all the books, smelling the newness of them, hefting them, riffling the pages with desire, like a miser with a row of doubloons.

There was a sales clerk about my age and I had noticed, in fact it was impossible not to, that he had a mad gleam in his eye. He was about six feet or so, thin, dark, and heavily five o'clock shadowed. It appeared as if he had slept in his dishevelled suit. His tie was askew and his shirt, the same one I had seen him in the day before, and the day before that, was not only wrinkled, it was filthy. Despite this, he maintained a superior air, bantering with the customers, quite often disparaging their taste in literature. Somehow, people seemed to enjoy this.

"It's not as good as *Cannery Row*, but it's readable," he said, when I took *Sweet Thursday* to the till, letting me know that he knew Steinbeck too, and he knew it was a sequel. Had I read *Tortilla Flat*? I told him I'd even read *Cup of Gold*, his first published novel, a very forgettable pirate adventure. He laughed. *Grapes of Wrath*, of course, but what about *In Dubious Battle*? Yep. And did he know about the book Steinbeck had written in between those two but had destroyed because it had been too bitter? Of course. And on it went. No different than two nerdy guys talking about video games.

Bill Hoffer and I took to one another instantly and, as one does, we soon had exchanged enough history to cement the friendship. What you don't know in meeting some people, is that you've just made a choice, and taken the first step down a road from which other doors may open, but there will be no turning back. We left the store together.

Hoffer had just started working at Classic's since arriving from Saskatoon. This was his entrée into the booksellers' world. He would go on to become a legendary curmudgeon in the antiquarian realm of used, old, and rare books. It was a perfect occupation for him. He was respected, feared, opened shop when he felt like it, and spoke his mind freely on the subject of one's adequacies or lack thereof as regards literary taste.

His first paycheque had yet to arrive, so I bought us smoked-meat sandwiches at Dunn's. We talked until our asses stuck to the red vinyl, and then wandered through the downtown streets, dreaming and scheming grandiose plans. Hoffer, I think, was always the kind of big-talking guy you didn't know whether to believe, but you didn't care because it was so much fun. One day, he said to me, sounding like a Broadway producer as was his habit, "Ralph, baby, I've got two thousand in cash," and he clutched the outside of his pocket with both hands, feigning a sizeable bulge. "Meet me after work. We're going to Europe." Well, as was often, if not always, the case, he'd barely have enough cash for a meal. The money wasn't quite in his hands. It was pending, always pending, via some con-voluted arrangement, with a guy who knew a guy. Europe was the Holy Land to young, literary hipsters — Callaghan had done it and Mordecai Richler was there as we spoke. So, like paupers every-where, we had a great time planning what we would do when the money came in. We wouldn't be like this guy we knew who did go to France and got so homesick the first night that he flew back the next day. What a waste, we exclaimed. Down deep, I knew how he felt. Perhaps Hoffer did too.

Neither of us had a fixed address, but Bill, who had been in Montréal only a few weeks longer than I, had an impressive array of comrades: student radicals from the prairies, unpublished poets, would-be playwrights, anarchists, communists, and drunks — all misfits, all from someplace else.

A space on the floor could be had in exchange for good conversation. Rooms, with bathroom down the hall, were going for twelve to fifteen dollars a week. Seven dollars got you a basement warren backed up against a filthy toilet, separated from your quarters by a wall of flimsy material barely thicker than two-ply cardboard. You could sit in the gloom and hear the various eructations of those worthies for whom these accommodations represented the end, not the beginning.

My brothers were living with my dad in Moncton. My mother was somewhere in Ontario. Hoffer and I were doing the usual midnight ramble after sharing a smoked meat and two coffees. One of the waitresses, a motherly type, had slipped us extra fries and a kosher dill. Hoffer had a guitar that he was just learning how to play. I hear, much to my incredulity, he eventually mastered it and became a decent blues player before he died. You would not have thought it possible that night when we were sitting in Dominion Square, under the new, continuous-line CN sign for which the designer had been paid an enormous sum. Bill was torturing a spiritual number — the easiest to play, some only needing one or two chords, full of "hallelujahs," "wayfarin's," and "lonesomes." He was just downslope from a howl, in that atonal, warbly moan of his, when I broke the news that I was going to Moncton. I would be coming back in the fall, to move in with the senator and Mrs. H. He stopped playing — a feat for which I silently congratulated myself — and stared at me.

"It'll never last, Ralph, baby," he said, finally. Then he confessed he was heading back to Saskatoon. I didn't say anything.

Westmount

By the time I got back from New Brunswick, Hoffer had gone. I registered at Westmount High, where the students seemed like kids all of a sudden — kids who were far more advanced in subjects like French, for example. I felt old and slow and out of my depth. Why was I doing this? It was hopeless.

At the senator's, I attended evening meals in a jacket they had bought for me, since one dressed for dinner. The Russian woman who lived in, cleaning and cooking, made fresh soups from scratch every day. The quality of her cooking, which was superb, belied her claim to be of the nobility. She was too adept in the kitchen, so much so that she was never called on it either. And, since there is only room for one Pretender in any given household, she wasted little time in campaigning for my ouster. She could see right through my nefarious Bolshevik scheme to murder them all in their beds and steal away with the silver, which she took to counting in my presence whenever she thought Mrs. H. wasn't looking. The paranoia made me wonder if perhaps she really was a Romanov after all.

After dinner, the senator and I would retire to the drawing room for a demitasse of coffee in decorative porcelain, which, after some weeks, the Russian woman refused to serve. How extraordinary. We must do for ourselves, there's no help for it. The delicate, gold-rimmed cups with their tiny handles practically begged me to stick my pinky in the air. I felt as if I were in a turn-of-the-century costume drama, and that Oscar Wilde was going to burst into the room at any moment, raving about Lord Douglas.

The sugar was another wonder, multicoloured rock crystals, of which the senator was inordinately fond. It was, however, Mrs. H., not Oscar, whose head would poke around the door with a reproving glare, in the way of good women everywhere, just as the senator dropped a second towering heap of rainbow-hued rocks into his cup, and stirred resolutely with a sterling silver spoon. Without a hint of guile he would, as good men will, stare vaguely into the middle distance, inquiring as to the nature of my day, betrayed only slightly by the merest glint of amusement, grateful, I think, for my presence.

The afternoons I had spent in the Saint John library, while waiting for the pool hall to open, had served me well. If I was too restless to read I'd look at pictures. It started with the hardcover art magazine, *Horizon*. Then I devoured all the back issues. From there it was a simple enough pleasure to work my way through the entire, smallish fine art section. Some days I wouldn't make it to the pool hall at all. I acquired a decent, if superficial, education in painterly matters and, before long, knew a Dali from a de Chirico. The names and periods of all the different schools and movements were end-lessly fascinating. Pre-Raphaelite, Renaissance, Romantic, Impressionist, Post-Impressionist, Fauvist, Dada, cubism, pointil-lism; Constable and Turner, Kahlo and Rivera, Gaugin and Van Gogh, Utrillo, who used to get beat up regularly, and his churches, Modigliani and his astigmatism-inspired women, Picasso, Pissaro, Monet, Manet, da Vinci, Goya, Michelangelo, Rousseau, Caravaggio, the macabre Daumier, Winslow Homer, Whistler, Bonnard, Delacroix, Bosch, Chagall, de Kooning, Pollock, Hopper, A.Y. Jackson, Lawren Harris. I was particularly fond of the Surrealists and confess a total lack of sophistication in my limited enthusiasm for abstract expressionism. So it was not without a cer-tain measure of awe and appreciation that I sat beside a Krieghoff while the senator and I chatted of this and that.

The time came, however, when he was required in Ottawa. Upon returning home after a pleasant evening with a classmate named Paula, I found the door chained and double-locked by a certain Slavic crone. Pounding loudly only served to rouse the police, who seemed particularly attentive to the wants of the neighbourhood. Eventually, the senator's son, Jim, who lived on the next block, came to my rescue. I moved in with him, Mary, and their three children. The Bolsheviks were routed, order was restored, and once again, if the breeze was right, the aroma of some of the finest soups ever made, wafted down the hill.

In the midst of using a knife and fork to polish off my reward of an open-face shrimp and egg sandwich at the Danish Food House in Toronto, now Cole-Haan's, at Bloor and St. Thomas, the girl I had been helping to move some pottery asked me where I had learned to eat — a telling question. At least she had not asked me how. I realized at once that she had come from a humbler background than her attendance at a private girl's school would seem to indicate. I knew she had been born in Nova Scotia, delivered as a confession, and had gone to Edgehill. But I had assumed, up to that moment, that her route had led from the manor.

That there was more to it than keeping your elbows off the table hadn't been a total revelation. I had read something somewhere, had seen English movies, but the first time I wished I had paid attention was at Haleen's, on the one occasion she had invited me to dinner. Haleen was the only serious relationship I had had in high school. She was a blonde, blue-eyed day girl at Netherwood, part tomboy, all lady, and naturally happy. After I had gotten out of jail Haleen had been the only one to call — even though I had broken it off between us some months before, for no good reason other than I thought I should. Actually, she left word with a buddy of mine that I was to call her since our phone had been cut off. I called at once, hoping, but she had only been asking how I was and to say that her father, who had grown up on the mean streets of

London before emigrating, had said if there was ever anything he could do I need only ask. I thanked her and we said goodbye.

Aside from my relatives, I had never been anywhere for dinner. Her father, mother, older sister, and two younger brothers were enthroned around a huge table in the dining room. I sat next to Haleen, feeling like a dog at the vet's. I had a plan: watch what everybody else does first, then imitate. What threw me, I think, was the way my knife and fork, held halfway between a tremble and a death grip, rattled like rain on a tin roof every time they touched down on the plate. Mere fanfare, as it turned out, to announce the launching of the pork chop which, after a clumsy thrust, went skittering off my plate and out onto the table.

You wouldn't have thought there'd be so many places to look in a room that size; eyes were casting about everywhere but at me while I retrieved the meat, having first to arrest its spin. Haleen's warm touch on my arm, and request that I pass the butter, set everyone to talking at once, as if nothing had happened. Even the boys, who were at an age to appreciate the gift they'd been handed, elected to take the high road — for the time being. After, there had been no sense of history that we had participated in the longest meal ever, just a mutual, backslapping hosanna of relief following dessert.

With the exception of spaghetti, which I pretended not to like, I learned how to dine properly at Jim and Mary's. I played the country cousin — a variant of bohemianism — and Jim, acting as the foil for my foolishness, served to correct my loutish ways. I was grateful. They were both lawyers and once, only once, I won an argument with Jim. Although he had the *gravitas* of someone who knew he was going a long way, and behaved accordingly, he enjoyed engaging and defeating me in debate. I brought this out in people. That there was nothing too preposterous for me to promote and vigorously defend was only part of it. The rest was a mystery.

I had been relating a tale of a broken cup, describing the pieces as shards, an appropriate word which, for some reason, had failed to attach itself to Jim's considerable vocabulary. Pronouncing it with a long, hard, double "r," as my people are wont to do, perhaps gave the word a certain regional, and therefore illegitimate, air. Sha*rr*ds. He pounced on it at once. A bet was struck and dictionaries — one wouldn't do — were consulted. Jim took the loss like a gentleman. Mary, not practising at the moment, and who, at six foot one or so, was the most easygoing, was amused, fuelling my crush.

The entire family was exceptionally good to me, in a manner that didn't ask for a lot in return, with the type of kindness that one can only repay to others — a debt from which there is no discharge, serviced as often as possible along the way. I felt at home there and, even when the results from Christmas exams confirmed that I had no business being in school, I was still welcome to stay. For a while, I did.

Atwater

The hub of the universe had spindly legs. It would have wobbled incessantly had not one end of its one-and-a-half-by-two-foot top been butted against, and fitting exactly, the eighteen-inch bulwark between two doorways that led, like parallel spokes, either down a long hallway to Wilson's room, or, through the old, swinging, dining room door, to mine. This made it, providing we ate in shifts, or on the diagonal, or with tiny plates and an air of forgiveness for those occasions when one chap's mash splashed on another's banger, a perfect table for three.

Archeological evidence, provided by the few remaining paint chips on a hardish wood of indeterminate origin, indicated it had once been green, and, before that, red. Likewise artifactual, the three attendant chairs were pigs of fat, stuffed, puffy, paint-splattered, permanently-dimpled, burgundy plastic, supported by pitted chrome legs that ended in cloven, black, polymer tips.

By an unwritten concord of mutual territorial consent, peculiar to nesting males, Wilson always sat south at the table, facing north, along one two-foot side. I held the north, along the other. Davies, or Tony, being the unacknowledged leader in an anarchy of three, thus rating two forms of nominal address, claimed the foot-and-a-half east end, whose shorter dimension nevertheless held dominion over the larger territory of the kitchen proper. This realm, spreading rearward behind him, contained the beer-laden refrigerator. Between it and the entrance to his small bedroom, the third spoke, stood an enormous, deep, chipped porcelain laundry sink, which, during festive gatherings, could nicely accommodate, in a slurry of ice and water, sixty bottles of ale or lager. The cupboards above, plastered in wild collage with labels from every possible brewery, proudly attested to the sink's well-stocked diversity, like celebrity photos in a deli.

There was never a fourth chair, just these three that sat, like gopher mounds, in front of our respective burrows, around the mesa where we had our tea, which we drank incessantly — Wilson and I, long after Tony had switched to Black Horse ale. It's a wonder, what with all the parading back and forth to the loo, the filling of the kettle, the warming of both pots — Wilson had his own; white and embossed with tiny violets, it held exactly two cups — the steeping, and the pouring, that any business was conducted at all. But this ongoing ceremony, precise as Zen, casual as camping out, was the heart of a process that stretches back into the mists to the first fire, and forward, one hopes, to infinity. Passages in certain books invoke the feeling: Mac and the boys on the banks of the Carmel River, speculating on the longevity of chickens before catching frogs to pay for Doc's party; Huck and Jim on a raft, pondering the origin of stars.

Moving into the basement apartment on Atwater, a block north of the legendary Forum, was the beginning of the life I would own, the one that was all mine. My two roommates, both older than I, were from the north of England, an area then regarded as being quaint and backward to Londoners — much like the Maritimes were seen by Lower and Upper Canadians.

Tony Davies, a shade under six feet, beanpole skinny, large nosed, and still faintly scarred from adolescent acne, was, at thirty, the elder. He had worked at Classic's with Hoffer. Tony had a soft border accent — not Irish, not Scottish — that made people ask where he was from. "Middlesbrough," he'd say, "up north, close to Yorkshire." He had been in Canada less than a year.

We would gather in our tiny kitchen at our small table. Tony, dressed in wide wale cords, one of those faintly checked English cellulose dress shirts, topped with a lambswool V-neck, and desert boots, would sit, his legs more intertwined than crossed, hunched forward foetally, with one arm resting crosswise on his lap. The other would either be holding a glass of beer, or fluttering as if shooing flies away, while he was making a point. I had never met anyone as brilliant as he, or as funny. Nightly, he would hold forth in that soft, beautiful voice while I laughed my guts out. At beer number seven he'd sing a bit of the hymn, "We Shall Gather at the River." It amused him no end. A brooding silence would descend at beer eight. He would then rise, lurch to the loo for a Guinness Book-of-Records piss and, with a woebegone, weary little wave, he'd stagger off to bed.

Wilson, just Wilson, grew up in Birkenhead, a ferry ride across the Mersey from Liverpool. He would say he was from "The Pool," putting on a thick Scouse accent for fun, or, since the Beatles had become heartthrobs, if he thought it would advance his romantic endeavours. Wilson was a diminutive five feet four. He was seriously into style and clothing and, at the time, inordinately fond of mauve. He wore his hair long and combed forward, à la early Beatles, and had suits custom-made with the pants zipper up the side instead of a fly in front. This amazed me. It was beyond daring.

"Those are like women's pants, Wilson," I'd say. "People will think you're gay."

He'd just look at me, bored like, and say, "Yeah, so?"

The truth is, Wilson didn't give a damn what people thought. He was a lover. He loved music, poetry, photography, fine clothing, and women. And women loved him. Man, did they love their cuddly little Wilson. He was hardly ever home. When he was, he'd sit around the table reading thick books held in the palm of one hand, like an actor treading the boards, reading from a script, and drinking tea from his special pot.

My English lessons, paid for just by listening — the aural equivalent of reading, and as nuanced — proceeded apace. I was learning accents, Cockney rhyming slang, odd foods (bubble and squeak, tripe and onions, Marmite), obscure words and expressions, prison slang and Royal Air Force terminology, all from Master Davies.

It was endlessly fascinating to me that a plate of meat in your boat (plate of meat = feet, boat race = face) had nothing to do with, and was far more unpleasant than, dining on the water. And, since I can scarce imagine a writerly moment where I would ever use the word "cuddywiffter," although thinking it quite splendid, I offer that it is a term for a left-hander, like southpaw. The English, it seemed, were more at liberty to play with the language than those of us who shared the mother tongue.

Occasionally, as with Bob Dylan lyrics, I was able to return the favour.

"Osborne," Tony asked one day, with Wilson straining forward to hear the answer, "What's a ck?"

"A what?"

"A ck — see kay?"

"I have no idea, Old Chaps," I said to their fallen faces.

"Well," Tony persisted, "In that song, Dylan's going: 'Ah'm walkin' down the highway, with muh ck's in muh hand' . . . so what's a ck?"

"Try suitcase," I laughed. "With my suitcase in my hand."

This became a running gag between us, particularly with Tony, who loved running gags — and accents. He claimed he could tell, within fifteen miles, where any Englishman had been raised, just by the way he spoke. That they had asked me to explain anything to them was an honour. I was the kid, the greenhorn, who had been introduced by them to Bob Dylan, Miles Davis, Thelonius Monk, Erik Satie, and Bach's fugues. But I could translate Dylan and was therefore cool.

One night I sat, alone, in the unlighted kitchen, my back facing east, in Tony's chair. I was drawing — something I had never done before — with my fake Waterman fountain pen, a genuine 'Waterman's' by IDEAL. "Never" did not include the Second World War tanks and planes of the middle grades, replete with dotted lines from the guns that ended in jagged-star explosions. Nor did it acknowledge the if-you-can-draw-this-you-can-be-an-artist bit of two-dimensional Irish setter profile I had sent to the address provided. "But, Dad, I won a scholarship," I had said to the back of his surly and muscular shoulders, as he chased the official representative of the academy down the stairs. I had been sure I could somehow raise the necessary "pennies per week" required. Realism, however, not having been distracted by the intoxicating possibilities of drawing a fifth heart for the flush, took the day.

There was more than enough light from the two-hundred watter in the hallway to see what I was doing. The long, definite shadows made it easier to draw the table, from which I had cleared everything, leaving it bare, and one chair, Wilson's, having placed mine out of sight. The drawing was simple, black ink on white paper. I moved my hand slowly and carefully. My paper supply was low, erasure or crumpling not an option. To my great surprise, the drawing actually resembled what I was looking at, which had to do with seeing, as if for the first time, since childhood at least, not the table but the qualities of light and dark from which it was composed. Drawing, then, was seeing things in a different way: enlightenment, in other words.

This is what Fossum couldn't or wouldn't tell me. Couldn't be bothered, that is. We'd had a lot of fun together since Hoffer had introduced us. "Ralph, baby, meet Marty Fossum. He's an artist." Physically, we resembled one another, perhaps vaguely. He was a year older and a little taller but, in the alley, you'd probably want your money riding on me. Marty was from Kitimat and had taken schooling on the Prairies where he had met Hoffer, and ran in the same crowd of radical, artistic, left-leaning, middle-class smartasses. He knew his literature, spoke French, was learning Spanish, and could argue with the irritating, almost Jesuitical, skill of a second-year logic student. Guys like this made you smarter. He also played decent guitar and was not embarrassed to sing.

Fossum's hands, smallish, delicate, were forever moving, as if a pair of sparrows had grown from his wrists. He was always drawing, coming at the paper from around the corner and over the top, like the cuddywiffter he was. Once, as we talked, he was fooling around with a child's watercolour set, making what looked like long lines straight up and down, of random widths and lengths. Five minutes later he turned his composition so I could see it right side up, and there, looking out from all the places he hadn't touched, as if from a streaky, multicoloured mirror, was me. Unmistakably me, attitude and all.

He said he wasn't an artist. He was dropping the whole thing. What, I wondered, would make him do that? Art school? Fossum pissed me off. Not because he was a tad too patronizing in encouraging me to give university a chance. Not because he was actually going to Europe while Hoffer and I weren't. Not because he was a little smug while speaking perfect French. And not, but almost, because he occasionally corrected my grammar when I spoke colloquially. No. Marty pissed me off because he had a definite and obvious talent that some would describe as God-given, and he was turning his back on it. How many of us are able to make that claim? How many are Mozarts instead of Moes, have the voice of an angel, Pavlova's grace, Bocuse's touch, Chaplin's athleticism? It was an identifiable ability that most of us hungered for and he just dropped it. It was too easy, perhaps. It took me a long time to realize, certainly longer than Marty, that facility is far from being the only quality brought to art.

The only work he travelled with was a series of pencil drawings on newsprint of a girl who, in the art at least, was stunning. They were different from the stuff he tossed off. These were of his unrequited love — except somehow I couldn't see Marty being able to commit like that, to throw himself into a thing headlong, emotionally naked, uncontrolled. She was, I learned, the wild doe of the north. The formidable, intellectual, long-haired beauty who crushed men's souls with the flick of an eyelash. The artist's daughter, who had even Hoffer agreeing with Fossum. "Stay away from her, Ralph, baby. She's trouble." Degen. What kind of a name is that? I just laughed at them.

So, indirectly, drawing was one of two things Fossum inspired me to do. I had to see how difficult it was. I thought, if I had had his talent I'd have had it made. At the very least, I could do quick sketches of people for small sums. Travel with the carny for a while. Maybe adopt a single name. As usual, I startled myself by laughing out loud. Ralphangelo, indeed.

I had been out west, to the Prairies and northern BC, back to Montréal, then to the Algonquin Hotel in St. Andrews, back to Montréal, west again, and back to Montréal — all since March. It was now the last week of November. Soon I'd be blown back to the Prairies for a considerably longer stay. Things were coming apart in my movie. I thought about all that as I drew.

Wilson's gift was to appreciate. He was a romantic, seeking beauty and finding it everywhere — in poems and books and records and old photographs and teapots; in Beardsley drawings, store windows, and second-hand clothing stores. He was a poet, a great poet, who never wrote anything down. But Wilson would talk with such enthusiasm about a thing — an old wooden rocking chair, or a passage from Henry Miller's *Remember to Remember*, or a saucy three-year-old with fire in her eyes, spitting from a balcony, at the boys who had chased her home — until you loved it, too.

I would miss our walks down the night streets to The Bistro. It had a name — Chez Lulu Des Bacchantes, I think — but was only ever called *The*, or *le*, Bistro, depending. Wilson almost belonged in nineteenth-century Paris, ducking when Verlaine shot Rimbaud, because that almost certainly would be the bar to which he would go. We'd hurry, in clothes too thin for the November wind, passing other people, blowing this way and that, standing and stamping our feet at the corner, waiting for the light to change. Then I'd follow Wilson's small body, his quick steps darting like a fencer, past the dullards and slow feet, on the way to find love. With the smell of roasting chestnuts hinting at the warmth to come, we'd sprint the last few yards, dashing down the steps below street level, through the French bistro door of rectangular panes, passing from the dark, windy tunnel of la rue de la Montagne into an updated Toulouse-Lautrec poster exploding with colour and noise.

English and French spoken at high volume created its own special music. Cool people, dressed in colours and black, with scarves wrapped schoolboy style, once around the neck, stood one and a half deep at the long marble bar. Bartenders with droopy moustaches, and waiters in black and white with striped aprons, moved quickly, imperiously serving the motley lot of us. Tip, or die of thirst. Local celebrities like Nick Auf der Mar stood here, maybe arguing a fine point of writing with Terry Heffernan. Ivy Carpenter, refusing to be Yves Carpentier for some forgotten reason, refusing to be French at all, would order his beer in accented English. I would, after practising over and over yet another thirty times, say to the waiter "twa zekes" with the stress on "zekes," eliminating the "un" in front and the "s'il vous plaît" that comes, if one is polite, after, lest my accent betray me. "Oui, m'sieur, a Three X coming up," he would invariably reply, exposing my charade.

Opposite the bar was a long, mirrored banquette stretching into another room. Above the mirrors, the walls were inhabited by caricatured figures painted with abandon, almost life sized, of various personalities, local and otherwise. Marble-topped tables surrounded by denizens in bistro chairs floated like orderly floes between two shores with visible shipping lanes where waiters plied their trade, and individuals tacked their way to a safe anchorage, listing more to starboard or port as the evening wore on. And, should a rusty tramp, say, the Graham McKean, heave into view, its captain, a once highly acclaimed pianist, whose most famous concert involved breaking into a downtown church to play "Slaughter on Tenth Avenue," on an organ that broadcast hymns to the street, the moustachioed harbour patrol would quickly escort the offending vessel through the breakwater and back to sea. Captain McKean, providing he did not holler loudly in either the French or English with which he was equally adept, would be permitted a moment to scan the crowd and cadge a sou or two before leaving, from those not quick enough to avoid his glazed, penetrating, baleful stare. After all, he is an artiste, n'est-ce que pas?

Wilson usually tried for the centre of the banquette, the better to peruse the room. Then, he'd work the mirrors. He had a technique. If he saw someone he fancied — and when did he not? — Wilson would stare at her with his big wet brown buttons, trying to catch her eye, shyly at first, then slyly as the evening lengthened. Who is this funny little fellow? Can he really be staring at me? Oh my, he certainly is persistent. Let's stay for another Pernod to see what happens.

"My God, Osborne, have you ever seen anything so beautiful in all your life? No, over there, in the corner, the one with the gorgeous long hair. She's so lovely. Look at her. Watch her hand bring the glass to her lips. How graceful, and such a perfect little mouth. Look. Don't stare with your gob open, you thick twit. Just look. See how she brushes her hair back, how it falls so softly. My God, she's blushing. Look at the colour in her cheeks. Have you ever seen anything so delicate?"

He could sit for hours like this, enraptured. He was steady and constant. The style for women was tending toward longer hair and very short skirts or dresses, accompanied by high leather boots that rose above the knee. An arresting enough combination, wrought to a fine art by the women of Montréal. No one had more style, or could do more with a bit of fabric, or a scarf, or a hat worn just so. I couldn't help but look at them all, especially Bobby, the most beautiful of many beauties, with close-cropped blonde hair, the tallest boots, the shortest skirt, her borzoi shivering, tied to the rail outside. It's just as well she was gay.

Davies called it the nurse's curse. I had had, being twenty, very little luck with women. It's a difficult age for a guy. During the summer at the Algonquin I had finally met some girls from Montréal who would be fun to spend time with. Then the news arrived by mail from Saskatoon. There was a scruffy dog that hung around the dorms, obviously interested in company but still keeping its distance. They took to calling him Ralph. He was a large shepherd cross, terrified of thunder and lightning, and he accepted my offer of shelter one night during a storm. Facing a corner in my room, he lay trembling with his paws over his eyes. He politely asked to leave when it was over and, after that, sat nearer to me than anyone. Ralph and I spent a lot of time together during the last few weeks of the season. After supper I'd sit on the lawn, chain-smoking and writing furiously. Ralph inched closer and closer until one day I was allowed to give him a scratch behind the ear. I told him I was about to become a father but it didn't seem to faze him. He just liked to hear me talk.

Go West,
Young Man

On St. Patrick's Day, I left Montréal. It had been an unusually warm week, with D-Day minus one being particularly stunning — blue sky, no wind, steady warmth, no cool pockets. The sap was rising. In my hometown, it used to be during the first warm days, girls in their teens and early twenties would suddenly appear on the streets wearing wide skirts and dresses puffed out with starched crinolines. It was common to put two or three of these on top of one another to get the right degree of volume, both in size as well as the audible swish that whispered with each step. In pairs or threes, they floated down the street, upturned blossoms swirling in a brook. Whatever the style happened to be, this was one fashion constant that lived for a brief week or so each year to signify the beginning of spring. In Montréal, the tradition seemed to be to ditch the thigh-high boots and long coats, but make the skirts even shorter. It was the most delicious agony.

I was sitting on the steps in front of the apartment watching the traffic cruise up and down Atwater, the afternoon sun on my face. I had been restless for days. I held a pen and a piece of paper, thinking I might write a poem or draw something. It was at least helping me to sit still. There was a convent across the street and I could see a group of nuns milling about the grounds. They appeared to be occupied with yard maintenance but I could tell they were only playing at it. Something in the way they moved, chatting and laughing, told me they had been smelling some of the same perfume I was. Here was a poem. No doubt we were all going to spend the night alone on our cots but theirs was a lifelong decision. I, at least, had a ticket in the lottery. Curious about what they must be feeling, I dodged cars and skittered across the street to ask.

One of my cousins on my mother's side had decided to become a nun. I didn't know her all that well, having been more or less ostracized by that half of the family since you could reckon my age in single digits. It was hard to figure — she was blonde and quite pretty, with no obvious defects, mentally or physically, no sordid past. They had a bride-of-Christ shower for her, or some such thing. I was my mother's stooge, the go-to guy when you needed someone to tell the bill collector at the doorway that no one was home while she was flattened against the wall in the next room. It fell upon me to deliver the offering of baked goods while extending her regrets. That she didn't want to deliver them herself was the tipoff that this was going to be a pretty grim affair. One of my mother's sisters was also hearing impaired, deaf as a post in fact, and all the girls, five of them, plus my grandmother, could sign, so Mum could really get in there and talk without having to use her considerable extrapolation skills for the stuff she hadn't quite heard. Normally, she would never pass this up.

There was the inevitable priest, in addition to a couple of nuns, casting a sanctimonious pall over the proceedings. They stood around with varying quantities of food in their mouths projecting piety. I was not expected to stay, of course. The gifts had been opened. Piled in front of my cousin, who herself was pale and dressed in black, were black socks, a black coat, several black missals, and a large black suitcase, all nestled in white tissue paper. A step up from being placed on a coral slab and having your heart ripped out with a stone knife, to be sure. But only just. The happy ending was that she snapped out of it. She was home less than a week after she had gone. She affected a hangdog expression for a few months or so, like she hadn't been worthy and was sorry about that. All I could see was relief. But, what of the girls that had stayed?

Should I have asked her to dance? My nerve faltered the minute I stepped off the sidewalk onto juju turf. A carefree, saucy poet had been replaced by a kid trying to sell a magazine subscription to the stern Mrs. Grundy. Perhaps, in completing the mission, the path to redemption could be found. The closest route was bent over an old flowerbed. I approached from the rear. Politely, I cleared my throat, causing my quarry to do a neat imitation of her cousin, the dervish. Her Mrs. Grundy wasn't bad either. Somehow she had looked younger from the sidewalk, but I was staring at an ageing face, oval framed in cotton, that had wary eyes behind a formidable pair of steel-rimmed glasses. Wimp meets wimple.

"Excuse me, do you speak English?" I asked. Perhaps there was a way out.

"Yes." Damn.

"Well," I continued lamely, "I was just wondering what you thought of today?"

"Huh?" She was genuinely perplexed.

"Today. I mean, it's a nice day. I was just wondering what you felt about it?"

"Ohh, I see." And I looked in her eyes as the gates slammed shut. "Well, I thank God for such a beautiful day."

And that was that. My retreat (not the part where I almost got run over, not being able to get away fast enough) came as a relief to both of us. I resettled on my steps as the traffic was slowing in the approaching rush. At once, I had a vision. Framed in the open window of an old beater, was the most beautiful creature I had ever seen. My jaw must have dropped because she looked at me and laughed, and gave a little wave as they drove off. The poem ended: "Today I blew a kiss to a girl in a passing car."

The first night out, in Sudbury, I had slept on a tavern floor. The next, in the later-to-become-famous black hole of hitching rides, Wawa, Bob Dylan sang in my head: "Tell yer Ma, tell yer Pa, our luck's a-gonna fail in Wa-oo-wa." This ditty would repeat itself maybe forty or fifty times between cars, over and over again, oo-wa-oo-wa. As it got colder I developed an appreciation for Russian folk dancing, stomping my feet rhythmically to keep warm; having time for long, elaborate, inventive routines in the lengthening intervals of hope. Out of the black, high beams would sweep toward me, slap me around a bit in the glare, and change to a pair of glowing, red pig eyes winking around the curve. Then Bob would sing in a Russian accent: "Tell your mama, and papa, too, you will be dead man, in Wa-oo-woo."

Finally, driven by my own silliness and a dearth of traffic, I backtracked a mile or so to a cheap motel. The old man had dropped me in Wawa. He and the collie had picked me up in Espanola. They were heading west for good in a '52 Fargo at a steady forty-five miles an hour. He was going to get some land in Peace River, and was looking for a partner if I was interested. He had even bought socks for me at Canadian Tire in the Soo. It was the westernmost, the last one, and he wanted to use up all his Canadian Tire money. "It's no good where I'm going, Boy." We parted amicably on our separate quests. The next afternoon I blew by him in a Volkswagen. There was another partner in the passenger seat, book-ending the dog. Stopping for the night at the Lakehead, I endured another hazard of the road. The fat Jehovah's Witness in the all-night laundromat in Fort William — or Port Arthur — was not much older than I, and not terrifically fervent. Last year he had been a Mormon. Could he possibly not have known that he was gay? At one point during his lecture, I noted, I had spent more than if I had taken the train.

Ten days later I had become a dharma bum. With "This Land Is Your Land" ringing in my ears, I had hitchhiked across the continent. Sitting in the northern shadows of the same mountain range that Gary Snyder (Japhy Ryder in *The Dharma Bums*) had written about in *Earth House Hold*, I mulled over Zen koans and the nuances of haiku, like Gary, while watching Fossum fill a cereal bowl with raw oatmeal, chopped walnuts, raisins, wheat germ, brown sugar and condensed milk. He had sampled this ur-granola, or something similar, in Europe. It would never do, I derided, failing to hear the call, although with real milk instead of Carnation, it wasn't half bad.

Fossum wanted to talk about Degen, hanging on my every word whenever I relented. This was the beginning of an observable phenomenon that has persisted to the present. People of all sexes always want to talk about Degen. She is a fulcrum for the kind of gossip usually reserved for celebrities. Amongst her own crowd, mostly the western arts community, she is a celebrity still, as well known as, say, Cher. Which would make me Sonny.

She had shown up as if by magic at Rainer von Köningslow's — dubbed Rainer von Umlaut by Marty — in Saskatoon. I had voluntarily, in a flirtation with whimsy, spent the night in jail in Regina. Apocryphal or no, someone, probably Hoffer, had told me that if you were really hard up for a place to stay the cops would put you up for the night. I had arrived in Regina by a bus I flagged down in a howling blizzard outside of Brandon. The desk sergeant had never heard of such a policy but, it being twenty-below and a slow night, gave me, after putting the contents of my pockets in an envelope, accommodation until six the next morning. Released, oddly cleansed somewhat from my stay, I shivered through the early morning swirl of rose-tinted boiler smoke, grey automobile exhaust, and ice crystals, along similarly coloured streets, to a diner. I had yet to actually see the prairie. It was not so flat as I had expected, and hard to look at with the sun bouncing off the blue-tinged, snow-drifted fields like high noon at a Jamaican beach.

Rainer lived in a crummy student pad above a shoe repair shop. His small room, doorless and off the kitchen, consisted of a sleeping bag on a mattress surrounded by books arranged on planks supported by concrete blocks, a decorating idea I hadn't seen before and therefore found clever, as even clichés were once newly minted. Vintage cushions of every shape and colour were strewn about so that one had to walk over them to enter. There was a small tabletop, a foot high, in the middle of the room, where one could have tea.

Every flat surface was covered by an array of collected detritus: candles, gutted in Chianti bottles, rocks, several different pipes, diverse brands of tobacco tins and pouches, incense, crusted ash-trays, enamelled tea tins, spent matches, dried orange peels, and a magnifying glass and maps. It was the messiest, most glorious room I had ever seen.

Rainer had acquired enough credits to graduate several times over but would choose, when nearly finished a course of studies, to switch disciplines, feeling he had not learned enough, which is to say, all, to merit a degree. In addition to text books, of which there were many, his library was, in a compact way, quite complete: including Huxley, Mann, Hardy, Joyce, Woolf, and Durrell's *Alexandria Quartet*, which everybody was reading. All the philoso-phers were there, alongside Freud and Jung, as were dense tomes on physics and Boolean algebra. Finally, I had met a true academic, a genuine intellectual, an astonishing and admirable breed.

Tall, thin, blonde and more déshabillé than scruffy, Rainer was an aristocrat and very, very German — not only having been born there, but evidenced by an aura of correctness and spinal rigidity that would not desert him no matter how hard he tried to nonchalantly slouch. One could, when introduced, practically perceive a slight bow and hear his heels click. Being in his early twenties, it was not difficult to see the schoolboy in him still, all enthusiasm, cowlick, and Oxfords, in grey flannel short pants. Yet he had the reasonable assurance that when he entered a room, regardless of how many were present, he would, by a large margin, be the smartest one there. He appeared to pay little heed to this, much as a seven-foot gentle giant might well not notice the difference in size of others. If provoked, Rainer would seek to enlighten rather than engage. It was neither surprising nor ironic that he shared this flat with the soiled, rumpled, irascible Hoffer who, at the moment, was away.

Rainer was doing his best to postulate: the more clever the male, the more complete the lovestruck dolt. My aloof and measured friend was, although trying not to, beaming like an idiot when the doe of the north dropped in to visit. She knew I was there just as I knew she'd show up. With one hand outstretched to hang her coat by the door, she reached under her chin with the other and shook her hair loose from a plain white scarf that had artfully displayed her heart-shaped face. The golden brown cascade was uncommonly long and shimmered as it fell to the small of her back. It was beautiful hair, shiny and natural and cared for, at a time when perms, cuts, backcombing and rollers were the norm. She was, by any standards, a beauty. And, as certain beauties do, she knew it. At her private high school she had been anointed as Miss Luther Lion.

I couldn't believe she had lowered her eyes shyly and had fluttered her long lashes during Rainer's introduction. Surely she was having fun at my expense — or was she? This was a girl that made you wary. In the two minutes it took to become totally enmeshed, I noted with some satisfaction that she was great looking, sure, and maybe she had the exotic name: Degen — rhymes with ray gun — and her ass was perfection, okay, but, man, she was in-your-face obnoxious. It would be easy to be immune to this one. Thank God she wasn't sultry like Fossum's drawings. That would have been hard to take. And her mouth! — not the full, red lips part, but the vocabulary of "fucking this" and "asshole that" with every second or third phrase, obviously for effect. It was way overdone. Even hard girls didn't talk like that. Approaching the midsixties, it was still automatic to tone one's language down in mixed company. It was part of the etiquette you learned as a kid, right along with the swear words.

She spent most of the evening talking to Rainer, whose Teutonic composure seemed to have gone AWOL. Flattered by the attention, he became tentative, too quick to leap to the argument, approaching the supercilious in his display of intellect. It was a mixture of undergraduate stuff that, not having taken the class, went over my head, and gossip. She challenged everything, no matter what. At one point, out of boredom, I interjected that my foot had fallen asleep, thinking that would be hard to refute. How dare I trivialize a legitimate discussion with such a trite observation, blah, blah, blah. Mercy. Eventually, Rainer — who had been patient to the point of doting in explaining that whether Nietzsche was a fucking bastard or not had nothing to do with the postulation that might is right — had to admit that, yes, Soren was an interesting given name of Kierkegaard's.

This was before I knew anything of auras so I couldn't describe Degen's as being a brilliant green glow that had, in its complex composition, something of the emerald and something of the swamp. She got away with all that because she was beautiful. If she had been even slightly less attractive no guy would have put up with her for any longer than it would take to cross the street. This is a sad fact. She pushed as far as she could push, and the more hoops you jumped through the more would appear. Of course, most women were aware of this, while men, as a rule, weren't — they ignored it, or didn't care.

The gossip, almost all of it sexual, was what various people had said or done to her or she had to them. I was hip enough to realize that although she had been telling stories to Rainer she was really talking to me, or at me. This was irritating and fascinating at the same time. Rainer deserved better, but making love to this guy or being attracted to that guy was interesting soap.

There was nothing soft about her. She sat in a short skirt, her leotard-clad legs crossed kindergarten style, chain-smoking menthol cigarettes while sucking on a candy. When she shifted positions it was hard not to look. I heard the story of some guy who was currently in an institution under sedation because she had dropped him, while his young wife, "a timid little thing," wasn't taking it very well. I was to learn later that when she used the term "making love" it meant necking, not that she had screwed half of Saskatoon, and the guy in the straight jacket had been her first and only sexual experience to involve penetration. And that she likely chose him because he was married and, therefore, temporary. (She had known that intellectually they weren't suited.) I was, apparently, her second — as she was mine — but, at the time, I thought she was way too experienced for me. Nor was I normally the one ordained to get the beauty queen. I resisted everything about her.

The wrapping on the package had hummed and glowed, crackling with electricity, shooting sparks so delightfully that one might never take an interest in the contents, or dwell there for long before returning to the sizzle. She had charisma. But, after an evening where I had learned far too much about the girl — her mother, who had abandoned her at the age of three, her much older artist father, the list of suitors — I had been glad to see the ass end of her, so to speak, when Rainer took her home. A few minutes after they had gone, with a toothbrush and paste in my mouth, I answered a soft knock on the door. Degen stood there, her face framed in virginal white, and said, almost shyly, "It really was nice to meet you." I was able, without swallowing the toothpaste, to sputter: "'ee too." Those eyes.

As I was telling him all this, Fossum kept his back to me, staring out the window. I told him how the next day, on a whim, Degen had decided to hitch-hike with me as far as Edmonton, where she would stay with Rainer — who had gone by rail — at his parents' house. She sent her regards, of course, as did the entire, blonde von Umlaut family, at whose home I had also spent the night before taking the train through the Rockies to Prince George. A young trainman, a skinny, ferret-faced guy, had been pretty nasty on the ride, calling me a "goddamned Beatle." I tried to interest Marty in how, when the train stopped in Jasper, I spotted the bastard and chased him around the station a few times. Had I gone for him on the train I knew I would have gotten kicked off.

Before I even reached Terrace I knew I wouldn't be staying for long. The mountains were magnificent but they kind of bore down on me. They loomed. One afternoon I walked along the rocky shore of the Skeena River and watched a lone snowflake spiral out of the grey sky and dissolve the moment it hit a smooth, rounded boulder. Marty said he wanted me to stay a while longer but I think he was relieved to see me go. I was thankful that Degen would not be in Saskatoon on the way back. She had gone to Toronto for the spring and summer.

The books had changed, and the low platform for tea had been replaced by a chair and card table. Hoffer had resumed occupancy of the student flat. I wrote my first novel at that table, one hundred and forty-three pages of single-spaced longhand in eight days. It was about a young guy who had taken a detour into a life of crime, only to be caught by a fluke. It ended sadly. It would be thirty-five years before I wrote another.

Hoffer, who had been taking a dozen pills a day ever since I had known him, stopped doing that. His father, Dr. Abe Hoffer, had been one of the first to assert that most, if not all, mental illnesses could be attributed to chemical imbalances and therefore could be controlled by drugs. He had done groundbreaking research on schizophrenia and was also one of the LSD pioneers. He found me at the pad when he had come to confront Bill. Never having met the man, I was astounded when he proceeded to tear a strip off me. Who is this guy? I thought he was nuts. There had been no pleasantries, just that I was a distraction to his little Billy. "Sorry about that, Ralph, baby, he's a little overprotective." Like Hoffer needed help to be distracted. Word had come from Montréal just in time that I had been accepted as beach supervisor at the Algonquin Hotel.

Although we kept tabs on one another for a while, I saw very little of Bill after that. When he died too soon a few years ago, many newspapers noted his passing, most with regret.

Early Regina

Degen, who had been at university in Saskatoon, was now in Regina. She and her father, whom she, and everybody else, always addressed as Ernie, thought it best that she spend a semester or two there, owing to her condition. People might talk. When I got off the train and went to the rooming house where she shared a space with her old private school roommate, she was five months pregnant. She was wearing a bright magenta maternity smock whose colour immediately transferred itself to my cheeks. I had been rendered suddenly bashful and could barely look her in the eye. She was quite demure herself, casting her gaze slightly downward, smiling enigmatically, relishing, perhaps, the tribute my awkwardness had paid.

Her roomie, Maureen, of whom I had been warned to be careful and, under no circumstances, was to never, ever be called "Mo," looked at me with a mixture of curiosity and . . . not pity, sympathy perhaps. She had the demeanour and grace of the superior athlete she was and, having lived with Degen for a couple of years, knew at least some of what lay in store for me. What had been billed as a sharp tongue was merely a lack of pretense and a propensity to dismiss bullshit whenever she came across it. I liked her immediately.

Up to that point, Degen and I had spent four or five days together, exchanged a handful of letters and had known one another barely half a year. We were strangers, and, had it been necessary to qualify, we would not have even approached the minimum requirements for parenthood. Welcome to the club. Ernie, asking the age-old question — "How could you be zo ztupid, Degen?" — had pushed for an abortion that he was gladly willing to fund. It would have meant flying to Sweden where it was legal and therefore safe. She was terrified of planes but, more importantly, she was much taken with the idea of motherhood as well, referring ponderously and often to "the child" within her. She made it very clear that it was her decision and we — Ernie, the child, and I — were, at her pleasure, along for the ride. There were no consultations, no collaborations.

Although close at times, it wasn't exactly ninety-three seconds of pleasure equals a lifetime of woe. The circus in which Degen was the ringmaster often proved highly amusing. There was not a lineup, as it seemed on occasion, of suitors stretching down the street and around the corner willing to plight their troth and rescue the fair maiden. But come they did, one by one, to state their case and make their earnest pleas. I just sat off to the side where I had been brushed, answering the door and assigning numbers. Maureen, if she were there — and it seemed not to matter whether she or I were there or not, such was the fever — would exchange glances with me or roll her eyes in mock despair. I was neither offended nor threatened by this. It was too bizarre and rather poignant, with my sympathies oddly engaged on behalf of the underdogs.

The madonna, who had yet to encounter a form of attention to which she was inured, would merely shrug and throw her hands up as if to say, "What can I do?" This was the beginning of a phenomenon that persists, I think, to this day. In the movies they call it foreshadowing but I knew shit about cinema.

Tauno — who had been named for a wild and handsome Baltic lad who used to visit our apartment on Atwater and sing folk songs in his native Estonian, who had, with his family, escaped the Soviets, and who had blown his brains out with an eighteenth-century flintlock pistol in what was hotly debated to have been an accident rather than a desperate act of melancholy — was born on February 15, 1965, the same day as the new Canadian flag. He had come close to being named Zapata by a mother determined that her child be saddled with a name as unconventional as her own. It had not only flown as an eleventh-hour compromise but was such a pleasing choice to her that I was granted the boon of further saddling him with the middle name of Geordie in honour of my North-of-England chums. However, the surname Lindner was entered on his birth certificate instead of Osborne, forever — and I know how stupid, chauvinistic and unimportant this is — sticking in my craw. It was more of that foreshadowing business.

On Sunday, Valentine's Day, we were at a film sponsored by the Regina Film Society since that was the only way to legally watch a movie on Sunday. Halfway through an iffy Bogart flick, *Beat The Devil*, we rushed to the hospital, stopping first for the suitcase we had prepared at home. We were scared. Our request that I be present during the delivery had been routinely denied and not just because we weren't married. It simply wasn't done. In fact one hospital official, a doctor, had gone on record to state that any man who wanted to be present during childbirth was not only deranged but quite possibly dangerous as well. This had been prompted by Myron Kuziak, a young local left-wing lawyer, who had not only attended the birth of his daughter but had the temerity to take photographs. This had created quite a scandal.

I waited with Degen lying on a hospital bed in a small green room as the sedatives kicked in, reducing her trembles. I read to her from *The Little Prince*, doing all the voices, until they took her away.

Six hours later — it had been a difficult delivery with the umbilical cord wrapped around the little guy's neck — the doctor walked right by me, shooting me a look that was by now familiar from the lineup of erstwhile swains, saying not a word. God, not him too. The two guys that had been pacing the night away with me had long since joined their wives. It was a nurse who took pity and gave me the good news. I was even permitted a moment with the proud, if exhausted, mother before they wheeled her away. Seeing my son had to wait until that afternoon, a moment I shared with Ernie, who had miraculously appeared.

Ernest Lindner, the grand old man of Saskatchewan art — then the Canadian hotbed, had been fifty when Degen was born. A disproportionate number of major artists were painting in Saskatchewan and the Regina Five of Art McKay, Ted Godwin, Ron Bloore, Ken Lochead, and Doug Morton dominated the national scene. They all looked up to Ernie. Also, the Emma Lake Workshop, his brainchild, sponsored by the University of Saskatchewan, was attracting major players from the U.S. art world, especially Clement Greenberg, then one of the world's most preeminent art critics. Ernie was a huge presence in this worldly scene. Meeting these guys — and the composer, John Cage, a sweet little man who talked to me about mushrooms and who summered at Emma Lake with his companion, also a fervent mycologist — taught me more about art and the language artists used to converse with one another. I could have passed.

A cherubic old guy, almost Santa-like, with a charming Austrian accent (Ernie smoked a pipe and was fond of aphorisms he translated from German — "Vat ve build up viss our handz, ve knock over viss our behindz") is pretty hard to resist. He was truly loveable to almost everyone. We played a lot of chess and he had helped to improve my game to the point where I was winning three out of five and on my way to four. One day, during one of those complex beauties that all chess players love in which it only matters to be a part, I called Ernie, out of affection, "lieber Ernst." He resigned suddenly. That evening, late, I was informed by Degen to never again be so presumptuous as to call Ernie "Ernst." That was a privilege, he had told her, reserved for his brother, Carl, with whom he used to play chess, and his old friends in Austria.

"You're joking, right?"

"He's very serious about this. So don't."

Ernie's house, Ernie's rules, Ernie's daughter. You wouldn't think he needed to compete. I had married a couple.

God was dead. I found myself being more careful. Had there ever been a child this rare, with so much promise? The first six months go by so quickly. Christ was really a mushroom. I grew a beard, a wispy thing, more hope than hair. Every day brought a gift. An old lady at the co-op, seeing me in black with glasses made from my grandfather's steel rims, asked me: "Are you religious or something?" Buddhist monks in Vietnam were immolating themselves in great pyres of protest against "the war." I resolved to drive more slowly.

We were set up on the top floor of the Beta Apartments, an old brick three-storey affair with thin walls and creaky hardwood floors. Against my better judgement, I had enrolled in a "mature" matriculation course at the brand new University of Regina. Halfway through his fifteenth month, Tauno was getting around pretty good. As part of perhaps his essential nature, he had, at eleven months, learned how to run before he could walk. The apartment was set up like a sleeping car on a train and Tauno would fly down the long hallway past the bedrooms and bathroom into my arms. It had been not so long ago that he'd expend great effort struggling to his feet by grasping the bars of his playpen only to burst into tears when he couldn't get back down. I'd help him, then he'd do it all over again. Eventually, as with walking, he mastered the art of the descent.

Old unframed oil paintings of Ernie's that he had done in the thirties and forties, and hadn't thought much of, were used to child-proof the flat. The one of him as a young man, painting a self-portrait in front of a mirror where the canvas reflected in another mirror and then back on the canvas and so on in diminishing images until his face turned into a skull, was always turned backside out so as not to traumatize the little guy. A nude woman, sensuous, beautifully painted — the one thing of his I had requested and been denied long before his death when they became worth thousands — was left facing out and used to wall off the garbage between the sink and the stove. This used to knock people out.

Nothing worked, of course. Like water, Tauno could find his way through anything. We had almost lost him the first day home from the hospital. I had turned to get a diaper and he almost flipped himself off the table. When I gave him his first baths, I was terrified of hurting his soft spot. Now he would run up to me, fling himself across my lap and sink his perfect little teeth into the flesh above my knee. Ow! Stop that. But he wouldn't, keeping it up for weeks, although sometimes letting a day or two slide by between bites. I had no idea what he was exploring. Finally, using an older form of mammalian instruction, I bit him back. Not hard. He cried a bit, he was never much for crying, more startled than anything. Well, what was I to do? It hadn't been covered in Dr. Spock.

She was sitting bolt upright in bed. Light from the street lamps bisected the bed leaving the top half of her in shadow. She stared off into space and rocked slowly back and forth. We were both prone to drama.

"Maybe I can't love anyone . . . you know . . . because of my mother."

"You love Tauno, don't you?"

"Of course I fucking do. What kind of a question is that? That's different. That's not what I meant."

"Okay. What then? Don't you love yourself?"

"Jesus."

"It's a valid question."

"We're from different classes, you and I. Maybe on some levels it can never work."

"Are you serious? Give me a break."

"Our backgrounds are totally different. And this pill! You try taking it. Who knows what it's doing to me?"

It had been the longest winter in the history of the universe. Finally, the weather broke. By mid-May the snow, which had fallen the previous September 15 and stayed, was gone. Even by prairie standards it had been a hard winter. The people were happy — downright frisky, in fact. We shared the back fire escape with two other couples. Clint Bomphray and Linda Rankin were right next door. Wayne Morgan and Norma Lundberg lived one apartment over. All of us were students and we had become friends — for life, as these things often turn out.

Morgan had the only TV. We'd all go there to watch "Batman." It was camp, like Andy Warhol's soup cans. There were chocolate cake bake-offs. Dinners and parties were given. There was a certain night with a Ouija board when we all freaked out. We were young and beautiful. We eyeballed one another. Morgan playfully kicked people when he drank. Norma, tall and blonde and Nordic, got on at the *Leader-Post*. Clint spent too much time with the guys in an effort to show he wasn't totally mad about Linda, which he was. Linda wore an electric blue dress one night, shining, in a room full of beauty. I could hardly keep my eyes off her.

On one of these early warm Saturdays we marched down 11th Ave., then south on Albert St. to the legislature. It had been the classic route since before the Regina Riot in 1935. Spirits were high. It was as much a celebration of spring as a protest against nuclear weapons. Ban the bomb. Marching on the legislature was not an uncommon event. Many of the student radicals in the crowd were the sons and daughters of people who had themselves been student radicals and progenitors of the co-operative movement. Lining the marching route with ranks of the opposition was also an old sport, as demonstrated by the enormous crowds either protesting or endorsing medicare a few years earlier.

We were not just students or radicals. There were professors and doctors and bus drivers and old people, all in all a healthy turnout from the community. The people lining the streets were not necessarily in opposition either, they just didn't feel like marching or wanted to see what was going on. Degen and I pushed Tauno in a stroller, feeling just a bit proud. There were crudely drawn signs and benign heckling could be heard from both camps.

I saw the guy immediately. He stood out because people around him had removed themselves farther away. He had a thin face under an orange hunting cap. He was wearing a nondescript jacket and chino pants. You wouldn't want to see a nastier smile. It was chilling. He wore a sign that said something like: "Help Yourself." He held aloft in one hand a red, two-gallon gas can and a shiny silver Zippo lighter in the other. I mean, our child was there and he was grinning.

Acid — The Beginning

Life under the Big Top is a thrill a minute. A beam of light shoots out of the dark from somewhere on high, illuminating the Ringmaster who, as it turns out, is me. "Laydees an' gennlemen . . ." A lion — massive, old — spills from a cage. He looks like my boss. I crack a whip and hold aloft a sheaf of papers in my other hand, shaking them until he leaps onto his pedestal in retreat. The crowd — also me — murmurs approval at first, then the note lowers, becoming ominous. A tigress had somehow sneaked behind me. She is in a crouch, tail flicking, ears flat, ready to pounce. I turn and duck just in time. She sails over my head, beautiful, deadly. I go wild with applause. I take a florid bow. Fool!

The ring begins to spin, quickly transforming into a giant whirlpool. Maelstrom. Frantic figures trapped in the vortex wave their arms. They are not me so much as incidents from my life. The closing of a cell door, the frosty end of a cold shoulder, acts of personal cowardice, accusations of abandonment, and an overwhelming almost whimpering sense of inadequacy and hopelessness, threaten to permanently imbed me in sorrow. In trying to resist I become more agitated, grinding my teeth. The feelings persist, grow uglier. Help me. I am so scared.

Who are you asking for help? I don't know. Who wants help? I don't know. Behind that voice, and mine, lurks a presence — paranoia perhaps — cruel, mocking. Heh, heh, heh. I become smaller, shrunk within myself, surrounded by something dark and nameless. And even farther behind, behind the behind the behind, I hear from somewhere slightly out of reach as if it were external (yet I *know has come from deep within), a disembodied consciousness as that of some sort of god, malevolent possibly, make a throat-clearing sound — ahem — as if it were watching me and wants me to know how trivial all that other nonsense had been compared to it. What have you been messing with? I could feel the hair rising on the backs of my arms. I am so small. Help me.*

It just becomes too much. Too much. I can no longer fight, no longer resist. There is nothing left but to forgive myself and show mercy. The crescendo rises, the space between the notes diminishes, the vortex spins faster, taking up all my thought. What am I to do but let go? I can no longer stay afloat, spinning in all this misery. I abandon myself to the raging funnel, whirling faster and faster. Transgressions, errors, unkind-nesses and quotidian irritations gather such momentum that it is a relief when they blur together, creating what seems like a paisley tornado.

Approaching the void, I offer no resistance. Voices and images dis-solve into a soft, floating darkness. At the end of a last dizzying spiral upward, my head explodes in a flash of relief. It is a big bang. Illumination, from a pinpoint to All, is instantaneous. And, like slowly falling plumes from a skyrocket, I become suffused with a golden feeling of clarity and calm. I am at peace, complete and whole, with a sense of well-being the like of which I could not ever have imagined. I am in a pure state of grace. In the background, I can once again hear the sitar music of Ravi Shankar, hear it instead of inhabiting it. The wailing notes ascend and descend an ancient scale in plangent tones I now implicitly under-stand to be the classic pattern of creation.

I had had only to have opened my eyes to make the maelstrom go away. But, as I would learn another time, the voices and discom-fort would have stuck to me for days, weeks, months, even years, like smeared shit. Had I seized upon my fear it would have stayed with me for the rest of the ride, settling in as a bad trip. Instinct or luck, or a combination of the two, enabled me to abandon all hope and accept whatever came next. It also helped to have a sufficiently powerful dosage to render the concept of control as being futile.

Death will come like this. I know it. The secret, then, is to not resist. Let go and embrace it if you can. Since I had been flying solo without a guide or instruction, my own nature had saved me. This was important. Somewhere, buried perhaps deeply within, was a strength I either didn't know I had or had forgotten. It was durable, something I could trust. I felt truly fortunate to have realized that, however briefly. There was a resource available to me — and it came from within. Hallelujah!

As a child of five, almost six, I had, according to my mother, been prescribed belladonna, an alkaloid also known poetically as "deadly nightshade." I'm not sure why, tonsils probably, since, a short while after, they were removed along with my adenoids, my consent having been bought by a mere bowl of ice cream. Nightshade has reddish, bell-shaped flowers and glossy black berries. But it's the roots and leaves that are deadly, whose extracts dilate the pupils and were once used by women to get that favoured doe-eyed look — hence, Bella Donna, Beautiful Lady. Atropine, being the active ingredient, is often used to relax muscles and sup-press glandular and mucous secretions. It's versatile — depending on strength of dosage — having been used as a sedative, a poison and, in medieval times, an hallucinogen.

That would explain the clown. I had been given a triple dose because, apparently, the pharmacist had typed the instructions incorrectly. After determining that I wasn't in mortal danger and that the effects would wear off, my mother, ever the curious one, was quite amused by my antics. All day, I ran and jumped and played hide-and-go-seek with an imaginary clown. By her account, I had had a happy time of it with Bozo Invisibilus. She also told me I had no memory of my playmate the next day. Indeed, I recall nothing. But I love the story. I had made a great choice of com-panion, for starters.

Ingesting the alkaloid, LSD, was something else. Nothing would ever be the same again. Aldous Huxley's "Doors of Perception" had been opened. I had seen the Garden. What I had seen, or realized, could not be dismissed as mere illusion or hallucination. I remembered everything. For me, nothing could ever be the same again — in a good way. It could just as easily have been in a bad way, or a nothing way, wholly unsatisfactory. One thing I knew for certain is that acid wasn't anything to idly mess around with.

After what I had just gone through, I saw LSD as a sacrament. I have never been persuaded otherwise. Creation had been revealed to me in startlingly clear form. Suddenly it was all there, and, at twenty-three or four, I had access. The cosmos was mine, although it almost seemed as if I had cheated somehow. Scholars had laboured until their hair had turned white, searching for answers through the weight of decades. Theologians had spent lifetimes in the service of faith in what could not be named, arriving at tentative proofs accepted by adherents, possibly ridiculed by competing theorists. Ascetics denied the flesh, or flayed it into either hell or ecstasy, in hopes of a tiny shred of enlightenment. Hermits lived silently in caves listening to rocks grow. Certain mathematicians cackled gleefully in rubble-strewn rooms with formulae that proved the existence of God. I had dropped a pill on a Saturday afternoon because I had to work all week. In an instant I had elbowed my way to the head of the line.

Later, in an upstairs bedroom, with Degen calling up from the living room from time to time to determine if I was all right, I felt like some sort of cosmic warrior who had survived an epic struggle. Hours before I had, as we say, dumped my garbage — one of the therapeutic benefits of acid, if done correctly, is to get rid of all the crap that sticks to you from inhabiting the world — and peaked, a few hours into the trip. Now, around hour nine, I was mellow but still sailing. I was sitting on the edge of the bed. My senses were acute and things were kind of sorting themselves out for me.

With my eyes shut I was sitting on a house-sized asteroid, on the rim of a small crater. My left leg stretched out and my right was bent at the knee. I was dressed like Robin Hood and in my right hand was a cap with a feather in it. Other asteroids occupied the blue-black void and ranged in colour from deep apricot, like the one I was sitting on, to a hard silver off in the distance. Windlessly, soundlessly, we whizzed through the void at great, but varying, speeds. Some were slowly sailing by, while others quietly fell away. Some kept the same pace. There were so many I could barely see the distant stars. I felt not so much old as timeless.

I needn't have worried about jumping the line. What I had searched for and found, I still seek. The difference being that I realize that the glow of enlightenment is, at best, temporary, transitory and fleeting. I wouldn't have it any other way. Then, I saw it as a state to be achieved and dwell in forever — like winning some sort of spiritual lottery. Find the grail and all will be well. Yet, all around me, the very ebb and flow of things that ebb and flow, egress and ingress — the natural way of things — contradicted the static nature of this desire. Knowing and not knowing, empty and full, inhale and exhale; the strength comes not from achieving a particular state but realizing that there is a rhythm. Down will eventually traverse its way to up, and back again. The circle will turn. Strength is having the sense not to grab on to any one part, good or bad, allowing respiration to occur. I suppose I had no right knowing any of that.

Wisdom is all well and good until the exigencies of something gnawing at your ass force you to abandon nirvana and embrace reflex. I had a job. Having failed the mature matriculation course, I would not be advancing to first-year university. I had learned bridge, improved my hearts game, and made a few interesting friends. Alec Cameron, a newspaperman from the old school, a crusty curmudgeon with a good heart, had taken a chance and hired me as an assistant in the publicity department of the Saskatchewan Wheat Pool. He taught me the five Ws of journalism: who, what, why, where, and when. I had my own column in the *Western Producer*, "Pool Notes," un-bylined and full of arcane little tidbits. I also covered cattle auctions and grain elevator openings, making sure to, "for God's sake, get the names right," and in the proper order. It was my first experience with the editing process. No matter how perfect I felt I had got it, I'd come from the bosses' offices with more red marks than words on the pages I had submitted.

The wage of four hundred per month was relatively decent. We moved to a house that was a five-minute walk to work. I wore a shirt and tie and still managed to look scruffy. One of my classmates became a boarder. I wrote poems in the evening at the plywood kitchen table I had built. It wobbled gloriously. I had been working on a series I called my "sewer poems," having been seduced by the way waste products were transported from the city.

Then Leonard Cohen came to town.

Comrade Cohen

In the early and mid-sixties Saskatchewan was one of a half-dozen places in the world where research was conducted on LSD. Who knew? Timothy Leary and Richard Alport, at Harvard, were getting all the headlines which, in the beginning, were of the cutesy filler sort. Dr. Humphrey Osmond, the British counterpart to Leary, had come over from England and worked with Dunc Blewett at the provincial hospital in Weyburn, about an hour's drive south of Regina. (I think Abe Hoffer was a significant partner in all this, since he was the guy who did groundbreaking research on schizophrenia.) As with Hollywood Hospital in Vancouver — run by a Doctor MacDonald and aided by Ted Poole — they were attempting, amongst other things, to determine whether or not LSD could cure alcoholism. All of these stars in the psychedelic firmament were pioneers and all, except for Poole, had the honorific of doctor.

Another American, a guy named Hubbard, was part of the group but I get the impression that he was something of a dark force — respected but viewed with a certain amount of circumspection. Ostensibly, he was deeply involved with the U.S. government in general, and the military in particular. One story has Hubbard inviting his fellows to witness a demonstration at a small, secluded lake. He sat in the stern of an old lap-straked dinghy that had once been a little put-put but whose motor had long since been removed. There was no wind and there were no oars. There was no method of propulsion in evidence save a greening brass propeller at the end of an old shaft that was attached to nothing. Hubbard said to the group: "Hey, fellas, what do you think of this?" He crossed his arms and the boat glided away from the dock. One might conclude the cause was some sort of current except the dinghy turned and came back the same way it had gone. Then it swung away again and, in a fifteen-minute demonstration, proceeded to do figure eights, turn wide circles and move back and forth with ease. At the end of the exhibition the craft was neatly docked and hauled from the water to show that the outer hull was devoid of any secret appliances. No explanation was sought or given as to the energy source behind the demonstration.

Part of me wants to believe in magic or, at least, in as yet untapped mental powers in that ninety percent of the brain we are reputed not to use. In my heart I know the story is bullshit, or some sort of trick was employed — if indeed the event happened as described. However, even if the story were true it would take focus away from the real power of LSD, which is inward, not external. Not much is known about lysergic acid diethylamide. It's synthesized from ergot, a disease primarily affecting rye grains, turning them purple. Rye, like rice in Asia, provided the people with their daily bread. During years of particularly bad infestations the ergot percentage in the flour would rise to toxic levels. Every so often, entire populations of afflicted villages would experience mass hallucinations — many would die.

A Swiss chemist named Hoffman researched this in the early nineteen-forties. He knew he was on to something when, cycling home after work, he perceived his bicycle to leave the pathway and become airborne. Since then, not much by way of science has come to light. LSD apparently triggers a release of large amounts of serotonin from the pineal gland — a.k.a. the third eye. It is taken in microscopic quantities and exits the body in less than an hour. That just about exhausts the scientific knowledge.

Twenty years after Hoffman's flight home, when the golden calf had taken the form of a station wagon parked in front of a sprawling, ranch-style bungalow, material prosperity had seldom been better. The prospects of a nuclear holocaust seemed equally bright. This occasioned a bunker mentality in some and, having eaten and drunk their fill, a search for meaning in others. It was perfect timing for Timothy Leary and fascinating accounts of his adventures in inner space made it to the newspapers and glossy magazines. The psychotherapeutic community originally had thought LSD to be psychotomimetic. The thinking was that madness could be induced in the short term, in order to study dementia. The subjects, however, were unable or unwilling to co-operate. They kept seeing paradise.

All heaven broke loose.

Clint took acid and it suddenly became less abstract. The list of people I knew who had tried it was growing. They were mostly connected to the psychology professor, Dr. Duncan Blewett, whose message was reaching me via my friends. I was not a joiner and, although curious, I rejected every attempt to be introduced. At the same time I had gotten a copy of *The Tibetan Book of the Dead*. It was not, as I had expected, like reading Zen koans, and it raised more questions than it answered. "It's like climbing out of your ego and seeing things as they really are," said Clint. I had no idea of what he meant, particularly being shaky on the entire concept of ego.

Then, Linda Rankin dropped. "It's beautiful," she said. "You have to try it."

I was a sceptic, a traveller of the road not taken. I didn't believe in much of anything, stopping just short of nihilism. Meanwhile, a new breed was emerging. These guys were plain silly, but courageous in a way. Regina, being the boondocks, had about six people who qualified. One of them was Gary Anweiler, a feisty, wiry little guy from Melville who was one of the few people around daring enough to get hold of marijuana. He was more prone to sweet laughter than taking umbrage — unless you knew which buttons to push — and my reticence about taking drugs had somehow become a personal challenge to him. He stormed off one day when I kidded him about just trying to expand his market. Anweiler was a believer and I don't think he ever made a cent from drugs. He, like many others in the early days, just wanted to get the word out. He was, in the strictest terms, a missionary.

A few weeks later, presumably cooled down, he dropped in only for a moment and handed me a white pill wrapped in foil. "When you take this, and you will, I want you to let me know. I'll come over just to see the smile wiped off your face." What made him think I'd even consider taking it? I put it away. I didn't know then that it was of the highest quality, the Sandoz stuff, manufactured legally by the giant pharmaceutical firm, and being used clinically in places like Weyburn.

Somehow Degen had become interested in Quakers and I had agreed to go to a meeting. They had a history of being opposed to violence and, more interesting to me, held meetings that were distinctly non-liturgical in form. A group of "Friends" would assemble, usually on Sunday, at someone's house. They would sit in silence for an hour, then have tea and "bickies" and go home. The idea was, during this hour of silence, if anyone had something to say they'd share it with the group. Normally, church gave me the willies, but, as a church experience, it had promise, a communion of a different sort. No fire and brimstone or preaching of any sort, no doctrine that had to be accepted without question, no "because that's the way it is." The silence would be powerful. And, had it lasted longer than a minute I'm sure it would have been.

After three sessions with the Quakers, it didn't take a brainiac to determine that the wife of one of the new American professors at the U of R would be dominating the gathering, using it as her own personal pulpit, showing her chops. "I'd like to say something," she'd begin. When, in fact, would she not?

Injecting a wonderfully subversive element into her ramblings, was a soft, utterly at peace snoring. It issued from a rumpled little guy in a tweed jacket who, but for a face that said forty or fifty, might well have been a tousle-haired twelve-year-old impersonating an adult. It proved a delightful antidote to the enveloping solemnity, particularly when his nicely timed bass notes punctuated, to her obvious annoyance, the monotone epiphanies of the professor's wife. Whereupon the entire room, save one, would be delivered.

This, I discovered, was Dunc Blewett. I had taken note of him before the meeting, before I was told who he was, because he had seemed so relaxed and easygoing. His expression ranged from a smile to a grin, even managing to project mirth while snoozing. He was not at all as I had imagined. At five six he was neither tall nor imposing. If he had a professorial air it was of the absent-minded, much-beloved sort from a different era. Dunc was, I suppose, one of the earliest acid gurus yet he didn't preach so much as ramble on — often incomprehensibly — to an alarmed body of straightlaced students in his Psych 100 classes. Whether you understood him or not, there was never any doubt that, what he was saying was positive and all-inclusive. When you parted company from Dunc, it was as a co-conspirator in a cosmic revolution whose main objective appeared to be to infect society with a sense of joy. He had a permanent twinkle in his eye. I could find no fault with his mission.

Still, I resisted the inner circle. There would be no gurus for me, no matter how benign. But I liked Dunc and I felt way better about him and about my friends — of whom I had felt protective — being part of his group. Polarity was becoming a societal norm. There was much choosing of sides and unsolicited declarations of where one stood. Some people meant Dunc harm. In that regard you could count me on his side. So, when a loud New Yorker appeared out of nowhere to reside in Dunc's orbit I became wary. Who was this guy?

Anything or anyone remotely exotic stands out on the prairie. Bank robbery was not a popular crime. Where are you going to run? Where will you hide? Small populations divided by vast expanses and connected by thin, grey ribbons of highway don't provide much cover. Even without the abrasive New York accent Bob Ochshorn would have stuck out. It would have been easier to hide an elephant in a flock of sheep. The natural order of things, such as long winters and a certain Slavic melancholy, encourages prairie folk to turn their personal flames lower. Flamboyance, while occasionally triumphant if you're just passing through, can, if it lingers, stick a burr under a lot of saddles.

Ochshorn skipped the grace period. He was irritating from the start, having long since realized that there would be many drawing rooms to which he would never be invited, and that he probably wouldn't enjoy it much if he were. Soft-bodied, balding, and powerful, he looked like a distant cousin of the comic Myron Cohen, and had the air of a stand-up performer who loved to bait hecklers. Had he a tattoo, it would have said: "Don't Fuck With Me." And yet, in his obvious effort to be accepted within a group of young adults a decade younger than he, Dunc's group, one could detect a faint whiff of vulnerability.

One of the prevalent theories of the time was that the phone company was plotting to take over the world. It was fantastic, one of those things that was believed and disbelieved all at the same time. (Would we have worried more — or less — if we could have flashed forward to the present day?) Ma Bell, the phone company, was part of an establishment coming under increased suspicion, not liked, not trusted. So it was not untoward to think that Ochshorn might be CIA when he suddenly appeared in 1966 and signed up for Dunc Blewett's class. For sure they were among us. Ochshorn spent a lot of time with Dunc, dropped a ton of acid, and hung with the campus lefties and arts community.

I ran into Dunc one day and I asked him: "Do you trust this Ochshorn guy?"

"Well," says Dunc, grinning widely as usual, "I figure it's the only way to keep him on our side."

It was the dawning, as well, of the age of No Shirt, No Shoes, No Service. Space was needed for people who didn't want to go to the bar and who were increasingly being harassed by staff and owners at coffee shops. So, Ochshorn converted an old second-floor office into a drop-in centre. The building owners got wind of this and evicted them. He then found another location and rebuilt, becoming a hero to a new constituency. However, questions persisted. Somehow it had been discovered that Ochshorn had been, or still was, a captain in the U.S. Army. Everyone knew the army was interested in LSD as a weapon. This looked bad for Bob.

On an evening where some were muttering at a party, ready to get the tar and feathers and run him out of town, Ochshorn arrived with a stunning blue-eyed blonde in the Grace Kelly mold, softened and made more accessible with touches of Sandy Dennis. She was warm, funny, beautifully dressed and had a smile that made Mona Lisa look surly.

"I'd like you all to meet my wife, Anne," he said coyly, almost humbly, the bastard. He knew full well her effect, and that she was genuine, unassailable, and provided him with an acceptance that would be harder won on his own. "She's a Toronto girl," he added as a clincher. She was irresistible, and one of our own. He was in. Was Ochshorn CIA? Who cares, we all thought. Even the women.

On the Thanksgiving long weekend, on a Friday afternoon, Ochshorn took a sledgehammer to Lori McKay's living room wall and proceeded to convert an unused carport into a slick, fully drywalled, insulated, wall-to-wall carpeted addition that looked better than the rest of the house. He told us it would be finished in time to watch the football game on Monday afternoon.

"Whaddya think?" he asked rhetorically, a wicked yer-lucky-I-love-ya smile playing at the corners of his mouth, as we settled in for the opening kickoff. Even those of us who had been pressed into service were impressed. And that was Ochshorn's trick — how he made his numerous fortunes — the perfect application of focus, untiring energy, and ability to mobilize others to get the job done. Somehow he would also contrive to lose everything periodically just so he could start up all over again. He had apparently been broke and just resting in Regina — rest being a relative term. He was serious about acid and was determined that Dunc should write a book about it, which he did. It was called *Frontiers of Being*.

Leonard Cohen was on tour and booked into one of the lecture halls at the university. It was an afternoon gig and I played hooky from work to attend. He was not just my hero as a poet. He was everybody's hero, and the fact that he would be right here, in Regina, was huge. I had a paperback copy of his novel, *The Favourite Game*, and had made a new cover for it since the original was pretty tacky and I was inclined to do that sort of thing if I liked a book. Now he was a singer, too.

Clint, who was the editor of the *Carillon*, the student newspaper, had gotten a call from a publicist in Winnipeg asking if he'd like to do an interview with Leonard Cohen. Clint and a couple of *Carillon* staffers who were real fans — Clint claims to have been somewhat vague as to who Cohen was — traipsed down to the old Drake Hotel in Regina. "Things very quickly became Leonard Cohenish, then he sang and I was totally blown away," Clint said. The subject of LSD came up and Clint told Leonard there was a local professor, Dunc Blewett, who had dropped acid hundreds of times, asking would he like to meet him. Yes. So, the night before his concert, Leonard Cohen arrived at a hastily convened soirée at Clint and Linda's. He presented Clint with a scroll. "Never come to a stranger's house without bearing a gift," he advised, with a big smile. It was a calendar from a Chinese restaurant.

Clint introduced me. Many people feel, when meeting their heroes, that something passes between them. I was no different. He was quickly surrounded, however, not being just my hero, and I ended up on the sidelines. When Dunc arrived and was presented to Cohen they wandered off to conspire in an ornate alcove of the old house, still grand despite years of being rented out to students. The emperor and sage conferred with much laughter whilst their faithful subjects cavorted to *Rubber Soul*. As was often the case, I left to relieve the babysitter while Degen stayed behind. It was disappointing not to have spent more time with Cohen but I would see more of him at his concert the next afternoon. I was curious to hear him sing.

It was magic.

A few years later, Dorrie Pelletier told me about the night she and Wilfred had gone to a Judy Garland concert in Detroit. The first half had been pretty much what people had expected, which is to say, great. After the intermission, the house lights dimmed and a single spotlight illuminated Judy as she emerged from the wings, without sequins or glitter, wearing only a simple dressing gown. She walked slowly to the edge of the stage and sat, her feet dangling over the orchestra pit. The murmuring crowd fell silent with the first aching notes of "Cry Me A River." People listened, spellbound, great lumps rising in their throats, eyes brimming with tears. I'll cry for you, Judy.

"It was so intimate," said Dorrie. "You felt like you could reach out and touch her, and that she was singing just for you." A campus lecture theatre is perhaps not the best venue for a troubadour, but the first thing Leonard Cohen did, without saying so much as a word, was to light several sticks of incense and pass them to people in the crowd. It was as unusual as Judy performing in a dressing gown. Incense was becoming a ceremonial part of the new order massing on the fringe. The whiff of sandalwood transported us away from the university as the lights were banked low. Just like that, an intimacy had been created. We were already in his hands when he began to sing. I had come, without knowing it, to hear "Suzanne" and have tea and oranges brought all the way from China. I was mesmerized. At the end of the concert, there was a stunned silence for two heartbeats or so before the place went wild. Had he nodded to me in recognition?

That evening, Clint, Linda, Degen, and I were garbling our accounts of the Cohen event to Morgan and Norma, who were leaving town, having been hired to do an art outreach program out of the Weyburn library. We had gathered at our house, unknowingly for the last time as a group, to celebrate. None of us drank much so we were high on herbal tea and each other's company. Around eleven, a knock at the door produced Dunc Blewett, all smiles as usual. Out of the night behind him, Leonard Cohen emerged. Nice touch.

"We are travellers seeking refuge," said Dunc. "May we come in?"

"Please, be welcome." I imitated Dunc's comic formality, bowing, throwing open the door to my caravan.

Had I experienced acid I would have known that our house was an ideal place for such travellers to find comfort. At an altitude of two thousand feet, Regina sits flat on the prairie. There are no hills. If it's of a mind, the wind blusters unimpeded through empty streets, kicking up dust and grit. It is not uncommon to see a tumbleweed lurch drunkenly through a downtown intersection, not bothering to wait for the light.

If you had just come from a second-rate hotel room not all that far from the tracks, the soft light from our living room window would have shone like a beacon. You would have perhaps shivered on the steps waiting for an answer to your knock, anticipating and receiving warmth. Our fireplace, a sculpted, white, stuccoed beauty with built-in shelves and cedar mantel, and banked low with crackling birch, promised cheer. There was art on the walls, handmade lamps, old sticks of furniture covered with East Indian bedspreads in reds and oranges, a jumble of mismatched cushions, a fraying wicker rocker no longer wanted at the cottage, one runner secured with tape, and Bach playing softly on the stereo. Three smart and beautiful women in their early twenties sat, all Gemini's and, like their doltish consorts, each a vessel of hope and good intentions. Be welcome indeed, friends.

In this room, this world, it was perfectly normal to have Leonard Cohen show up on your doorstep, to feed him tea and oranges that came all the way from the co-op. For one brief moment, however, it would have been a toss-up as to whose pupils were more dilated — the six of us who were amazed, or the two who were soaring on the wings of LSD. Not that we knew they were tripping — not that I knew. Clint and Linda, knowing Dunc as they did, and having tried it themselves, would have at least suspected.

Very quickly, perhaps surreally, we bonded as a group, our two new members inheriting and enhancing the peaceful feeling that had existed the entire evening.

Dunc radiated glee and goodwill like a pot-bellied stove, babbling delightful nonsense. Leonard talked to each of us in turn, drawing us out. We knew who he was, now he knew a little of us. We were getting stoned off their vibes, not uncommon in the presence of acid-takers. Upstairs, Tauno, all of two, laughed in his sleep.

Spying Degen's nylon-stringed guitar, Leonard politely asked, as musicians will, might he try it? Of course, will you sing for us? Perhaps in a while, I need to feel it out first. He took it around the corner and halfway up the stairs where he sat and played. Degen followed shortly, sitting at the foot of the stairs at a private concert of her own. "Suzanne takes you down . . ."

If you have a picnic you've got to have ants, Ochshorn's cue to pound at the front door. He was wild eyed, agitated — not his usual self, the suave mover of mountains before lunch. He seemed a trifle miffed with Dunc. From that, I had the impression that the acid session was supposed to have been a threesome, or even had been until some parting of the ways. The music from the stairwell drew Ochshorn to his target. He had the air of a skeptic informed by jealousy and was out to expose Cohen as a fraud. Degen came back into the living room, throwing me a look. She was not pleased, having her moment stolen like that. I shrugged, what can I do?

Leonard continued to sing, then you could hear low talking for a while. In the living room Dunc was conducting what he called "sermons." This consisted of him shutting his eyes and miming facial expressions of what he felt was the essence of someone you knew — non-verbal impersonations, the object being to guess who it was. He had been doing Ochshorn — we had guessed immediately — who appeared much calmer when he and Leonard rejoined our company, but not totally won over. Out of the blue, Leonard asked Ochshorn if he had ever run across a book called *God's Man?*

He was startled by the question, blinking furiously, holding hard to a frozen grin. Clearly amazed, he asked, "You know *God's Man*"? From their conversation we discerned that *God's Man* is what is now called a graphic novel, one of the first, from sometime in the first half of the twentieth century. In a hundred odd pages a series of linocuts or woodcuts tell the story of an innocent young man corrupted by greed, envy and lust — and what transpires as a result. There is no text, but by the pair's accounts the stark illustrations were powerful enough to sear themselves forever into the brain of a thirteen-year-old. It was the first time either of them had run into anyone else that knew of it. They talked of the book as old friends might have recalled a fishing trip, lingering on this image or that. Although we weren't sure as to the nature of the conflict between the two, it was apparent that Cohen had, by being the genuine article, passed a difficult muster from a man not used to losing, or being wrong. Ochshorn left as abruptly as he had come, this time as a man who needed some time alone.

At two or three in the morning — time was elusive and our living room had become like a comfortable, shared campsite where people wandered in and out on their way to the kitchen or bathroom — I found myself in the basement working at a rickety little table saw I had picked up for twenty bucks, sawing a short piece of quarter-inch cedar. It didn't strike me as being bizarre, although I suppose it was. At the time, I had been making small wooden boxes with lids, crudely, and giving them to my friends. Leonard had admired the one I had just given to Morgan and Norma so I decided to make one for him.

The idea of these boxes was certainly not the finished product. They were roughly sanded, sloppily put together, unfinished, and unique in that no two saw cuts were alike — although the lids all fit perfectly. In my mind their value was that they were something I had made with my hands for a particular person, my version of primitive art, wooden poems. It was just a notion.

Earlier, I had shown Leonard the cover I had fashioned for *The Favourite Game*, a girl in the wind, long black hair blowing. He was pleased. I had declined to show him my series of sewer poems, feeling too humble. He didn't press it. The cedar box would have to do. I heard him come down the stairs while I was gluing the last bit. I looked up and he was standing in front of me.

"I made this for you but you can't have it for twenty minutes. The glue has to set."

"It's beautiful."

He looked at me silently. His eyes were big, his expression loving. I felt no discomfort. We held each other's gaze, having some sort of conversation without words. He smiled.

"Have you tried acid?"

"No. Not yet."

"You have to. Especially you."

I didn't know what to say.

"It's important. We have to see these things. We need to see the world this way."

"Okay."

"People like you and me . . . it's important that we share. Our help is needed. We have a duty. The people upstairs are important. We are needed. Will you help?"

I could barely croak out a "yes."

We embraced. Now, there are a number of men, old friends, with whom I share hugs when we meet, usually after a long absence. Then, the only other time I could recall having embraced a man was the time my father had broken my cheap guitar over a chair-back — I had provoked him by verbally defending my mother, whereupon we both collapsed in great wracking sobs in each other's arms, with my dad saying, "I'm sorry, I'm sorry." In the cluttered basement, lit by a bare bulb, standing in fresh sawdust, Leonard and I clasped our arms stoutly around one another, warmed and full of the proper emotion. I was almost overcome for the joy of it.

"Shall we go up?"

"Yes."

It had not occurred to me that to someone upstairs, particularly if sensitized by LSD, my little saw might well have sounded like a scream of anguish. No matter. It had stopped.

"You must let me know how it goes when you drop acid," Leonard said on the way back to the living room. "I'd be interested to hear what you experienced."

"I'll tell you."

"Good."

One thing I discovered in the early days of acid was that it was difficult not to express a missionary zeal. You wanted others to feel as you had felt, to see as you had seen, to be liberated, to experience what could scarcely be described as the paradise that resided within. It *was* important. The world could be a better place. The term "recreational drug" had not yet been invented. If it had, the thought of applying it to LSD would be absurd, except in a truer meaning — as re-creation.

We sat as a group until morning, announced by a chirping Tauno unaccustomed at having anything more than one sleepy adult for company, let alone a whole roomful. He could not yet talk in what we call English but nevertheless chatted away in a language of his own device, conveying to us that he was delighted with such a good turnout for the day.

It was decided that we would all have breakfast at Smitty's Pancake House. We sat at an enormous round table. Dunc beamed throughout the meal, after which he offered cigars all around. Only Leonard took him up on it.

"Ahhh," sighed Dunc, twinkling as he fired up a match. "This puts an entirely different light on things." The two travellers collapsed in laughter.

Several weeks after Cohen's visit, I finally took the pill Anweiler had given me. I had been very afraid. The prospect of losing control didn't appeal to me. Not that I had been doing such a great job of being "in control." Help was needed. Appropriately, it had been a Saturday afternoon, the day I was born. I would have preferred to be fair of face like Monday, or to have Tuesday's grace, but Saturday's child must work for a living, something that had always seemed ironic in my case. By then I had had several jobs, enough to know that I would always hate going to work, and being at work. From the beginning, the entire concept had struck me as being such a crock of shit. School, too. There had to be a better way. Nevertheless, during the week I wore ties and wrote copy. At night I'd put my old Underwood on the plywood table, rattling, clacking, and wobbling out words of a more intimate nature. Always, I'd be thinking furiously in the back of my mind. Why hadn't I shown my poems to Cohen? Because they weren't good enough, and written by a fraud? At least, as promised, I had tried LSD.

My second or third trip also took place on a Saturday afternoon. I lay flat on my back upstairs, on top of the bed. Tauno clambered up and lay beside me. He folded his hands across his stomach as I had done. His head was on my pillow and he was yakking away in that language of his, telling a story as he might have seen me do. He had all the inflections and pauses of a storyteller. As his tale reached a conclusion, and by now we were both tuned into one another, he moved his head to face me at the same time I was turning toward him. Our noses and foreheads touched just as he fired off his punch line. I found myself staring into a very merry pair of large brown eyes that were staring back at me. We pushed our noses closer and opened our eyes wider, making a game of it. Simultaneously we exploded into a huge laugh. It felt like the top of my head had blown off. A rush of good feeling washed over me like a wave. Even if I had known how soon we would lose one another it could not have been a more precious moment.

Everything was eroding — not slow and steady with perhaps some dignity, like rust. It was more like a school of piranha on a floundering buffalo. The storyline could have been so simple: a young man with a shaky beginning gets married, has a child, lands a decent job, a writing job with room to advance, and, despite the odd setback here and there, advances. May your fields be free of rocks and your furrows straight.

Trouble was brewing at work. It was not the usual sort, of feeling like the steer end of an electric prod. I knew it was a good job, a great job. Any fool who had ever split limestone in a meadow with a sledgehammer knew that . . . or shovelled frozen fish into bins, or hauled garbage, or filled and folded until called upon to tally, ring, and wrap. My boss and mentor, who, never knowing for sure whether it was Alec or Alex, I always called Mr. Cameron, was due to retire shortly. Slouching with undisguised impatience in the wings, his successor, the assistant director of publicity, was waiting to get even for my calling him merely by his first name. The assistant director had written a play once that had not been produced. This made him bitter and therefore dangerous. Taking heed, I kept a low profile by spending more time in the dusty basement archives where I picked out all the purple kernels from the ergot-infested rye samples. You never know.

It hadn't occurred to me that I might appear as something of a menace. I spent almost two hours inhabiting the short block, pacing back and forth on a grey afternoon, huddling in doorways during intermittent bursts of rain. All the while, I watched the second-floor window with a smouldering intensity. Once, I saw a blonde girl looking out. I imagined her to be beautiful, despite the watery lack of definition. She seemed to see me looking up and withdrew quickly, the wet pane fading to glistening black. There might have been someone else in the frame as well, a man, standing back in the shadows. All hope of seeing if it was him was obliterated by another downpour. What had I been thinking — that no one would notice? Aside from an old lady with a battered, black parapluie I had been the only thing moving in an otherwise deserted street. I was hoping that perhaps he would deliver me by stepping out on his way for a walk, or a pack of cigarettes at the dépanneur. I wouldn't be forced to knock, to be bold, to take a chance.

Who would have thought that my indecision — unresolved,

stopping in mid-step, spinning around to quit the madness and walk away, then, in an instant, resolved again, turning slowly, reluctantly back toward the target — gave me the appearance of a lunatic alternately stalking and retreating from demons. Nor did I consider that this might not be the first time someone had waited, perhaps in hope, perhaps in ambush, bearding the lion in his den. A vicious poet, having been too long stranded in Winnipeg. A jealous lover. A desperate fan. It hadn't occurred to me that, after the first hour, having gone for a brisk walk to a nearby greasy spoon for a few minutes of coffee and warmth, that someone might have glanced out the window and said, "My God, he's back, should we call the police?"

In the end I had to retrieve at least some of my effort. I had to complete the mission. I had to be able to pass a mirror or a darkened shop window without having to look down and away in disgust. My friends would give me leave, find excuses, knowing I would torture myself far more than they ever could. What was I doing here? Why had I set up this impossible event? Worse, why had I told everyone? The only way out was to do the job.

In a scenario that once again confirmed that I would never succeed in door-to-door sales, I knocked softly, barely compressing the air between my knuckles and the wood. No fair bolting. No saying you tried but, alas, no one was at home. First, a proper knock and a proper wait, *then* you may take off. The door opened before I had a chance to produce a louder summons. It was as if he had anticipated my being there, as if he had seen my final approach and hurried stealthily down the stairs to beat me to the punch.

The door hadn't just opened either — it flew open aggressively, stopping abruptly about a foot into its swing. A dark-haired guy in jeans and a khaki shirt stood there, sizing me up. He was about my size. Behind him was a dog, the black snout and alert ears of a large German shepherd — neutral but intently staring — head slightly tilted, poised on the cusp, ready to stand down or attack. The guy saw me take in the dog, maybe my Adam's apple bob. Perhaps I was not dangerous.

"Yes?" His eyebrows arched, plowing furrows into his forehead.

This was not how it was supposed to go. I had gone over the moment on the train, practising variations on a theme. First, I would talk about acid, saying, "You were right." Or, "I'm glad you convinced me to try it." Then, "Oh, by the way, I brought some of my poems if you'd care to see them." Lame, but how else does one do these things? "Dunc sends his regards." When, in fact, Dunc had not. Besides, it implied that I was riding on his coattails, that I had nothing of my own. Humour, possibly, being ever close at hand. I could key off the improbable form Degen's flirtation had taken after Ochshorn had stolen her moment.

Emerging out of the archetypal Teutonic mists — or possibly she had some Celtic blood — was her challenge to arm-wrestle our country's finest poet. I could crack, "Degen wants a rematch." Then, realizing that perhaps, weak from travel or hunger, or being at peace and lacking a warrior's resolve, he had been in dead earnest for the several strenuous minutes it had taken to best her. It might have been a difficult contest, not an enjoyment of contact, an attempt to enter her body via interlocked palms. No, better let that one go. Let him bring it up. But there was no "him." He wasn't at the door. Just this guy and the Alsatian that I would not refer to sardonically, saying, "Nice dog," implying, "Gee, Pal, would you be so in charge without your four-legged friend? Who the fuck are you anyway?"

"Uh, I'm looking for Leonard Cohen. Is he in?" I was matter of fact. No big deal, I do this all the time.

"Do you have an appointment?"

"What?"

"Do you have an appointment with Leonard?"

"An appointment?" My eyes widened, my mouth a sideways oval of incredulity, almost spitting at pronouncing both *p*s, letting him know that I thought this was very uncool. It had not dawned on me, even once, that I might have been the third guy this month, that it had been a slow month. He was unmoved.

"That's right, an appointment."

"I'm here from Regina. He told me to drop in any time." Not precisely correct, but I had convinced myself that it had been implied. For sure it had. I hadn't interpreted his lyrics in a book as an invitation. I hadn't heard him bid me welcome at a performance where I had sat in the third row. He had come to my house and now I was at his. Thus my voice rang true.

"Sorry, he's not around."

Did I detect an element of doubt, a softening? "Is he liable to be here in the next day or so?" Might as well push it.

"He's away right now." He was paying closer attention to me, maybe memorizing my face, seeing what I might do next.

"Too bad." Unfortunately sounding like Holly Golightly saying, "quel bummer." "Well, tell him that Ralph dropped by to say hello. Another time, perhaps." You know, if our schedules permit.

"Sure. Ralph, you say?" Ralph is a funny name. He kept a straight face.

"Ralph," I confirmed gravely.

"Okay." Nodding his head sagely, thoughtfully.

"Thanks." I spun and walked away quickly, before the door could close, before being mocked, before the red flush crept from my neck to my face, before saying, "Nice dog."

"An appointment? My God, Osborne," exclaimed Wilson in sympathy.

"An appointment? Friggin' 'ell, Wack," said Davies in a silly accent to cheer me up. "Who the bloody 'ell does he think he is?" Well, I had to laugh. In his subtle way, Davies was poking fun — not necessarily at me, but certainly at ill-timed, half-assed plans of unfocussed ambition. The three of us had come from similar neighbourhoods. We had all been exposed to the umbrage taken by the dispossessed, coaxed by drink or bitterness, dancing to a tune of shadowy logic. "I'd have been an artist, too, if big shots hadn't blocked my view." Who did I think I was?

"Did I tell you guys how great it is to see you again?"

Summer, 1968

Late one afternoon, all fucked up and wandering through the streets of Montréal, I bumped into Graham McKean. It was the second time I had run into him that summer and, improbably, he was sober — as he almost had been a few weeks before. Then, he was just beginning a day of drink at the Swiss Hut and to say he was almost sober would be perhaps putting too fine an edge on it. He was cogent and reasonably lucid, although one could detect that he was sitting on a greased toboggan and pointed downhill.

You can see Graham about twelve minutes into the film *Ladies and Gentlemen, Mr. Leonard Cohen.* Leonard has just walked into The Bistro and offers to buy. Graham orders a double cognac, pushing. He rants about having been cut off and ignores the sweet girl beside him, who has attached herself to something dangerous. He really had been a promising musician and had been coasting on that for some time. But Graham was one of these guys who, with their first drink, seemingly transform in front of your eyes from Jekyll into Hyde. He was also, I had discovered, a New Brunswicker, which, oddly, counted for something with me, and from a genteel family no less. He had, when in his cups, what is called a gravelly voice but, in reality, is more like a hacksaw cutting through tin. It's a hoarse, desperate kind of sound that sprouts up like a cactus in a pansy patch in taverns around the world. Graham was just coming into his voice that afternoon at the Hut when he squeezed into our booth.

"God spoke to me the other day," Graham said. "And he asked

me, Graham, do you speak bullshit? So I said to God, I ought to, Pops, because you taught me."

It had the air of a scripted quote, one he used to cadge beer from the novices. It went nowhere with Tony and Wilson, who had brought me there to settle me down. I had been packing a big load that had started to unravel. As a testament as to how far gone I was, I bought Graham a quart of Trois X for at least making the attempt. The waiter hadn't recognized him or he might well have been asked to leave. As it was, he looked furtively around the room every minute or so. I had once been sceptical until Tony confirmed that Graham was indeed an old friend of Leonard Cohen's, or at least an acquaintance of some standing. Even so, I thought Graham was stretching it a bit when he said he was on the way to the airport to meet Leonard. Somehow the story came out about my visit to Leonard's house.

"Fuck, a German shepherd, eh? I think I know who that was. Well, I'll get to the bottom of that."

Sure you will, Graham. And might I buy you another?

That next time I ran into Graham, several weeks later on Ste-Catherine St. outside of Dunn's Delicatessen, I was still lost in my head. I had been to Regina and back. When I had first arrived in Montréal in mid-May it was to spend the summer writing, but I was guilty of artifice here — on two counts if you include the writing.

Secretly, after a winter of clandestine meetings, Lee-Ann, a Regina girl of whom I had become greatly enamoured was to meet up with me in Montréal. Alone on the train, I began to have doubts around Chapleau or Marathon or some such place. My thought processes were suspect and I experienced a surge of fear — terror, in fact. What was I doing? True, I had had it with Degen and all the attendant bullshit — a mutually shared sentiment by all accounts since she had spent the night of my early-morning departure dancing cheek-to-cheek with an older guy of thirty-five who worked for the National Film Board in Montréal. It must have been like shooting fish in a barrel for him. But this sneaking around business didn't feel quite right. It was a sly way to hedge my bets. I got to thinking about all that and phoned the minute I arrived in Montréal to say that I was on the way back, that we needed to discuss some things. She informed me that things were beyond talking, having become quite close with film board guy. Mine had not been the only clandestine activity that spring. I, the doer, got done.

I had not handled it well. The day after I had been in the Swiss Hut, I flew back to Regina. These things are nearly always messy and it seems I had made it incumbent upon myself to provide the sticky emotional bits as a foil to her irritatingly calm, smug behaviour. There's a certain type of emotional anguish that comes over people in these situations that is not far from madness. I have mostly observed the phenomenon in other men. It's an indulgence, really, but a nasty one along the lines of self-mutilation. You keep asking why, failing to listen to the answer you already know. One is somewhat ashamed when one comes around, having behaved badly. Following a week or so of wallowing in my own swill, I again took the train back to Montréal, this time with Lee-Ann.

The day before bumping into Graham at Dunn's, a familiar voice called up from the street to the small apartment Lee-Ann and I had been sharing. Degen had come to town, visiting Film Board Guy. I stuck my head out the window and Tauno hollered, "Hi, Ralphie." I had not expected this. He ran to me when I opened the door. He jumped up and wrapped his arms tightly around my neck, as if to let go would be death. He said not a word, keeping his arms locked and his face buried. I took in his familiar little-boy smell, the rough texture of his favourite sweater. We clung to one another for the longest time.

"You look a little down," Graham observed, looking quite spiffy himself and as sober as I had ever seen him. He was all cleaned up. I mumbled something.

"Never mind," he said. "I ran into an old friend of yours. He said to give you this."

Graham handed me a square of paper that had come from a pocket-sized notebook. It had been folded twice. The name "Ralph" was written on the outside. I opened it and read the message. Simply, it said, "Hello, Comrade," and was signed, "Leonard." The timing could not have been better. I felt good. I looked in the distance for a moment and saw another path that perhaps would be more suitable to travel. Graham mysteriously turned down my offer of a beer and continued on his way.

The earth tilted in the fall, once again effecting that mysterious gravitational pull that summons people back to the prairie. It exudes a force and pressure that can take years, and sufficient will, to overcome. The previous winter and spring I had been a teacher in a free school that a group of us had started. We didn't want our children in the school system and my lack of formal education proved irresistible to the hiring committee. All I had to go on was the work of A.S. Neill as described in his book *Summerhill*, an inspiring account of his free school in England. Not knowing what to do has never been an impediment to me leaping blindly into an enterprise. It was the one serious qualification I owned. How else does one learn? This time I got a real job.

I heard about Rochdale College from Clint. I was wearing a shirt with my name on it and mopping floors at the University of Regina on the five p.m. to one a.m. shift. It was winter. It was Saskatchewan. It was cold. Clint and other Regina people were in Toronto. I'd think of them as I was taking the garbage out to the loading platform with a minus-forty-degree wind whipping me into a rigid, chattering thing stiffly clawing for the door back in. Lucky bastards, I thought.

It was a grey time, sort of like being stranded on an ice floe. I'd get home around one-thirty, fall asleep anywhere from four to six, if I was lucky, and wake up at two in the afternoon. After I had bathed, eaten, and changed into my uniform, it would be time to make the ten-block walk to pick up my ride in a car pool of fellow blue-clad custodians. Since everybody I knew was in bed when I got off work, and preoccupied with the tasks of the day when I awakened, I lived a solitary existence. Weekends were only slightly more animated.

At one point I developed a sleeping disorder and was given sleeping pills by the doctor. I was living in a one-room apartment a few blocks up the street from Tauno and his mummy. She appeared to be doing well. For one thing she was getting a lot of attention from the San Diego crowd who had swept into town in the fall to become radical teaching assistants at the U of R — as well as avoiding the draft.

Tauno was, I think, adjusting. One afternoon I left his house after one of our visits. He had been caught up in something that didn't require much from me. I saw, for the first time, that he had to survive regardless, and that he would have to make the kind of choices that kids are sometimes forced into making. I left for work in a black mood, especially when he hadn't even looked up when I said goodbye. He must have sensed my vibe because suddenly he was out on the doorstep hollering, "Ralphie, Ralphie," and when I turned and waved he shouted, "I really like you, Ralphie." I told him I liked him too, and he went back inside. I asked myself, who was taking care of whom?

The pills put me out, but they were interfering with my dream sleep. As a result, I became even more morose and was experiencing feelings that were new to me, at least in the wakened state. I didn't exactly want to harm anyone, but I would sometimes look at an irritating person's throat and wonder what it would be like to bite his or her windpipe. I stopped taking the pills and embraced insomnia.

Big John, the large-bellied, crewcut, Ukrainian foreman of the custodial staff, had given me every dirty job in the book to try and get me to quit. Part of the deal was never learning my name. "Irwin," he'd say, "I got a little job for you. Not pretty, but has to be done." And off I'd go with him to muck out some shit or other, not bothering to tell him, after a few unsuccessful attempts, that my name wasn't Irwin. It was nothing personal with Big John. It's just that my hair was a bit long and I had a beard, which pretty much told him everything he needed to know. He used to sneak up to watch me work, hoping to catch me at something. First, you'd see his belly sticking out from behind a corner, and then the big, black, size-thirteen boots. He'd hide like that for a while, listening. You couldn't miss him. By the time he poked his head out I'd be working away furiously, pretending I'd never noticed him standing there.

After three months I passed probation and became a full-fledged union member. I was now untouchable and got a shirt with my name on it — "Ralph," it proclaimed boldly. Big John, not really all that bad of a guy, knew he had failed. Looking at my new shirt and, more pointedly, my name tag, he said, "Dats not how you spell Irwin," and walked away. Nearing the end of a glorious career, he was saddled with having, on his crew, the only bearded custodial engineer in the province.

As jobs go, it's not all that bad being a janitor. You start out with a dirty floor, sweep it, mop it, wax it, and go over it with a buffer until it shines. You can see the end of your labours, giving you at least some satisfaction in a job well done. There's a short and brutal learning curve figuring out how to balance the buffing machine so it doesn't wrap the cord around your legs and throw you to the floor. The rest is pride. You want your floors looking good. I had my own section off the beaten track in the back halls by the chemistry labs — Big John's final attempt to banish me — which suited me fine. But I wasn't talking to many people. (The secret to invisibility, especially in a university, is to wear a uniform with your name over the pocket. Even though you're asking them to lift their feet, and they comply, nobody will see you.) Nor was I experiencing many hours of daylight. David French was about the only person who ever visited my apartment. I had met him in Montréal through Leslie Gray, Lee-Ann's best friend, who had travelled with us on the train and shared the little apartment with us for a few days. David would come over and maybe show me something he had written. Or we'd talk about writing, each of us dreaming.

Clint, now single like me, was pursuing a film career. Linda was also living in Toronto with a guy named Rick at Rochdale College. When Clint had written to me about Rochdale, shortly after it had opened in the fall, he told me it was a free university, and a totally amazing place. He saw it as a giant beacon calling us all together.

In the way these things happen, I moved to Toronto suddenly, on a whim. I had considered Toronto to be not very interesting, being a Montréal man, but Robert Holmes told me he had had a lot of fun there and wouldn't mind going back. We made a pact, one day at the Sask — the legendary pub in the basement of the Hotel Saskatchewan — that one of us would go secure a beachhead and send for the other. Spring had come and shed enough light to lift me out of my depression. It's a prairie phenomenon. The days get longer, classes end, and everybody who is young and rootless takes off, only to return in the fall and submit to another glacial grind. Lee-Ann and I were sort of not together.

I left by plane to break the cycle and arrived in Toronto on the first of June, 1969. For all I knew, I'd be back in September. Finally, I had taken Dunc Blewett's advice. He said he wanted to send a telegram to everyone he knew. The message would read: "ALL IS DIS-COVERED. FLEE."

Rochdale,
Summer of '69

In great grey slabs of concrete, striated with rows of plate glass, rose Rochdale College — eighteen stories high on the west wing that was set back from the street, and seventeen on the east wing that ran along the sidewalk. The patio created from the offset monoliths — Rochdale's town square — contained a massive bronze figure on a pedestal of a rotund nude, seated cross-legged and hunched forward. Titled *The Unknown Student*, its posterior cheekily pointed toward the street, it faced inward to see all the antics in the front yard, and through the plate glass windows into the Rochdale restaurant.

I had strolled up Spadina from just south of College to meet Clint. I was crashing at Ed Fitzgerald's top-floor, three-storey walkup, across the street from a bar with a palm tree sign lined in neon that proclaimed it to be the El Mocambo. Ed was a Regina filmmaker drawn, like many, to Toronto. Having just arrived from the almost rural simplicity of Regina, and not yet realizing that these places along that stretch of Spadina were considered the epitome of urban cool, I thought it was quite a dump — something of which I had had considerable experience. Nevertheless, I was grateful for the pallet on the worn, dusty, hardwood. In the five or so nights I spent there, I read, by the apocalyptic glow coming from the street and a small, under-watted lamp placed on the floor, Frank Herbert's *Dune* and most of Heinlein's *Stranger in a Strange Land*. I was ever the sucker for the "Christ" story, no matter how badly written.

Waiting for Clint, I felt great. It was muggy; traffic of incredible density whizzed by. The streets roared, buildings hummed, throngs of people gathered at the lights. I used to love this about Montréal, and Toronto seemed to be even busier. Either you like the city or you don't. It had put a bounce in my step. I assessed the building looming above me in the twilight. Like Ed's apartment, it was not quite what I had imagined, but what ever is?

A multiplicity of window coverings with no apparent uniformity of design gave the building a somewhat shabby air. An off-red, faintly striped drape predominated and, I supposed correctly, would have originally covered all the windows. (I would later see this patterned material turn up in the form of sheets, blankets, dresses, ponchos, and, in one case, a pair of pants. These curtains had not so much been rejected but transformed into objects of greater need.) The net effect, with most of the lights on, punctuated by the dark rectangles of unoccupied rooms, was that of a giant Indian corn, or row upon row of Cheshire cat grins with any number of missing teeth.

A steady flow of people in ones and twos and threes, entered and exited at random. Tie-dyed T-shirts, sleeveless vests, denim shirts — with and without beads, spangles, or sequins — and assorted tops of every hue presided over the ubiquitous bell-bottomed jeans. It seems I had been somewhat short sighted in predicting their quick demise, looking, as it did, like some sort of scruffy, unisex navy had landed.

Clint and I entered the restaurant whose 1960s high-tech interior consisted of a maze of galvanized pipe resembling monkey bars in a playground, a long cafeteria counter, and a jukebox. The pipes were set up to accommodate aerated, grey metal benches and glass tabletops between definable aisles. They were sturdy enough, having at least two people swinging from them. One of them, clad only in jeans half-falling off his ass, as if exchanging greetings with

The Unknown Student, was shouting "again?" in three syllables —
"ah-geh-enn?" — to a wasted-looking guy feeding quarters to the
Wurlitzer. He gave the finger without turning around. Maybe a
dozen people were inside at any given time, there being frequent
entering and exiting. Nobody seemed to be buying anything.

"Revolution" began to play. Behind the cafeteria counter, the
lone employee, as denoted by a splotchy apron, shook his head and,
looking up from a book, frowned. I understood when it played
again, and then again after that, and again, driving us out to the
street. (By October another Beatles tune had replaced it. I would
learn and come to dread that "Come Together" as if it were possible
— would play every time I set foot in the restaurant. It had become
an anthem for speeders who hung out all day plugging the box.) We
had learned one thing, there was to be an important council
meeting the next afternoon. Elections were to be held.

"You have to see that," Clint said.

"So far, I'm not impressed, my dear chap."

"Nonsense. It's theatre at its finest."

In truth, I was feeling a little disappointed. I had made the mistake of having expectations.

Saturday afternoon matinees at the "Bughouse" came to mind
at the council meeting. Popcorn throwing, hair pulling, loud whispering, and the ingress and egress of groups of fellow kids changing
seats, had actually been more civilized affairs. Admittedly, there
were no stern-faced ushers with flashlights to impose an order of
sorts. And I was an outsider not privy to the sensibilities of the
flock, much as an adult would have been at the Saturday double
bills. But I was reminded of performances ascribed to the original
Globe Theatre, replete with boos, hisses, catcalls — everything but
projectiles of fruit. Put everyone in codpieces and conical hats and
it would have been a scene out of Breughel.

From what I could gather, with help from Clint, this was a piv-
otal moment. A group of reformers, led by a bushy black-bearded,
bespectacled A-type in the striped pants, puffy shirt, and black hat

of a pirate, was in the process of throwing the current rascals out of office. Standing beside him on stage was a frizzy-haired, red-headed guy with the type of wispy beard in which each whisker could be seen individually. He had the disdainful sneer of campus radicals everywhere and, though no doubt smarter than everyone, appeared to lack the necessary diplomacy and tact required for leadership. He was clearly of the breed that has a sufficient taste for power, and the wiles with which to achieve it, to become an éminence grise. They look awkward in the light, as he did. The duo, John Bradford and Paul Evitts respectively, had themselves been the rascals in power prior to having resigned in favour of the current lot who were now being swept out in a fervour of reform.

Accusations peppered the air like grass from a mower. Rants, occasionally encouraged, were shouted down after a certain length of time had been breached. Hoots of derision, cheers, and cries of "shame," vied for attention with the numerous calls for order. One couple danced throughout, their principal move appearing to be the do-si-do of square dance fame. Clint and I endured the brief speeches by the candidates but left halfway through the election, which was conducted by show of hands. It was tempting to weigh in, apparently being an eligible voter by having the ability to raise my arm, and having the sense of entitlement of being in the room where the election was taking place. You could have taken a wrong turn on your way to the bank and ended up on the winning side of the landslide that brought Bradford and Evitts back into the executive fold. Voter momentum of this magnitude ensured they would have a firm grip on the reigns of power, literally for months.

Ed said to meet him on Bloor St. outside the Royal Conservatory of Music at one sharp. He had only booked the room for an hour. He was there with a cameraman to make a documentary on speed freaks that he would pitch to one of the networks. His subject, Chico, arrived just before two. While Ed and camera guy scrambled around for another room, Chico took pains to explain to me that he was Big Chico, not Little Chico, who, apparently, was running around Yorkville looking to stab some guy. I duly admired a leather article he had proffered, about the size of a saucer, which had a rudimentary horse's head gouged out of it and had been spray-painted metallic silver. Sorry, no, I didn't want to buy it.

It was Chico's art. He was gaunt, dressed in black, hollow cheeked, moustachioed and red eyed. He spoke in short sentence fragments punctuated by the non-word, "bzzst," which occasioned him to jerk his head from side to side as if something very quick had just passed, and passed again. Like an overworked typewriter carriage, he repeated himself over and over until bumped into another groove. Hurry up, Ed.

It was a glorious day. Sunbeams shot into the room overlooking Philosophers' Walk. A muffled French horn puffed through the bars of Handel's *Water Music*. Chico, who had jabbed himself eight times in as many different locales, was having trouble finding a vein to crank up the stuff Ed had given him. "Fuckers have all collapsed. Bzzst." When the horror finally outweighed the humour, I told Eddie to let me know how it turned out. "No rush," I said. We both laughed at the pun.

At my job interview the day before, I had spent five minutes with Stephen van Beek, one of the new council members. It seems that Rochdale had failed every health inspection since it had opened, and was thought to be in danger of being shut down altogether by the city. Could I get the place cleaned up? Absolutely. I was, after all, a professional. When could I start? Is tomorrow all right? Good answer, but lets make it Monday. I had made quite the career move, becoming Rochdale's head of maintenance, just like that. All that remained was to move into the building.

On the top floor of Rochdale, the eighteenth, there was no east wing, just a laundromat tucked behind the east elevators. Looking all the way down Bloor St. to the Danforth and beyond, encompassing Varsity Stadium, the Royal Conservatory of Music, Queen's

Park and much of the University of Toronto, it had, probably, the best view of any laundromat ever built in Canada — a little known fact to all but the initiated.

Opposite the laundromat was an opaque glass door that led to the seven apartments that made up the west wing, also known as the Eighteenth Floor Commune. Like the seventeenth floor, which was operated by the Indian, or, Nishnawbe Institute, a block-rental agreement gave both floors control over tenancy. I had the good fortune to arrive at Rochdale just as Matt Cohen was moving out, leaving someone named Stan Bevington short one roommate. I had heard of Matt because he had published a novel, *Korsonilov*, with the upstart publishing house, Anansi. I had not heard of Coach House Press, which Stan ran, but gathered instantly that it was very highly regarded. It didn't take long to discover that Coach House, and its horde of mindless acid freaks, was in a class all by itself.

Linda Rankin had arranged the whole thing. As with the Beta Apartments in Regina, we were about to become top-floor neighbours again. I had no idea how lucky I had been for her sponsorship until I was well into my residency. I had had to be approved by a quorum of the other residents. At the time, I remembered being somewhat aloof from her companion, Rick Waern. He wasn't Clint, and, as Clint's friend, that was that.

Linda and Rick's Aphrodite (one-bedroom apartment) was the first of three on the south side. Next door to them, Rick's twin sister Brynn Waern, lived with David Humphrey. Seeing Brynn, a psychiatrist clad entirely in leather, roar away from Rochdale on her big BMW motorcycle was an impressive sight. David was an army dentist who operated out of the base at Downsview. The third, last, westernmost apartment on the south side, the one before the door to the exit stairwell was the one I would share with Stan Bevington.

My room — nominally the living room since Stan had the bedroom — was an airy, sun-filled space with a wall-to-wall window overlooking U of T and the downtown skyscrapers. On a clear day you could see across the lake. We shared the tiny kitchen and bathroom, but the large storage closet off the front entrance ended up mostly being mine. Save for a small table and chair, my new room was empty. Matt had left a gigantic poster of a war movie that spilled around a corner from one wall to another. We met when he arrived to collect it several days later. Except for a brief introduction, it was several days before I saw Stan again, a pattern that would prove to be etched in stone.

There were four apartments on the north side, three Aphrodites and a two-bedroom Zeus at the far, western end of the hall that was held by the reclusive Jack Dimond and his wife. In a row, from the entrance door to the Dimond residence, there was Rose Marie Harrop's place that she shared with Stan Troyer; next door lived Martin Wall (Marty) and Rochelle Glazer (Shelley) and, between them and Jack, stood the lair of Jim Garrard and his wife, Susan.

Rose Marie worked at the University of Toronto's Student Advisory Bureau, and lived with the madman, Troyer. The bureau, amongst other things, provided counselling to U of T students and anyone else that needed help. It was run by an amazing man, Farrell Toombs, and was therefore an amazing place. Among the variety of staff — full, part-time, and voluntary — you could sometimes spot Shelley Wagner, a.k.a. Dr. Sheldon Wagner. It was possible to know Shelley for several weeks, as happened to me, without clueing in to the fact that he was actually a medical doctor. That kind of modesty is still rare. Doctors have a way of letting you know they are amongst the chosen ones. The bureau folk were a quasi-subversive group, definitely on the side of students in particular and youth in general.

Marty Wall worked at the U of T as a professor in its psychology department, becoming its chair at a later date. Jack Dimond, one of the Campus Co-op movers and shakers who founded Rochdale, ended up as registrar of the University of Toronto. (Linda Rankin went on to become executive vice president of Telesat, before becoming the first president of wtv, The Women's Network, and current ceo of the Green Channel on digital.) But none of us, especially Rose Marie, Marty, or Jack were aware that, twenty-five years later, during a ceremony in which they were being honoured for providing exemplary service to the university, the three would be identified as being former alumni of Rochdale College. To their delight, this occasioned a hearty cheer from an otherwise appropriately sedate audience.

Back then, however, the cheers were reserved for when Marty got his harpsichord. It was a big deal; none of us had television. Not only do I love the harpsichord, it was also a great excuse to hang around and gape at the stunning and luminous Shelley Glazer who could, with a smile, tie the tongues and paint blush on the faces of any male within a certain radius. That she was one of the most caring and genuinely kind humans on the planet as well as possessing great beauty only deepened the cheek's hue.

I didn't know any of this, of course, prior to moving in but I knew and trusted Linda.

She said, "You're going to love it here. You'll be right at home."

The next day, having secured a mattress and an abandoned wicker chair, I moved into Rochdale. I tried to buy an ounce of grass to celebrate. I also thought I should probably have some on hand, much as you might keep beer in the fridge for unexpected company — Dunc Blewett, for example. Earlier, I had escorted Clint and Dunc past security in the lobby. They were looking for a guy named Troyer, one of my neighbours I had yet to meet — an ex-Reginan who had been one of the first subjects who had tried LSD therapy at the provincial hospital in Weyburn.

One minute Dunc was standing beside us on the elevator, the next he had disappeared, having dropped on all fours to the floor. He was searching for something as perhaps one might for a contact lens, sniffing around like a dog at the park. Apart from his hair, slightly mussed up and curling around his shirt collar, he was dressed more or less normally for a professor. As the elevator lurched its way to the top, people of both sexes got on and off at the various floors, stepping around Dunc and generally paying no more attention to him than if he were a Labrador retriever. No one patted him at least.

I remember feeling a little proud of him at that moment and, if anything, more intrigued. Even after the Leonard Cohen visit I had not sought out Dunc's company. It had been a delight, however, to happen upon him on a dreary Regina street in late winter and join him for a coffee. His supercharged energy and wild talk would totally charm me as door after door opened in my mind. I used to wonder how he could be so positive and happy all the time. I was about to discover, if not the probable cause, at least a viable suspect.

"Aha," he said, picking up a small object as he got to his feet, grinning as only Dunc can grin, like a lovesick Leprechaun. "Somebody give me a match."

I handed him my lighter. He held the flame under a small piece of paper until it began to smoke. Then, pinched between thumb and forefinger, he held it to his lips and sucked in air with a great amount of gusto. He sputtered and coughed and flicked the flattened roll-your-own cigarette butt back onto the floor.

"Damn," he said, his eyes twinkling, "I thought it was a roach."

"Come back this evening," I said, having responded to one of the broadest hints ever. "I should have something by then."

Nothing doing. Despite media reports, it wasn't like you could just go down to the lobby and buy some weed — not then, anyway. That came later. You had to know somebody, or at least what floor to go to. I had so few contacts at that point that I couldn't even find someone to rip me off let alone score. Enter Clint's brother, Kieth, to the rescue. For ten bucks he gave me a foil-wrapped sandy lump roughly the size of my baby fingernail cubed.

"So, this is hashish," I said, holding it to my nose and sniffing delicately. I squeezed it and there was a bit of give, like an extremely hard Kraft caramel. I smelled it again. It had a faint pungency, like pine resin, but overall was fragrant and spicy, and seemed oddly, perhaps archetypally, familiar.

"Red Lebanese," said Kieth, "about three grams. Ten bucks is a really good deal, you know," he added somewhat unnecessarily.

The small bit of reticence he was picking up was more my not knowing quite what to do with it. My only other experience with hash had been two years earlier when Anweiler and a buddy of his had furtively brought some to my place on a wintry Sunday afternoon. It had been a bigger piece but harder, and darker, and had no definable smell. They cut a chunk off, put it in a little pipe on top of a copper screen, applied flame, and we took turns trying to get a hit. The inert lump needed to be relighted for each person, as it kept going out. Even when you got it going you could barely get any smoke at all. I finally gave up and decided right then and there that hashish would never be anything I would seek out. I hear the gods laughing even now.

"Wanna smoke some?" I offered, giving Keith the ten, and hoping to get some hash-smoking tips without seeming like the neophyte I was.

"Nah. Gotta run," said my best friend's kid brother. "I'm jamming with some guys. I play better straight." And off he went to become a rock star.

I lifted the lump out of the tinfoil and smelled it again, a long, slow, olfactory perusal. Its aroma was compelling, particularly after becoming warmed by the heat of my fingers. Again, I sensed a familiarity. It lingered on the edge of consciousness, like a word on the tip of one's tongue, like an old friend of distant memory, like a vestigial organ whose function had once again been rendered necessary. Perhaps it had to do with a resemblance to the incense used in church — not quite like it, but of that family.

How odd, I thought, that my mother's tribe, the Irish Catholics, and my father's tribe, the Anglicans, both had high masses where billowing clouds of perfumed smoke would issue forth from a perforated brass censer swinging on a chain. Frankincense, I assumed, but had never asked. There were far too many black-clad people all too willing to explain everything in the struggle to claim my immortal soul for the one, true religion. And, from what little I had seen of both churches — the orderly pews, the gothic arches, the beatific stained glass Jesuses, the hymns, the missals, the common books of prayer, the stern-faced rows of clean-shaven paragons and solemn ladies in hats, the communion rails, chalices and chasubled priests in the pulpit — this fragrant incense, frankincense, would be the only thing I would keep. All the rest would have to go.

It was the colour of old bricks mixed with a dash of soot. I rolled the hash between my fingers, fondling it until it became warmer, releasing more fragrance. It became malleable to the point where I could slightly alter its shape, softly rounding the edges. Each time I placed it back in the foil, a delicate sniff of my fingertips implored me to pick it up once more. Again and again I'd position it close to my nostrils, taking great, gusty snorts, fascinated by its mystery.

I might have gone on for hours like that but for a knock at the door. Its author was a grey-bearded, middle-aged guy, wearing what looked to be old British army shorts, the kind that flare out dramat-ically like tepee bottoms. He was shod in sandals and, in keeping with the military look, wore a greenish shirt with epaulets that was perforated with BB-sized holes charred around the edges. Hmmm, where had I seen that before? His eyes were slightly glazed and played at being amused. His lips, however, were pursed almost primly. They twitched at length before he spoke.

"Hello," he said, "I'm Stan Troyer, your neighbour from down the hall. Dunc told me I should look you up. Is that hash I see? Well, what are you waiting for, man, lets fire it up. Hippety hop." He had said "man" army style as well, not like a laid back hipster.

"Come in," I stammered to the apparition and then, before I had time to regain my social balance, we were cutting tiny squares off the block of red Lebanese, placing them on the tip of a burning cigarette, and sucking the smoke up through a straw. I was wary of this guy — and you would do well, as I soon discovered, to always be alert around Troyer — but mostly what I remember is laughing my way through the rest of the afternoon. That, and making sure I would have enough hash left over to entertain Dunc.

Troyer told me about how he had met Dunc, and his first acid trip. It was at the Weyburn Mental Institution, about an hour south of Regina. He had been part of a group being treated for alcoholism with LSD therapy.

"They took me into this hospital room," he said, "and strapped me into a cot. The room had a white ceiling, white walls, and a white tiled floor. They even wore white lab coats. I was handed a pill and a glass of water. Even the fucking pill was white. I took it, feeling, naturally, quite apprehensive.

"So, I was lying there, on the white sheets, with my head on the white pillow and they turned on a tape recorder, one of those big reel-to-reel ones, and began asking questions. How did I feel? What was I thinking about now? I had gathered that the point of all this white was to provide an environment that was not distracting, pre-sumably so I could concentrate fully on the questions.

"The tape recorder was a subdued grey, and the spools were clear plastic. But, and here's the damnedest thing, the light in the room was hitting the spools and creating a prism effect. I could see a rainbow spinning off them and splashing every colour of the spec-trum all over the room. It was bloody marvellous. By the time they got to: 'Who are you?' I was gone, really tripping out. 'I'll bet you'd really like to know' or some such thing I said to them, and then I added, 'And, by God, so would I.' I saw they were slightly perturbed by all this, and I wanted to help them, they were so serious and all. But I couldn't. I was laughing too hard."

For nine months, from the day it had first opened, with only seven of eighteen floors reasonably complete, Rochdale College had failed every health inspection conducted by the City of Toronto. There was talk of the city shutting it down. At my interview I had been asked if I could get the place cleaned up. "Of course," I had replied. It was not quite like an equinophobic actor saying he loved horses and could ride dressage to get the part. I had some experi-ence. It was a building, therefore it could be cleaned. All that remained was to do it.

By then, I had heard the stories. The building, designed for a population of 800 students, had been overwhelmed by at least twice that many people. Because it had opened late, many of the original applicants had made other arrangements. The streets at the time were teeming with young people who had left home, voluntarily and otherwise, in search of peace, love, and groovy. A free university where I am my own teacher and my own student? Sign me up. The vacuum that nature abhors soon had a surfeit of bodies piled up to the top of the now more-or-less completed high-rise. There had been a strike by one of the trades and people just moved in around the debris. Every floor was packed, particularly the lower-rent east wing, designed more for communal living than the west-wing apartments.

On almost every floor there was a six-by-eight storage closet beside the elevators. They were dark and almost airless with no windows or electrical outlets, and nothing was ever stored in them. At the height of the population explosion, these were occupied twenty-four hours a day — in shifts. Eight hours would go by and a young couple would politely knock on the door. In a few minutes another couple, with maybe a dog or a cat, would emerge blinking into the light. "Sorry, man, time's up." "Cool." The new couple would punch in for their shift. Below, in the basement and sub-basement, people were living and sleeping in raucously decorated vintage beaters and vans.

These were the crashers, the more enterprising of whom actually lived in some of the Ashrams (multi-unit bedrooms sharing a common bathroom and kitchen/lounge area), Gnostics (two rooms sharing a bath) and the Kafkas (single room and bath). Perhaps at one time there had been intent to pay but, with a collections process that was glacial, and a population as mobile as a raiding party, money from this group did not often find its way to the rental office. Many of the crashers were speed freaks, a particularly volatile and messy group. Swaggering through the masses were the bikers who were quick to sense a market and an opportunity for dominance. They had a hierarchy, rules, and a somewhat wide-ranging sense of purpose. They also had a total lack of respect for a council of students who spent endless amounts of time debating what form structure should take — should there be structure at all.

Bikers were hired to evict the bikers. Crashers were given ultimatums. Speeders were thrown out. The detritus of war piled up beside the normal garbage resulting from plugged garbage chutes, and the excrement untended by pet owners who felt free to not be bothered. Freedom, not license, was an idea slow to be embraced. By the time I had arrived at the end of the school year, the dust had, literally, settled. A thousand people had gone, some with itchy feet — again, literally — and those who were disillusioned. You had to feel sorry for the founders, Dennis Lee in particular, who had had a magnificent idea. But, with Rochdale now only three-quarters full, it was time to start again.

Four guys remained on the cleaning staff, still reeling from the impossibility of it all, and prone to picking their own hours in the absence of consensus. Now they were faced with me looking to put a notch in my gun butt. Only the poet Bob Flanagan was reluctant to cede his independence. I fired him a couple of times to get his attention but instead of coming back to work a third time he chose to take the high road. I liked Flanagan. He was gentle, witty, highly intelligent and sorely missed. Consensus, however, was finally achieved. Robert Holmes, as promised, showed up from Regina and we were in business after adding two more bodies to the crew.

We all had some laughs during the serio-comic janitor seminar I insisted on giving. The buffing machine, previously having been mastered by only one guy who was no longer around, was good for the most laughs. It looks so easy, and it is, provided you learn a little balancing trick. Until you do, the cord is going to wrap itself around your legs and hog-tie you like a dogie. Corrections were also made in mopping techniques, a simple enough adjustment. Squeegee most of the water out before slopping it on the floor, otherwise you'll be all day trying to get it back into the pail. Sweep the mop in even strokes from side to side, not back and forth as if you were at shuffleboard. Use a one-to-one mixture of wax and water to buff out scuff marks with the machine. Oil the rag before using it as a dust mop. These were elementary things.

By the end of our first week we had, marginally and provisionally, passed the city's health inspection. We were as surprised as the civic officials. During the entire time I was at Rochdale, we never failed another. This helped to legitimize the reform movement on council. Politically, and I was woefully naïve and uninformed when it came to politics, for the longest time it also gave me a free ride. What didn't hurt was the fact that, owing to an uncanny ability to be able to spot one another, it took about five minutes for the health inspector — let's call him Norm — and I to discover we were both from New Brunswick. That, alone, might have sufficed.

This, however, was a year or two before Sinsemilla (sin = without; semilla = seeds) showed up from California and revolutionized the marketplace. Most grass was Mexican unless you were lucky enough to get Columbian, for which you gladly paid a small premium. The Mexican stuff was full of seeds and stems and twigs. There were any number of techniques employed to clean one's grass. Troyer, for example, had several and was only too happy to put you to sleep while he explained all of them to you in minute detail. All the methods had a short tedium quotient, leading to what could be summed up as the "aw-fuck-it-that's-good-enough" moment. This impatience to get on with it led to certain inefficiencies. Grass seeds, when heated, explode, wreaking havoc — particularly on newsprint and synthetic fabrics. To the trained eye, those telltale, charred, BB-sized holes in Norm's polyester shirt, provided a wealth of information.

He saw me looking at those little seed burns and grinned; I knew we'd be able to work with this guy. Not that he laid down and died, but he was friendly, well disposed toward us and, seeing that we were making an effort, prepared to cut us some slack. After several months of weekly inspections, I got a phone call from Norm. Our inspection was due that afternoon but he wanted to play golf.

Would it be all right if he flagged us for a couple of minor infrac-
tions and submit a report as if he had been there? Yes. The building
had achieved a state of normalcy that Norm and I could count on.
Soon, the inspections were cut back to every two weeks and then,
finally, once a month.

Todd Ward had requested a meeting on my second day of work,
prior to our first health inspection. He was the new general manager
and, since I had been hired by council and not by him, he wanted
some sort of action plan from me to establish that he was the boss.
He had taken over from Bernie Bomers who, by all accounts, had
been overextended. Bernie — who went on to fame as Bernie-the-
Beanbagger, purveyor of the newly conceived beanbag chairs — was
a frat boy, right wing and conservative, who spoke English with a
Dutch lilt and smiled all the time. He was good natured, Todd was
more brusque. I managed to tune out most of his lecture, beginning
with why it was important that he sat in the middle of the room
with his desk against the wall, and ending with the need for him
and all departments to "interface," the term currently being kicked
around Harvard Business School. Todd really talked the talk. He
gave me homework.

Because we had passed our inspection so quickly, Todd couldn't
really take credit. I ignored the homework and was pretty much left
alone. A small fiefdom was established in which I became thane,
and from which I got a clear look at the innards of bureaucracy. This
and politics became a small but significant part of my education at
Rochdale. Todd left in frustration after six weeks or so, not being
able to get any clear direction from council. I settled into the
second floor maintenance office, sitting behind my desk with the
door open, enjoying the endless parade of freaks going to and from
the various offices, or running up to catch the elevators on the days
they wouldn't descend to the main floor.

I'm not the only one who still has dreams about the Rochdale elevators. They were perfect vehicles for nightmares expressing a range

of emotion from mild anxiety to absolute terror. Jung, especially, would have had a great time interpreting these unconscious moments of being trapped in a box, sliding up and down a shaft, surrounded by sinister forces. There were four of them, arranged two abreast, facing each other across the lobby that separated the east wing from the west. Beneath the surface of their function as transportation — and, almost more importantly, as the principal communications centre for the hive — lurked a deep-seated mechanical malevolence that proved impossible to fully exorcise.

Elevators are delicate, sensitive, and neurotic things requiring constant reassurance. These were ill treated from the beginning and had never worked properly. Normal, acceptable, par for the course operation would be two cars able to function at any given time. Optimum would be two cars working, with a third kicking in and out as whimsy would dictate. Rare would be all four in a mood to transport passengers, regardless of the rate of speed or a predilection to stop at some floors but not others. All four in operation would be duly noted and pointed out eagerly, a sign that perhaps it was an auspicious day. The most common pose in the ground-floor lobby was that of neck craned upward to watch a winking bank of lights ascend and descend erratically until one would break through an invisible barrier to land at one. Cheers were not uncommon. The Otis repairman, Al from Australia, never failed to appear. In fact, after my time, he quit the company and moved into Rochdale to join the maintenance staff. One wonders if some sort of syndrome were not at work here.

Since the elevators were in my jurisdiction I got to hear about some of the more dramatic rescues. People got trapped in them all the time. They'd ring the bell and one of the guys would go up with a special tool that cranked the doors open. Halfway up, the opening would be all light and legs and bent-over faces. From the midpoint down was a black void, a long drop to the bottom which, according to rumour, was not bottomless so much as being a secret passage that led from the elevator shafts. Some of the speeders and marginal

Rochdalians, perpetual hallucinators, and the truly benighted, believed it was aliens who were hijacking the elevators and spiriting people to their hideout in the sub-basement.

On the benefit side, there was no shortage of reading material if you happened to be stuck in a car for longer than you had anticipated. The walls were plastered with messages, notices, advertisements, horoscopes, snippets of philosophy, photos of lost animals, and statements of a deeply religious nature. They were removed every Monday to make room for the new lot. More often than not it was like a carnival ride with the freaks in the car with you instead of on stage. People talked and were friendly, none of this staring at the door until your floor arrived. Etiquette demanded that any joint that was lit in a car had to be passed around. Even if you turned it down, the space was confined enough to give you, after riding for a floor or two, a pretty decent buzz.

However, underneath it all was the darkness in the shafts. Cars full of bodies plunged toward the ground; lights would suddenly shut off and you'd come to a halt, feeling like a blind eel trapped in a milk carton. One sanguine opportunist was miffed at being rescued. He figured he'd be there until morning, making it a great place to crash. Every step into the elevators was a leap of faith. You never knew what would happen, or whether the fates would take human or mechanical form. Each and every one of us had experienced a moment of panic or fear in elevators where the exception would be to have an uneventful journey. The elevators were an inside joke, a bonding element, one of the things that made Rochdale different.

In my first week, I discovered another feature of a society whose members were hardly ever on the same page — the capacity for spontaneous action, almost like a flock of geese. Even as alderman Tony O'Donahue was railing against the unwashed hippie hordes, a group of Christian youth were marching in orderly rows past the building on Bloor St., on their way to a rally at Varsity Stadium. It was a sunny day. The Christians were fresh faced, scrubbed and, since it seemed to matter so much, neatly dressed. Some carried signs or banners proclaiming a variety of virtues. Nearly all of them, good kids one and all, were smiling as they served the Lord. Clint and I were standing amongst the crowd that had poured out of Rochdale to watch a parade that, without quite proclaiming it, was obviously aimed at them, the godless and nihilistic. In an outburst of solidarity, the Rochdalians began to cheer and clap on the sidelines. Many V signs were flashed. Cries of "Love" and "Peace, Brothers and Sisters" issued forth. To their credit, most of the smilers kept smiling. A group of women from the building rushed onto the street with plates of cookies (they had been prepared for a bake sale — not an uncommon event) and pitchers of water for the marchers. To show how innocent some of these kids were, they took the cookies. A few of them were appropriately offended and refused. Christian organizers tried to restore order but it was too late. A large group from Rochdale had joined the march.

The rows were now a bit ragged as they quickened their pace down the street and through the open gates of the stadium. A platform had been set up on the grass where a sombre guy in dark pants, a white shirt, and striped tie spoke into a microphone, welcoming the crusaders. He encouraged them to sit in the stands for the rally. Bringing up the rear was an unruly mob of fifty or so, colourfully attired, long haired and dancing. They were in no mood to sit, instead forming a big circle and dancing around the small stage. Some of the Christians, confused perhaps, or not being able to make out the squawking pleas for order, or not wanting to come to order at all, came down from the stands and joined in. Clint and I, who had marched down the streets, passed on dancing but watched from the stands for half an hour. They were still dancing when we left. I remember feeling very pleased by that demonstration. There had been a vivacious, dark-haired girl, one of the more active dancers, who resembled Olivia Hussey of Romeo and Juliet fame. I had gotten her name and a promise to meet later.

Clark Stewart, in his early twenties, had shoulder-length hair that was about halfway prematurely grey. He was a gentle, intellectual sort of guy with granny glasses and a somewhat distracted air. Clark, one of the original cleaning crew, had been going on about how he had smoked so much hashish that, if anyone were to give him a nickname, it should be "The Brown Stain." Could he, I wonder, tell me where I might get some? Yes. He had a friend who, outraged by the high prices — anywhere from seventy-five to ninety dollars an ounce — had decided to buy a pound and become his own over-head. A neophyte dealer was about to make his first deal with a rookie buyer whose last crumb had gone to a certain professor of psychology from a western university. The moment positively cried out for a discount.

After what seemed like an hour of waiting in my room I began to think he was a no-show. I had fifty dollars of Rick Waern's, Clint's nemesis. Rick, who had been Rochdale's first registrar (whatever that entailed), asked if I could get him half an ounce and had himself arrived at the fifty-dollar figure, pledging more should it be necessary. Clark arrived. His friend should have been here by now. This was almost immediately followed by a knock on the door. A nervous little guy with shortish, recently cut hair and a neatly trimmed moustache, burst into the room, locking the door behind him. He was wearing an untucked Hawaiian shirt that showed a significant bulge in the belt buckle area. There was an almost pubescent odour surrounding him. He was pouring sweat.

"Fucking elevators," he said. "I got stuck in one for fifteen min-utes. All those bodies, the hash warmed up and started to smell. Everybody was kinda sniffing the air and looking around. Jesus. Finally it opened on eight and I just ran up the stairs."

Clark introduced us. The bulge turned out to be an air pistol. "You never know," he said, undoing his belt and fly to get at the package that had been strapped to his inner thigh. That explained the limp and the big pants. I figure if you're going into the dope business you should look at least a little like you could handle yourself. This

guy was a mess. I might have laughed out loud, had I not become mesmerized by the sight of an actual pound of hash. Clark had been
rendered practically cross-eyed with desire. We both asked to touch it.

Dimensionally, it was like a double-thick Fudgesicle, about nine
inches long, three and a half inches wide, encased in a coarse, white,
cotton cloth. Both ends were slightly rounded and puckered like flattened salami. A seductive aroma filled the room. Clark and I took
turns pressing our noses onto the cotton wrapper and inhaling deeply.

"I feel like I could levitate," Clark said.

"Blonde Leb," said Clark's friend, calmer now. He turned to me.
"You want an oh zee, right?" I nodded yes.

He hesitated, thinking about something.

"You wouldn't have a scale would ya?" I shook my head no.

"Clark?" Clark shook his head.

"Fuck." The little guy was starting to lose his composure again.
I looked at Clark and could tell he was as perversely amused as I
was. We kept quiet to see where it would go. His brow was furrowed
for a moment. You could see the idea hit.

"Okay, here's what we do. We measure. This is a pound, right?
So if we cut it in half it'd be a half a pound, see? Except we won't
cut in the middle, we'll just measure it into sixteen and slice an
ounce off the end." His salvaged dignity was then assaulted by a
nagging thought.

"Do you, um, have a ruler?" I nodded yes. I had a tape measure
I had borrowed from Troyer. In fact I could have borrowed a scale
from Troyer, who had everything, but this was more fun.

His relief was evident as he went about making pencil marks on
the wrapper.

"There," he said, pleased, I think. "How does that look?"

I took a moment.

"Well, the ends are rounded. There'd be less hash in those
ones." I said. Clark actually tittered.

"Fuck!" exclaimed his frustrated friend. "I need a scale. Jesus.
Never mind. Here, this is what we do." He drew another line

angrily, increasing the end piece by a sixteenth of an inch. "We'll cut it here and call it an ounce, okay, man?"

I took another moment, more for fun than anything. It looked good to me.

"I'll only charge you fifty-five bucks." There was a take it or leave it quality to his voice. I told him, "Sure, that'll be cool." He calmed down immediately, and then another cloud welled up in his eyes. He turned, wordless, looking at me almost helplessly.

"Hey," I said. "There's an old butcher knife in the kitchen. Why don't we use that?" I saw gratitude.

"That'd be great, man. Could we heat the knife on the stove? They cut better that way."

"Sure, man."

"You're a good guy, man. Sorry about the hassle."

"It's no hassle, man. Thanks for coming over."

He cut the hash evenly along the line, except on a slight bias in my favour. Clark edged forward during the operation to inhale a stray wisp of smoke that had been generated by the heated knife. The bottom part of my "ounce" had ended up wider than the top. He looked at it, shrugged, and handed it over. I put a five of my own with the fifty Rick had given me and gave him the money.

Later, after a short sermon on the necessity of having precision instruments with which to measure, Troyer lent me a small postage scale. Even after trimming the bias, giving the residue to Clark for a finder's fee, the lump of hash weighed in at just over an ounce and a quarter. I cut half an ounce off for Rick, not shorting it too badly, leaving me with a lovely, aromatic chunk of Blonde Lebanese that was so fresh it was slightly sticky to the touch. Quickly, I sawed a smaller piece off and put the main stash away. Troyer knocked at the door to inquire if all was well. I invited him in.

Having grown up during the fifties, I knew how bad I was being by smoking hashish. Most of the fuss centred on marijuana. Juvenile delinquents smoked sticks and bombers (skinny or fat joints, according to one book I had read — terms I have yet to encounter in real life) and it generally was intimated to be the first step on ruin's road. Nor was much distinction made between cannabis and heroin, the two being virtually interchangeable. It was bad, bad, bad. However, my first experience with marijuana, in Montréal, had not seemed like much of anything.

I was twenty, living with Tony and Wilson at the apartment on Atwater. Wilson, still into his mauve period, announced one evening that he was going to Toronto for a day or two. He had come to Canada in his teens when his family had immigrated. It was a well-known fact that, for whatever reason, he hated Toronto.

"Everything all right, mate?" asked Tony.

Wilson said, "Yup."

We knew better than to ask any further. Wilson never explained. The next day he packed a small eggplant-coloured suitcase and left.

Early the following evening, Tony and I sat round our little table. He was on beer two or three, well before the hymn sing. We heard the rapid click of black Wellington heels rushing down the hall, followed by the frantic scratching of a key that couldn't quite find the hole. At last, the door flew open, admitting a breathless Wilson. He slammed it shut, slipped the chain on, staggered three steps to the kitchen, and collapsed into his chair. We stared at him, saying nothing. He looked at me, then Tony, at our smug faces trying not to grin.

"Get stuffed. The pair of you," he said, smiling, quite pleased about something. He reached into the inside pocket of his suit jacket and pulled out a small, much-handled envelope.

"Gentlemen," he said reverently, "meet Miss Mary Jane."

"Who?" I said, slow to get it. Tony, who always got it, chuckled.

"Marijuana, you twit," said Wilson, with mock ferocity.

Wilson placed the envelope on the table and the three of us just stared at it for a while. It had been one of the great moments in my life to date. There I was, a year out of New Brunswick, just having tried garlic for the first time a few months earlier, looking at something impossibly exotic.

Marijuana. The name alone had invoked certain images. In addition to gang kids, ultra-hip, ultra-cool Beats smoked it, and rambled on in wild orgies of poetry. Jazz musicians used it to get high, and played bebop all night long. It was from the world of Kerouac, Ginsberg, Henry Miller, Jean Genet and Nelson Algren, all of whom I had just begun to read. It was then, for the first time, I realized that the underground had been calling to me as Bay Street would to a budding financier. Marijuana, not yet mainstream, was of that subterranean world — mysterious, compelling, and magical. Simple possession of even a pathetically meagre amount, meant jail if you were caught.

Wilson interrupted our private reveries to relate the harrowing tale of buying a nickel bag in Toronto and transporting it by train back to Montréal. Paranoia-induced terror accompanied him every step of the way. Whenever he saw a cop, or even a cop car, his knees turned to water and he could barely walk. Twice, he almost flushed it on the train because he thought the conductor looked at him funny. We had a good laugh, our eyes straying to the envelope, sitting there — practically throbbing — on the table.

"So?" I finally asked, looking at Wilson, and not being able to stand it much longer. "What's it like?"

"Have a look," he said, opening the envelope.

Tony and I nearly bumped heads rushing forward to gawk at a scrawny, brownish-green twig, around which was clustered a slightly darker tangle of dried leaves and seeds.

"I mean, what's it like to smoke?" I asked.

"Dunno," said Wilson. "Never tried it."

Well, who had? Hardly anyone, except for an irritating clique of so-called hipsters that Wilson sometimes hung with. They'd talk about the new group, The Rolling Stones, and vacuum cleaners as metaphors — laughing at things only they found humorous, while spending entire parties in the host's dimly lit bedroom.

Somehow we all knew that it would fall upon me to explore the mysterious. It wasn't just that I could translate Dylan lyrics. I also knew my way around cigarette papers and raw tobacco. So I rolled the "reefer." It hadn't been much more difficult than working with the powdery dregs of old tobacco, except the seeds were bumpy, and a piece of stem kept poking a hole through the paper. Wilson helped, telling me. "For Chrissakes, be careful," and "watch out, it's going to spill." As did Tony, by telling Wilson to stuff it and let me work. Three tries and the job was done. Nonchalantly, I tossed the joint onto the table. We stared at it for a while.

Crossing the line between "good" and "bad" behaviour had, by then, become so logarithmically easy that this new turn posed no impediment whatsoever. My hesitancy, I recall, had been out of concern for my psychic hide. The first time I had taken alcohol — chug-a-lugging a twenty-six of vodka with two other seventeen-year-olds, had been horrific. The world spun around in a most unpleasant manner. I had no control, staggering, falling, and lurching to my feet. There were tears, angry shouts, fist fights, and friendships tainted forever. There was nothing to suppose that smoking dope would be any better. Booze was legal, marijuana wasn't. Shouldn't that have told me something? Apparently not, because soon enough, I had fired it up.

Nothing happened. It was easy to inhale, no big deal at all, Wilson telling me you're supposed to hold the smoke in before exhaling. Okay. Still nothing, the big thrill being the "crack" of seeds exploding, leaving perfectly round holes the size of BBS, charred brown around the edges, in Tony's *Manchester Guardian*, airmail edition.

The taste was unfamiliar, easier to take than tobacco. I remember persevering for a couple of months to get past the nausea induced by the sickly sweet Player's Plain. One had to, to become a smoker, to become a sophisticate. Nothing in this smoke required perseverance. It went down easy. A tad dry, I found myself thinking, with a rather pedestrian bouquet that would not overwhelm one with its presumption. No legs. Well. I guess you'd have to say, considering the subject matter, no wings. I found that funny and laughed out loud.

Wilson and Tony, who weren't in on the joke, were watching me like scientists — curious, concerned. They hadn't smoked, preferring instead to observe.

"Where are your lab coats?" I asked, and laughed again.

"What's happening?" They wanted to know.

"Nothing." I told them. "Not a thing. Zippety doo dah. Nada. Fuck all and a donut." Then, with my eyes bulged out in what I thought was a great Peter Lorre imitation, looking first over my right shoulder and then my left, I hunched forward conspiratorially and hissed, "Less zan nossing. Minus zero." Which I also found inordinately funny.

My mates were barely amused at all. They kept exchanging covert glances, looking puzzled.

"Tell me," I said, "you're at least happy that I'm in such a good mood."

"Oh, we are, we are," they chimed in unison, a little too quickly, a bit too over-solicitously. This got me laughing again. This time they were more relaxed and laughed along with me.

When it became apparent that there would be no grand mal seizure, or coma, or talking in tongues, things resumed a semblance of normality. Tony and Wilson were still watching with clinical interest, but their intensity had eased considerably.

A symptom finally appeared when I got up to go to the bathroom. The floor seemed slanted, sloping away from me. Whatever direction I took, it felt like I was walking downhill, just like when I'd put my father's thick glasses on as a kid. I shared this information with Professor Zook and Doctor Zardoff, after I had taken a quick piss and returned to the kitchen. They seemed more interested in what I had been doing for the half-hour I was gone. I hadn't the faintest idea as to what they were talking about. Sure, I had made a few faces in the mirror but . . . the hell with it. I felt too great to care.

And that was it. I remember being quite disappointed, really. Here was this illicit, naughty, bad boy thing I had done, and all that had happened, I figured, could have been replicated by looking through a chunky lens. Oh well.

Tony sang the hymn, fell silent, and went to bed. Wilson whisked the marijuana away, never to be seen or spoken of again. He put Sketches of Spain on the stereo, tossed me a mauve blanket, and retired to read. I flopped on my couch. Eleven notes into "Concierto de Aranjuez," I hitched a ride, down into the deep, soft, purple folds of dreamland.

Of course I had been stoned, but I had not been aware of it. Because being stoned is a subtle distinction, I thought nothing of it. It hadn't occurred to me that there was anything unusual in finding everything hilarious or, indeed, in observing that I had been exceptionally witty that evening. When you're on, you're on.

This is such a common reaction the first time people get stoned, it's a staple of Middle Eastern folk tales. The apocryphal story is that of a rather serious merchant who berates a friend, demanding to know why he wastes so much time at the baths smoking hashish. What possible use could it be? Well, it being difficult to describe the pleasant experience, the man's friend suggested he try it himself before making any judgement. The merchant, overcome with curiosity, agreed. He gave his friend fifty drachmas for a small quantity and headed out on his own to the baths. He had observed how his friend had done it, and sent the attendant for a pipe. The merchant smoked the hashish and waited. It seemed hotter in the baths, but nothing else appeared unusual. He waited a while, becoming somewhat impatient. He began to feel annoyed, then outright anger. He had been cheated. Not wanting to waste any more time, he set out immediately to give his friend the comeuppance he deserved.

The merchant was not one minute into his journey when he spied his friend. I'll show this fellow that he had been ill advised to trifle with me. After all, he had noted, people in the street have been quick to get out of my way. They can see how angry I am. In high dudgeon he accosted the rascal.

"You, who call yourself a friend, have cheated me," he shouted, shaking his fist.

"Peace, brother," said the friend. "What has upset you so?"

"You know very well that you have sold me a useless piece of dung. I have smoked it, and waited, and nothing has happened."

"Nothing at all?" his friend asked.

"Nothing. I insist that you return the money at once."

"Of course, brother, but would it not be best if we first return to the baths so that you shall have some place to keep it?"

"Whatever do you mean?" asked the merchant. And then, following his friend's eyes, he looked down to discover, horrified, that he was stark naked.

When I finally walked down this road, centuries after the folk tale, I was following in the footsteps of many. Like the merchant, I had taken my time to get there. In the early sixties, when I had first tried marijuana, it was not something to advertise. Maybe your best friends would know and that would be it. By the late sixties, the climate had changed. Psychedelia was in, and had even gone mainstream in movies and song.

The relevant question is how long did it take to become less like the merchant and more like his friend? First, you must want to. Like ducks with water, I would prove a quick study. It helped that Rochdale, an asylum in which I had very quickly become an inmate, was a microcosm in which smoking dope was the norm. It was safe to do that and, therefore, to explore freely the altered state of consciousness that went along with it. One could assume that nearly everyone in the building was stoned, or about to be, or had been, or would like to be.

My fortuitous, blonde, Lebanese acquisition babbled away to me from its hiding place, "Unwrap me, squeeze me, gaze upon my sandy hue, inhale my perfume." I scarce could leave it be and, due to excessive fondling, had to frequently change its creased and crumpled foil garment. When I finally toked up, I could feel the hit as if a switch had been thrown. The light softened as I relaxed. My mind slowed down enough for me to see details that had previously sped by scarcely noticed. It was as if I had gone from driving on a busy expressway to meandering along a country lane. I could see clearly. Whatever problems I had became solvable to the point of hardly mattering. I felt empowered by this clarity of vision. I was on top of it all.

Standing in front of my south-facing wall-to-wall windows, a glimmer of understanding seeped into my consciousness like an old friend. Beyond the backdrop of downtown skyscrapers, the lake stretched out to become the horizon. I could look below at the rooftops and the crowns of trees dipping into the last rays of sun. Pigeons, in perhaps their one graceful gesture, took a final aerial stretch before roosting for the night. If only everyone could see this way.

A group of French writers, artists, and intellectuals in the mid-nineteenth century had formed "Le Club des Hashishiens." I had come upon a reference to it in Montréal. Members of the club, like Verlaine and probably Rimbaud, would eat spoonfuls of a cooked decoction of hashish described as a "greenish jam." They had fantastic visions. Fanciful accounts of their hallucinations — written largely by people in the description business — inspired envy. One would think that either the hashish of the day was far superior to, and more potent than, the varieties we now encounter — or the method of preparation employed a secret step, alas now lost.

A contributing factor might well have been a competitive one, since everyone had been encouraged to share their experiences. These sessions engendered musings such as: "How many angels could dance on the head of a pin?" — which, today, is a more familiar philosophical query. In fact, some of them had seen those very angels and set about counting them, each coming up with a different number. They were artists, after all, who trafficked in imagination. Their approach was also more social than that of their reclusive English confreres, who tended to lone, opium-induced explorations. Was this due to national character or — with British ships returning from the Orient, laden with soporific wares, and Southern France a short hop, as it were, from Morocco — proximity? An amusing debate for le club, n'est-ce pas?

I almost envied their visions. Even on the few occasions I had taken acid, I hadn't even come close to the intricacy of their visual hallucinations. Perhaps it was some sort of "secret of the ages" kind of thing where more intelligent, stronger, taller men were naturally more attuned to the cosmic mystery. In truth, the method I had been using to smoke hashish was in need of a tuneup.

To put approximately one-eighth-inch squares of hash on the end of a cigarette required not only a certain amount of dexterity but they had to be cut exactly the right size for one person. Once started it burned quickly and you had to be ready, bent over with the straw close to the smoke. If the piece was too big it kept burning after you could no longer inhale. A comic sort of gesturing would ensue for the other chap to take the straw and finish it off. Much, if not all, would be lost during this exchange. You could have two straws but that led to other imbalances, cosmic or otherwise. A person could come in a beat or two too soon or, after loosening up after a few tokes, they might forget, having been distracted by the sound of their own voice eulogizing on stray sunbeams. Troyer and I illustrated these failings a number of times, nattering and chastising one another like prickly octogenarians. Accidentally hitting the cigarette and knocking the hash onto the floor or into the ashtray could also provoke a spirited debate. And only the purchase of an Ex-acto scalpel spared me more lectures on the importance of keeping one's knife sharp.

Then there was the accompanying thin plume of smoke from the tobacco itself. It could scarcely be avoided, was harsh, and made the eyes water if you got too close. There were people who were more than willing to try hashish but could not abide tobacco, like a girl from Cleveland I had invited up. For her, I had to form a little ball of hash, stick it on the end of a pin, and apply flame until it started to smoke. Straws weren't necessary for this method, you just held it close to your mouth and inhaled, having frequently to relight the mass. This was even more wasteful than falling asleep at the straw; no better than those head-shop pipes with the copper screens.

A few people had told me that, to save the smoke — the end product of combustion, the active ingredient — a water pipe was best. I had tried it once. There was something about it I could never love. Drawing the smoke through water not only turned it a dirty grey but created an unpleasant odour. What I needed, I thought one evening while staring at an empty, one-pound Maxwell House coffee can, was an air pipe. Bingo. I cut two holes in the translucent plastic lid, opposite one another, close to the edge. Into the larger hole I placed an indented piece of foil that had been perforated with a safety pin. I used masking tape to make it airtight around the edges. A plastic straw was inserted and taped into the smaller hole.

I had observed, on the many occasions a piece had dropped off the tip of a cigarette, that when heated, hashish crumbles between one's fingers like fine, wet sand. So, with more foil I made a tiny spoon, dropped a piece of hash on it and heated it with my lighter from underneath. When it began to smoke I removed it from the spoon and crumbled it into the perforated foil pipe bowl. I sucked through the straw as I lit the hash. Not only did I get a prodigious amount of smoke but I could see it billow into the can, swirl around and stay there. You could still puff on the can after the hash had burnt out. There was little waste, therefore less product per person was required. Eureka! Archimedes could not have been more elated. It sounds simple, but this type of pipe was my invention. I have never seen another like Max, in Rochdale, or anywhere else. Troyer, although enjoying its performance, did not take it well, producing at various times some ridiculous device or other until he gave up and concentrated on blending diverse types of cannabis, attesting to different effects that could be produced. In his mind, perhaps.

In secret laboratories all through the building, a number of mad scientists were on the trail of the perfect toke. It was a sweet, almost innocent time. There were several variations on the "bong" theme, to which, in a way, my pipe was related. One day, as I was sitting in my office, a line snaked by the open doorway. About twenty people were waiting their turn for a hit off a cardboard tube about five feet long with a diameter of six inches or so. Two guys manned the tube bazooka style, one holding it steady on his shoulder and the other keeping it filled with grass and providing ignition. You stepped up and stuck your face into the open end and inhaled. When you created a sufficient vacuum, bazooka guy would open a small air hole and a blast of smoke would smack you in the face. Your knees would then buckle to the accompaniment of cheers.

It's possible that I may have only been the third or fourth reason for people to trek to my room. But, come they did, showing up in ones and twos after the supper hour, and staying until Clint would ask me "Have you even left the building today?" To which I might reply, "Not since lunch at Zumburger," which was just across the street. Sometimes Clint would visit early but, more often than not — since he rarely toked up, he'd come by around ten and haul me off to Palmer's drug store on Bloor St., opposite the entrance to Philosophers' Walk between the ROM and the conservatory.

Palmer's featured an old-fashioned lunch counter of veined green marble and brass, so meticulously maintained that it almost looked new. They served fresh-baked pies, particularly a tart cherry offering that had attained almost legendary status. Late in the evening, the counter would be lined with salivating young supplicants in various mental states, punctuated with senior citizens who knew what good baking was about, all of whom appeared to be in tune with their ecstatic natures. Like most businesses in the area, the folks at Palmer's — not getting any younger themselves — treated the hirsute, beaded, and elderly with benign indifference.

Back in my room with Clint gone home, I'd have a booster toke and sift through the ashes of the day. I had shared my coffee, my view, my music, and my hash — everything, in fact, but the pie.

I had a tremendous desire to share every new thing I had discovered, to have the entire world see as I had seen. That's how good I felt. Nor was this unusual. A lot of people had opened up, sharing what they had experienced as well. It was as if a new religion had sprung up spontaneously. Everyone who was a part of it was a proselyte, hell bent on converting the rest of the world. "I want," as the Beatles sang, "to turn you on." We wanted our parents in on it, our siblings, businessmen, cops, politicians, everyone. Peace would surely follow, children would receive what they needed, while order and good government would reign.

The first time I had seen a guy with long hair up close was in Regina while I was with the Wheat Pool. His name was Desi. He had exceptionally long hair at the time, falling below his shoulders, unrestrained by headband or ponytail. At the time, I was getting a bit of flack at work because of my hair (slightly past my ears) and the way I dressed (black corduroy sports jacket, striped shirt, paisley tie, shiny, light blue pants, and brown shoes). I'd see the odd nudge and wink in the crowd at rural elevator openings as I gathered names for the *Pool Notes* column. Those big city journalists from Regina, eh? But Desi, I had concluded with a total lack of irony, was taking things a bit far. I tried disliking him but he was a very sweet guy, no harm in him whatsoever. He would do things like show up after I got off work and present me with one of two peashooters and a bag of split peas. Next, we'd be running around the front yard in full battle, laughing. I don't remember when he had initially appeared, nor when he stopped coming. He didn't say much, preferring instead to smile, and seemed totally oblivious to the excitement his hair caused.

I thought I spied him tacking up a poster at Rochdale but it was a different guy. So, instead of greeting an old friend to tell him I had finally seen the light on the hair thing, I ended up reading a poster on the wall outside my office. It was an invitation to attend a "What Does It Mean To Be Stoned?" seminar at the Indian Institute, which occupied the seventeenth floor. As a recent convert, I felt almost duty bound to attend. I had met Wilf Pelletier, the institute's director, at the weekly council meetings. He was also, as a mortgage requirement of CMHC, contracted to be a designated resource person to Rochdale College along with the Reverend Ian McKenzie. I had noted that when Wilf spoke, people listened closely to what he had to say. He had been involved with the Company of Young Canadians and was therefore cool, CYC having been highly regarded at the time. He and Ian, an Anglican priest, were each paid a salary of ten thousand dollars a year as well as being members of the governing council.

I had heard Wilf talk about education in regards to the now legendary maple sugar caper. A group of Rochdalians had secured a grant from council to go into the maple syrup business as a fundraiser for the college. This happened a few months before I had arrived but was such a famous fuckup that the debate was still raging. There had been a dearth of organization. The group's initial foray into the woods had been too soon. The trees weren't ready, accommodation had not been totally worked out and they nearly froze. So they returned to the city. By the time the now smaller group made it back to the woods it was too late. Not only that, but of the remaining equipment that had not been stolen or lost, hardly any of it was suitable to the task. Eventually, the dispirited group returned to Rochdale with four gallons of watery stuff they claimed was maple syrup.

The project had been a huge failure. Council money had been wasted. Accusations flew fast and furious. The lone, dissenting voice was Wilf's.

"It was, more than anything, supposed to be an educational project, right?"

"Yes."

"So these guys went north to learn about maple syrup and just about everything that could go wrong went wrong."

"Right."

"They went too soon; they went too late; the equipment wasn't up to the job."

"Yeah."

"See, by doing everything wrong they learned all the things you need to know if you want to collect maple syrup. There's a season for it; this piece of equipment doesn't work because you need this one instead, and so on. It seems to me that these guys learned more about maple syrup than they ever thought possible. Each mistake added to their education. The thing about failure is that you can't have success without it. If you head from A to B in a straight line, see, and everything goes without a hitch, not only have you not learned anything but you've eliminated any number of possible discoveries along the way. It could be you need to get from A to B in a hurry and that's fine, but in terms of education you haven't learned a thing. Nobody in this room knows more about maple syrup than these guys."

Well, amen. I was completely sold. What was blowing me away was the different perspective of failure. I knew a fair bit about that. I had failed at school, at church, at work, at marriage, and at parenthood. I had been to jail, failing as a son and as a role model to my younger brothers. Now, I could maybe have another look at all that with an eye toward redemption. What else has this Pelletier guy got to say?

There were maybe a dozen people at the seminar, but none of them was Wilf. I was disappointed. An older guy was there, seeming to radiate authority, but saying very little. I took a good look at him. He wasn't real old, about mid-fifties, but his longish hair and neatly trimmed beard were absolutely white. He wore blue jeans and a denim shirt, looking, with a straw cowboy hat beside him, like some sort of hip rancher. This was Ted Poole and the seminar was his. He must be some sort of professor like Dunc, I thought. He caught me looking at him and returned my gaze. Before I turned away I had noted a slight twinkle of amusement.

Jay Jordan, a familiar face from Regina, was there. I said hello to her and she laughed hello back. Laughter was her principal mode of communication. Had she been in town long? No, ha ha, she hadn't. Where are you staying? That provoked another bout of hilarity. Right here, she said. At Rochdale? Yes. What floor? Right here. This is going to be my room when the seminar is over. We both found that funny. Jay and Gary Anweiler were a couple, off and on. I didn't ask which it was. She knew a bit about what it meant to be stoned. Things were looking up.

I sat on the floor beside a paunchy little guy with long curly hair who was sporting round, steel-rimmed glasses. He was stretched out, legs crossed, propped up on one shoulder, smiling almost beatifically. We nodded hello. His name was Shelley. Cool, man. Let the seminar begin. Right away, the people who were used to talking at these sorts of things began talking. Rick Waern was there, leading the charge, and I very quickly became bored. Being stoned is like a tree. No, it's like an elephant. Well, my theory, harrumph. . . . Somehow I felt I should liven up the proceedings. After fifteen minutes, I jumped up and left.

My room was only a floor above. With borrowed tights from Linda, over which I wore my Speedo bathing suit, a tight T-shirt, a sign on my chest that said Captain Supertoke, a motorcycle helmet and goggles, and a red towel for a cape, I returned to the meeting. Jay clapped her hands over her mouth, turning beet red with merriment. Shelley was grinning, Ted laughed, and Rick stopped talking. I had brought with me a blue coffee can that obviously functioned as a pipe, and a quantity of hash. I implored all and sundry to have a deeper look at the meaning of being stoned. With one or two dissenters, all and sundry did. It turned into a pretty decent event.

It was not typical of me to dress in costume. I had been making some discoveries by getting stoned. I didn't want to neuter that by turning it into a lecture. Besides, it promised a bit of fun and I was becoming tuned in to fun again the longer I stayed in the building. Shelley had been the first to join me in a toke. Ted, not appearing put out at all by having his seminar hijacked, took some healthy hits from the can himself.

The next day, heels dug in, I perched on the low concrete fence across the street. The noon hour foot traffic in and out of Rochdale drew my attention as I waited for my fashion consultant, Robert Holmes. Because of his recent fearless choice of wardrobe, I saw him as a trend-setter. The marketing concept known as Unisex was to blame for the skin-tight, one-piece, bell-bottomed jumpsuit that only fit taller, skinny guys (Holmes), or women who could pass as Emma Peel, seldom looking good on either. As with sack dresses and Nehru jackets, the jumpsuit's moment was fortuitously brief.

Holmes accessorized his dark green terry cloth number with a wide, brown leather belt. It had a large golden "O" for a buckle. Robert also wore the suit with its crotch-to-neck zipper at half-mast, exposing a tangled growth of chest hair, and drawing the eye away from other body parts whose bulges had little place to hide. This was Holmes's cruising outfit in which, with his blonde goatee and long hair, he looked like a hatless, futuristic George Armstrong Custer. In truth, the general fared not too badly, getup and all. But the items I had my eye on were his Swedish brown suede clogs, replete with wooden soles.

Worrying about height was one of the vanities I wasted time on. If someone were describing a beauty they had seen — and when were they not? — my one question would be: "How tall is she?" One should have outgrown this, especially if one were five eight and not exactly a midget. Even though I had yet to master flip-flops, or anything without an encasement for the heel, I was drawn to Holmes's clogs and determined to have a pair of my own. He would show me where to buy them. They were going to look good with my new button-fly, flared-leg jeans. The mystery of how Dutch kids could walk in sabots was about to be revealed, and I was going to be two inches taller.

Also without a hat, perhaps resembling what Custer might have looked like had he survived long enough to approach sixty, Ted Poole appeared. I watched him walk across the patio, past "The Unknown Student," to the corner of Huron St. The crosswalk, what used to be Rochdale's crosswalk, is now governed by a set of traffic lights. Its capabilities as a method of protest have been seriously compromised by the conversion. Budding civil libertarians from the building used to tie up traffic regularly, having been suitably provoked. They'd gather in a group of thirty or so and, one by one, stick their arms out and walk, skip or dance across the intersection, backing up cars in both directions, from Avenue Rd. to Bathurst St. These precipitate squalls of spontaneity were an organic, urban guerrilla tactic that gave the authorities pause, the desired effect.

Indoors or out, Ted had a glow about him, some mysterious light seeming to radiate from under his skin, so that when he was in a group you saw him first, like the shining nucleus of an atom surrounded by a cloud of electrons. He reminded me of a god — Zeus, maybe, or a dried-off, civvies-clad Poseidon, charming us mortals. Poole, I later discovered, was extremely fond of hats. He owned many: several Stetsons; a Greek fisherman's cap; a pith helmet that had spawned many puns; and beanies adorned with bottle caps or propellers. He had a deer stalker cap like Sherlock Holmes, which he said he wore whenever he had to see a bank manager. He maintained it really troubled them. "Wearing it says: 'Life is a mystery.' Bankers hate mystery, you know, anything that doesn't fit comfortably into a slot with a number that you can add up." He used hats for the usual reasons, but he loved their potential as costume or disguise. I had unwittingly tapped into that when I had appeared as Captain Supertoke.

As he approached, his smile went a long ways toward easing a slight wariness I had felt, not knowing why. My last bit of reserve flew away when, for no apparent reason, he made a gift to me of a pocket knife. It was a beauty, bone handled and blued steel, slightly old fashioned. "I want you to have this," he said. "It's a genuine Barlow knife, like the one in Tom Sawyer." I had no idea why he was giving it to me, but I accepted. It was plain to see he was one of the good guys. Any reservations I might have had had completely vanished.

Thanks to Dunc Blewett's example, it wasn't all that surprising to see a number of Rochdalians over thirty, the age at which people apparently could no longer be trusted. Most of them were thirty-something professionals, like the members of my commune. But there were several, like Dunc, in their early forties to mid-fifties. They were no more or no less part of the community like everyone else.

The soft-spoken Elliot Rose, a curly-haired, beefy, moustachioed U of T professor was a fixture at council meetings, frequently being called upon to calmly, almost apologetically, recite the appropriate text from *Robert's Rules of Order*, which he knew, seemingly, verbatim. Judy Merrill brought her own cachet, being an author and archivist. With her iron grey hair, steely eyes, and ferociously bushy eyebrows usually wreathed in cigarette smoke, she would pronounce on matters with her gravelly voice in such a way that you had better listen. She had a throaty laugh, like the actress, Anne Bancroft. Jack Jones strode through the halls like a beer-bellied Viking, creating drama. His long hair and bushy beard were a flaming red. Talking like a hipster, he often mentioned how he had walked away from the really big bread in advertising, using the word "like" in a manner and frequency that would put a current teen to, like, shame. The tall, ascetic Kent Gooderham was designated as being watchable because, as a sociologist, we weren't sure if he was on team or just studying us. There was also a sixtyish minister, fond of wearing his collar (it may have been his only shirt), who grinned much, but said very little, if anything at all.

Closer to home was Troyer, who periodically claimed to have invented the McBee System, a line-by-line accounting method for dummies using carbon paper. He also had been a distributor of Toro lawn mowers. Like Ted Poole, he was a minister's son. Ian McKenzie, the Anglican priest, was from the wealthy enclave of Rosedale and had always seemed more adept at business than spiritual matters. And, of course, Wilf Pelletier, who lived on the seventh floor with his wife, Dorrie, their two kids, Jennifer and Greg, and, in the cold months, his Aunt Grace would join them from the reserve.

Having almost mastered the art of striding without the new clogs flying off the end of my feet, I took a giant step past Troyer's open door. He caught me fumbling for the key to mine.

"Oh, it's you," he said. "For a minute I thought you were someone else."

Some old feelings were momentarily stirred as I was asked whether or not I were afraid of falling off. Were they cheaper without the backs? And so on. If Troyer found a sore spot he'd probe it until you bled.

To truly appreciate Stan Troyer and set him apart from, say, a raving lunatic, it is almost necessary to create a pantheon of gods to give him his due. In this cosmogony he would be like the cunning Loki, or the drunken reveller, Bacchus, or perhaps Pan, his pipes full of hash instead of music — inferior, low-grade hash. Troyer, the punster, master of ribald limericks and riddles, would exist as a trans-god, skipping across mythologies like a distant and difficult theological cousin. An Aquarian in the Age of Aquarius, he is the Water Bearer, Bringer of Tears, Spiller of Drinks. A would-be Denizen of the Dark, he, despite all his efforts, usually ends up tumbling into the light, dumped in a puddle, and only too happy to laugh at the joke, whether he be the butt of it or no.

The LSD therapy Troyer hoped would cure his alcoholism had created a strange hybrid. As the flip side of Dunc's happy song, Stan would try to down you out. Handling him socially was a poor strategy. When Wilf and Ted launched their book (*No Foreign Land*) at a church, Troyer stood on the sales table and mooned the crowd during the bishop's speech. There had been no provocation save it had been an evening of good cheer. He also has the distinction of having once been ejected from his own going away-party — one that he had organized himself. He couldn't be handled. You had to defeat Troyer, put him in total rout if you were to make an evening of it. Even then, like a newly trained lion, or a just-extinguished fire still smouldering in secret places, he had to be watched diligently for outbreaks of recidivism.

If you've ever read Mark Twain's story about the good little boy and the bad little boy, you will know that while the good little boy sat in church on a glorious Sunday morning, the bad little boy went fishing and had all the fun. Although it's great to wander around in solitude discovering new things, it's also a fine thing to have company that appreciates at least some of the same mysteries. Bad little boys seldom have trouble in recognizing one of their own. Despite Troyer's prickliness, I got a great abdominal workout from all the laughs we shared. He served as a litmus test for my own good mental health. To be centred is to endure.

So I asked Stan how the Rochdale inventory was proceeding. How long exactly would it take to count what was surely a modest number of goods, a number of weeks having passed? This was a sore spot with him. Somehow he had convinced the reformers that not only was an inventory necessary, but that he, with his business experience and, in an unspoken way, his maturity, was the man for the job. He was paid weekly, leading some of us to believe it would be a lengthy task indeed.

The east-wing units had been sparsely furnished: built-in desks and beds with storage, chairs, swing lamps, and burgundy and navy blankets. Each twin-sized bed had a foam mattress of a kind and quality that you must now pay a premium for, if they are even available. They were covered in striped ticking, also of good quality, and extremely portable. Beginning at the sixteenth floor, Troyer proceeded to count.

To aid him in the task, he had the Rochdale equivalent of Frodo's ring, a key that would unlock every door in the building, the all-powerful Grand Master. As head of maintenance, I had a mere Red Master that opened all non-residential doors. Ian Argue, as head of rentals, had two keys, one for the residential units in the east wing and one for those in the west. There were supposed to be two Grand Masters, one for the general manager and one for council president. The latter had been seconded for Troyer's use, creating some inequities in the power game and not a few resentments.

A third Grand Master was uncovered when the guy entrusted to cut the keys was caught red handed, using it in a compromising situation. Even so, like Frodo, he was reluctant to give it up, requiring the direst of threats to let it go. We were all thankful that security had not got its hands on it. They had been creating enough havoc with their Red Master and the east-wing key. Security had their finger on the beating pulse of where most of the dope stashes were liable to be. This proved a boon to the cleaning staff, who frequently stumbled upon stashes in non-secured areas not patrolled by the black shirts.

R.E. Bruce Martin, who would introduce himself at council meetings or on the telephone as "R.E. Bruce Martin here, fire marshal," was indeed the dedicated, diligent, volunteer liaison between the fire department and Rochdale. The prototypical nerd, pocket protector and all, he could be spotted at various times in dress pants, short-sleeved shirt and shiny black shoes rushing from one place to another, often carrying a briefcase. He had an odd walk, leaning forward with his head off to one side, as he lifted off on his toes with each step, giving the appearance of bouncing. He spoke in a nasal monotone and, if he had a sense of humour, it was buried deeply. He was the serious fellow no one ever took seriously.

A benign Gollum, R.E. Bruce sought the One Key. He was relentless in his single-minded pursuit of the Grand Master. He had an imposing ring of two dozen or more keys that sat in his pants pocket like a baseball, which gave him access to anywhere, almost. But he knew the power of the One far surpassed that of the twenty or so he freighted around daily. Every change of council executive, or department head, or minor coup would result in a new petition from R.E. Bruce. His argument was unassailable. As fire marshal, he, perhaps more than anyone, needed access to every space with a lock.

R.E. Bruce was trustworthy, wore his hair short, went to work every day and neither drank nor did drugs. Possibly he was seen as a geek among the super hip, but he was Rochdale's geek and no more or no less a misfit than anyone else. Even though most of us sought to avoid being trapped in a room with him, he was regarded with affection. Yet all his entreaties were rebuffed, out of perversity perhaps. A group of us did get together to present R.E. Bruce with a sealed envelope bearing the words: Grand Master Keyhole. He was merely puzzled by the empty envelope, causing our joke to fall a little flat. That Stan Troyer had a Grand Master and R.E. Bruce Martin did not, was one of the thousand demonstrations that life is not even close to being fair. Quite simply, he had wanted it too much.

Meanwhile, the McBee man had troubles of his own. He never got past the upper floors, really. Armed with a clipboard and a form he had devised, Troyer, having first knocked, would enter a unit and proceed with the tally. That one room might be missing a lamp or chair while another had double the requisite amount was not a problem. There was a reconciliation column built into the form to accommodate these anomalies. You would be pardoned for falling asleep during the explanation as to how cleverly it worked. However, a hitch developed almost right away, one that proved to be the norm.

Halfway through any given room's inventory, someone was liable to enter, exchange pleasantries — How's it going, man? — and pick up, say, a mattress, and stagger out into the corridor, carrying it off with all the deliberation of a leafcutter ant. Then, somebody else would arrive with a chair and a lamp and see there was no mattress. Bummer, man. They would disappear for a few minutes before returning with one that possibly had no ticking but still delivered the desired quality of sleep. The entire building entertained the constant motion of goods being ferried north and south and east and west at all hours of the day or night. Troyer kept a brave face for the first few weeks but he could be touchy when asked if things were proceeding apace. Occasionally he'd threaten me with exposure for having a chair, a lamp, and blankets that had no right to be in my room.

Later that evening, I answered a soft knock at my door. A young woman stood there in the outfit of a film noir cigarette girl:

pillbox hat, rouged cheeks, blue satin tutu dress, and fishnet stockings. Instead of stilettos, she displayed the unisex nature of clogs — hers were blue, and suede like mine. Her tray held a variety of goods for sale, including cigarettes, half-bottles of Chianti, cookies, joints, and silver-foiled grams of hash, none of which cost much more than five dollars.

Holyoke, Aunt Grace, and Nana

He was a ward of the court, barely seventeen, unmanageable, and a misfit. But he was able to live at Rochdale, where he had not only found a home but was one of its more exalted citizens. His engine was fuelled by the defiance of the wounded fighting their way to health. From the children who played with him for hours, and loved him, through the twenty-something Turks running the show, to the older people in the building who thought him to be splendid, Don Holyoke was the spirit of that community in the early days. He was the child in all of us who speaks the truth. He was Rochdale.

Talking to Holyoke, however, was weirdly incongruous, like exchanging recipes with a Supreme Court judge in a liquor store lineup. Only part of your mind would be on the basil trick you do with tomato sauce. It took but a sentence or two to broach Holyoke's comfort level, leaving you both looking for an exit. His preferred method of communication was dance, punctuated with theatrical asides, usually in a high falsetto. Standing out amidst the cinematic dramas that were our lives, his life was a musical.

He danced all the time. He danced in the elevators, the halls, and in and out of offices. He danced to the laundromat and danced to the store. He danced to music heard and unheard. Still in his teens, he had retained the natural ability of children to move spontaneously. In movement he was beauty, a frisky, wanton

Arabian colt. Holyoke, out of Isadora, sired by Nijinsky.

He was the worst nightmare of the restaurant owners stampeding to sign painters for a "No Shirt No Shoes No Service" special. Tall, and skinny as a riding crop, all Holyoke ever wore was a pair of thin denim button-fly jeans. Plastered to his hips, skin tight to the knees, they flared out to enormous bells, frayed and forever trailing, like Sweet Pea, considerably behind his bare and callused feet. Above the waistband was a supple rendition of high-definition abs, low-volume pecs of steel and whipcord arms. His oddly aristocratic face was usually betrayed by a loopy, gap-toothed grin, framed by a humongous, frizzy, honey-blonde, Jimi Hendrix afro. Even standing perfectly still Holyoke was an event.

He was particularly effective at council meetings. For one thing he didn't always need the stage or have to have his say like the regular hecklers, malcontents, naysayers and semi-pro contrarians. He picked his spots, illuminating Rochdale Council with his portrayal of Truth masquerading as Puck. Holyoke's constituency was among the marginal Rochdalians who would be most affected by some proposed bit of draconian legislation, like spot ID or residency checks, aimed at controlling speeders and crashers. He would dance around, pointing at the offending legislator, ridiculing anyone who had become self-important. When he trilled in his high-pitched girly voice, "somebodee's ly-ing" or "the truth will set you free-ee" you were toast. People trusted Holyoke because he had no particular axe to grind. In a way, he epitomized all the waifs who came to Rochdale because no one else would have them. The prototypical squeegee kid, he was their hero. Late one Sunday afternoon he became mine.

It was trying to be the first really warm day of spring but, under a wispy haze, there was still a nip to the breeze and icy fingers of cold were lurking in the shadows. Some heads who were trying to put a band together had dragged out a battered old speaker from one of the empty storefronts beside the bank — prime Bloor St. real estate that had never been developed or rented out. An impromptu concert began. Troyer, who had just left my place, returned to tell me that he could see from his window that a crowd was gathering on the front patio. It had been a long winter. The people were restless.

I took my usual spot at the corner of the building by the entrance, just under the second-floor office where I played at being general manager. I was standing tall in my clogs and very pleasantly stoned on a new batch of blonde Lebanese. There were twenty or so kids grooving to the music, Holyoke, of course, among them. As a concession to the chill, or perhaps as a prop, he was wearing a tattered blanket over his bare shoulders, flicking it about like Gypsy Rose's boa.

Two chicks were bopping, eyelids half-closed and swaying their hips, moving their arms, dancing with each other and totally ignoring some goofy freak with purple wire-rimmed shades, a Zapata moustache and one of those godawful floppy leather hats, who was trying way too hard to dance with them. Holyoke slipped in behind the guy and aped his efforts. We laughed. In the interest of fair play he circled around and imitated the girls ignoring the guy. When they turned to dance with Holyoke he stuck his nose in the air and spun away. More laughter. Karma was served. Some passersby stopped to watch. More people came out of the building. The crowd grew.

Cars full of Sunday gawkers drove past slowly. Rochdale was moving up to second place on the circuit, after Yorkville, as *the* place to show uncle Irv and cousin Mary some hippies when they came to town. People were, essentially, watching the antics of their own children as if they were another species. It was Holyoke's show entirely now. Everybody fell back to give him room. The sidewalk was his.

He took long, graceful leaps up the street, fluttering his blanket like butterfly wings. Back he came, whirling like a dervish, to wrap himself into a cocoon, from which he would metamorphose again, and career into the spectators. He would pull people out of the crowd, hide his face in his hands, play peekaboo, dance a little parody of whoever he singled out, and skip away. Fred Astaire gone mad, in a joyful sort of way.

On the street, vehicular traffic had slowed to a crawl when the ants arrived at the picnic. A bright yellow police cruiser disgorged two of Toronto's finest to restore order. Holyoke danced around them looking awed and mimed a small child looking up at a giant. One of the cops was appropriately affronted and made a grab for him. We all booed. Effortlessly, he pirouetted out of reach. Yays all around. To a wail of catcalls, they ordered the music turned down. As the cops turned to face the crowd Holyoke crept in behind them, hunched over, his blanket held up to his eyes like Dracula's cape. With exaggerated stealth he tiptoed to the speaker, cranked it up full blast, and jumped triumphantly to his feet, legs spread, arms thrust skyward, shedding his cape to a chorus of cheers.

It took two more cruisers, with four policemen in each, before the speaker was silenced. All the while the two original cops were trying to stop Holyoke, without looking too stupid, as they went about grabbing at this wisp, who would always be tantalizingly just out of reach. Although visibly tiring, Holyoke kept right on dancing to our rhythmic claps. He was nabbed taking a bow after a particularly spectacular jeté. He offered no resistance and they were reasonable about putting him in the back seat of the cruiser. They hadn't even bothered with handcuffs. It was chilly now and I turned to leave.

Just as I was thinking the good guys had lost another skirmish in the war against spontaneous joy, a huge cheer erupted. I looked up to see Holyoke sticking out of the rear passenger door of the police car. Somehow he had got the window down far enough to squeeze his skinny frame through the opening. "Yoo-hoo," he trilled in triumph, his naked torso still writhing and dancing. Both hands were waving, alternately blowing kisses and flashing the V sign, as they drove him down to the station. Ebullience 1 — Forces of Darkness 0.

I can see Aunt Grace standing at the living room window of Wilf and Dorrie's seventh-floor Zeus, one of the lone two-bedroom apartments that occupied the northeast corner of each residential floor. She would position her tiny frame just by the curtain, leaning slightly on her cane, and spend hours watching the activity on Bloor St. and the action on the front patio. You would hardly even know she was there but for her sudden gleeful exclamations. "Oh ho. There's that dancing guy again." She loved observing the young at play and Holyoke was one of her favourites. "Hee. Look at him go." And then she would absently mutter a phrase in Odawa. Wilf would catch her and respond in their Ojibway dialect, making his aunt laugh.

When tea was made Aunt Grace would hobble back to her stuffed chair. She always had something on the go, knitting or crocheting, and she'd put it in her lap, occasionally doing a stitch or two while she'd visit. She spent summers on her reserve at Wikwemikong on Manitoulin Island; the rest of the time she was Rochdale's oldest resident.

I had no cutesy notions regarding the ostensible wisdom of the elderly. I grew up in a time and place where old people were not particularly wise or accessible. For the most part they were disapproving tyrants who believed that professional wrestling was real. Even the benign were more than a little daffy, and smelled odd, like a meld of lavender and sour stomachs. Moments in their company were unbearably long. Aunt Grace helped me with that.

"Oh yes," she'd say. "These young people from the universities would come to the reserve in the summer. Well, I'd tell them . . . maybe they would ask me about this flower or that plant . . . I'd say, well, I'm just an ignorant old woman really. I don't know much. Not like you. You kids are smart and you go to university. But that plant, now. . . ." And she would proceed to explain everything about the plant: how it grew, where, whether it was used for something, and how to use it. She would give them everything but the Latin name. The simplicity of her next remark was startling to me, providing an epiphanic moment that has deepened and widened over time.

"No, I'm not educated, not smart like you. I'm just an old woman. But you know. . . ." She would pause here, with impeccable timing. "At least I put in the years." And then she would throw her head back and laugh.

Even though she was Wilfred's aunt, everybody called her Aunt Grace. That's how she was known in Wikwemikong, or to Ottawa bureaucrats visiting Wilf, or to kids from other reserves passing through Rochdale via the Nishnawbe Institute. If you were lucky enough to go to dinner at Wilf and Dorrie's, and she was present, you would go home later and you would have an Aunt Grace as well. Somehow you would also feel more connected to an older world of less frantic rhythms.

"A man from the hydro was at Wiki one time," she'd say, "checking lines or something. And he said to me, 'Boy, this is the friendliest place I ever been. Wherever I go everybody just smiles and calls me honey.' Well I had to laugh. 'Ah nee,' I told him. They're saying 'ah nee' to you. That's how you say hello in my language."

Thus were many of us taught our first word in Odawa. Our second might well be learned at dinner. "Please pass the peneeks," she would say. "Oops, I mean the potatoes."

Coming from a culture that embraced the oral tradition it was only natural to her that she pass on what she knew in whatever fashion circumstances would allow. She made no distinction regarding people, whether black, white, Asian, or First Nations. The one thing she insisted upon, however, was that she was Canadian, sure, but she was, because of her heritage, "One hundred and ten percent Canadian. One hundred and ten percent!" She declared this often, and firmly, so that there was no mistake. The declaration was followed of course, by a laugh.

Her Catholicism gave me pause, remembering as I did, being forced to sit in other rooms while grace was said before being summoned to the table, an abomination of a protestant lad at my mother's Irish Catholic parents. But I learned it was a manifestation of a larger, deeper, more all-inclusive spirituality. It was good to gather with people and give thanks to the Creator.

Aunt Grace's knowledge of plants and flowers also went deeper than horticulture. In a typically unassuming way she was a healer, a medicine woman. You would never hear her say that, and it took me way past Rochdale until I found out she was.

Wilf and Dorrie were out of town. A young woman, Elaine, was staying with Aunt Grace and I would drop by each evening to see if they needed anything. I'd have some tea, chat a bit and usually leave when Aunt Grace went to bed. One evening I fished out a joint and shared it with Elaine before I left.

"You know," said Aunt Grace the next evening, "I almost lost this leg when I broke my hip one time. It got infected where they operated. It was too deep, the doctor said, right down to the bone. He gave me some pills but he told me they likely wouldn't work, that they'd probably have to operate again, maybe cut it off." She paused and sipped her tea. "So, when I got home, I got one of the boys to go get me some spruce gum off the tree. Any kind is good . . . fir or pine . . . but spruce is the best. I heated it up. See, you put a pot of water on to boil and you take the gum and fold it into a strip of gauze or even cheesecloth. Then you hold the cloth over the steam until everything is nice and hot. Not too hot, but hot. When it's ready, you just put it on the wound and it draws out the poison." She laughed. "Hee. I went to see the doctor three weeks later. I gave him back his pills. No more infection, it was gone, and he was amazed. 'I don't understand how this can be,' he said. 'It's all cleared up. How did you do that?' Well, I used Indian medicine, I told him. 'What did you use?' he asked me. And I said, that's for me to know, doctor, and you to find out. Hee." Then Aunt Grace looked me right in the eye. "You don't just tell anybody these things."

She had just told me, however, and therein lay my cue. I produced a joint. I didn't ask if anybody wanted to smoke some pot. It wasn't referred to at all, not as pot, weed, smoke, or marijuana. Aunt Grace knew that pot was illegal and therefore wrong to use. One hundred and ten percent Canadians, people of integrity, do not knowingly break the law. She was curious about it but to offer her marijuana would have compromised her. She would have had to refuse. Without stating what it was, I offered a plant that exhibited certain qualities that she wished to explore. If she wanted further knowledge such as its name, or where I had got it, she would ask. Until then I would say nothing. I learned this from Wilfred. It is the Indian way.

I took two drags and passed the joint to Elaine. She took a couple of tokes and, without hesitation, offered it to her elder. Aunt Grace, who was not a smoker of tobacco except perhaps in ceremonies, took it, in fingers thickened from stitching a thousand quilts, and did exactly as Elaine and I had done, holding the smoke in for a time before exhaling a huge cloud. She was a natural. After all, the concept of passing a smoking herb around a circle, to be shared by all, was not exactly unknown to her. We put on a record of powwow-type music, some songs with English lyrics, some in Indian. We hardly talked but it felt good sitting there — comfortable. In time Aunt Grace got up and went to bed.

Twice more we had our little ceremony: on the following evening, which was uneventful, and the one after that, when Aunt Grace gave us a wonderful account of girlhood summers on the reserve — full of sights and sounds, and vivid characters, and the smell of new mown hay. She went on for a long time, taking many sips of tea, commenting on the dryness of her throat. On the fourth evening, the night before Wilf and Dorrie were due back, Aunt Grace said she was too tired to have tea but she wanted to tell me something. I kept the joint in my pocket. I would give it to Elaine later.

Aunt Grace gave me another medicine, this one more complex. Her instruction was a classic exposition of the oral tradition. "There's just one thing you have to remember," she would say. The simple fact would be soaked readily into your brain. Then she would go over it again, adding something else. "See, there's just these two things you need to know." And so on. By the time she was finished, the seven or eight steps needed to make this medicine — having told the story at least that many times — would be firmly lodged in your mind.

I knew it would be the last time that Aunt Grace would smoke. She had explored the matter to her satisfaction. We would not so much as even refer to it again. When she finished giving the lesson she got up to go to her room. I got up to leave as well.

"Megwitch, Aunt Grace," I said.

"Ah ha," she laughed, clapping her hands. "You're very welcome."

Clint, who knows everything, agreed to guide me to the airport to pick up my mother and my grandmother. They were on their way to Florida. Something screwed up and they were forced to overnight in Toronto. Could I please come and get them and, if it's no trouble, dear, they would just spend the night at my place. We went to Wilf's to borrow his International Harvester Travelall. Clint was wearing his fancy moosehide jacket from northern Saskatchewan. With his shoulder-length, naturally curly, almost ringleted hair he looked like Louis the Fourteenth on his way to a powwow. I had to drag him away from Aunt Grace, who was admiring the fancy beadwork.

I was wondering whether or not Nana was up to a visit to Rochdale but decided it was my mother's problem, not mine. I hadn't seen my grandmother in years. My memory served up a prim, disapproving, humourless woman who constantly tended to my grandfather's needs. And, the Captain, master of the tugboat *Ocean Hawk*, was a man of many needs. We were not close.

One sign of encouragement was that, since my grandfather's death, Nana, at eighty, took up drinking and smoking — something that would never have been allowed under Grampy's quasi-despotic rule. I was further astonished to learn that she was not only born a Scotch Protestant, but that there was also some urgency involved in terms of her and the Captain making it to the altar. The very humanness of that impressed me. Still, I thought, she was no Aunt Grace.

We drove off the Gardiner and straight up Spadina on the way back to Rochdale — me and Louis Quatorze in the front seat, ma and grandma in the rear. Just before we turned right onto Bloor, Nana pointed to a couple of freaks truckin' along.

"Look, Lillian," she shouted, since my mother is hearing impaired. "There's another boy with long hair!"

"Yes, I see that," humoured my mother.

Clint and I looked straight ahead.

It was a few days before Judy Merrill's Sci-Fi conference and space was at a premium. Ian Argue somehow found an available room, east wing, of course, with shared facilities, but on one of the less rowdy floors. I took Mom and Nana up to my place to settle them a bit before delivering them to their ashram. Nana was looking around a little sniffily, so I tried distracting her with the view long enough to grab my coffee-can hash pipe, and whisk it out to the hall closet. My mother's eyes were brimming with enjoyment at my discomfort — parental Karma. She nodded toward the bed. Neatly folded on my mattress on the floor was a pleated, plaid, wool skirt, a white silk blouse, and a navy cashmere cardigan.

"Are you seeing someone, dear," she asked, "Or is there something we should know?"

I had forgotten about Anne Ochshorn — not an easy thing to do. She and Bob had driven up from New York City where he was now the wealthy owner of a property management company. It hadn't taken him long to rise up after his Regina days. He and Anne had come to visit her mother on the same weekend that Mom and Nana ended up at Rochdale.

Ochshorn had become intrigued, seeing a pile of multicoloured rods and hubs on Rochdale's front patio. A geodesic dome had been planned for a science fiction conference organized by Judy Merril. Some of the serious players of the genre, including Judy, who was highly esteemed, would be there. Judy was concerned that it wouldn't be finished in time. I told her not to worry. As soon as she heard Ochshorn's "Noo Yawk" accent she relaxed. This, she concluded rightly, was a guy who could get stuff done.

Anne had come by just before Clint and I went to the airport.

She wanted to help with the dome and could she borrow a pair of jeans and a T-shirt? "Sure," I replied offhandedly, betrayed by trembling hands and a quaver in my voice. Later, according to my mother, she burst into my room, introduced herself, changed in the bathroom and dashed off. "Bye-bye. Tell Ralphie thanks. Mwah." When I returned with Mom and Nana's key, the folded jeans and shirt mutely testified that I had missed her.

"Too bad," said Mom, not ever being one to miss much.

"Ah, well," I shrugged, privately noting that it would be a while before I did laundry.

Later I took my mother for a Singapore Sling. We went to the only bar I knew — apart from Grossman's Tavern — the old Pilot on Yonge St. at Bloor. Nana, pleading fatigue, stayed at Rochdale. They were in a Kafka, which was a lockable unit of two bed/study rooms with a shared bath. Nana would be fine. I had Mom home by eleven, after unsuccessfully trying to get her to join me in a toke of hash. "Maybe next time, when I'm not with your grandmother."

I arranged for a cab to take them back to the airport the next morning. We made our goodbyes on the patio. The dome was almost complete. Ochshorn waved; I waved back. Anne was no doubt in Rosedale somewhere. Mom was watching everything and missing nothing from behind the curtain of her semi-deafness. Nana seemed quite perky.

A young couple came out of the building: she, brunette and tousled, he, scruffy and bearded. I knew them from around — decent vibes. They looked straight at my grandmother and the girl said, "Goodbye, Mrs. Hurley, have a great time in Florida."

"Thank you, dear. Bye-bye," said Nana.

My mother looked at me with furrowed brows. I shrugged, equally puzzled.

"I see you met some people, Nana."

"Yes, dear."

"When?"

"Last night. After you and Lil went out. I wanted a cigarette but I couldn't find any matches. So I went to that little lounge at the end of the hall and those kids helped me out. Nice kids, too. We talked awhile, shared some cigarettes, roll-yer-owns, and then I went to bed. I had the best sleep!"

"Oh." I looked at Mom. She got most of it. Enough.

"You know," Nana went on, "the hair takes getting used to, but I like the beards. Reminds me of when I was a girl."

The high falsetto rang out as I was ushering them into the back seat of the cab. It was Holyoke, dancing in front of the dome, waving at us like mad.

"Goodby-eee, Nana Hurley."

Nana's hand shot up and she gave a very vigorous wave.

"Goodbye, Don," she called back. And then, to me, with a big grin on her face, "That boy is such a rascal!"

Jéfé

José Garcia, the name, is — according to José himself — the Latin American equivalent of John Smith. I know a John Smith, now Doctor John Smith, courtesy of a University of Toronto graduate degree in physics which, at the time, seemed to have taken an indecently long while to acquire. I first met Smitty when Susan Sutherland brought him to my room in Rochdale as an unwitting trump card in her successful bid to end my romantic pursuit of her, even though it was obvious she had led me on. With Susan we were all more or less unwitting, which could be the German word for "putty."

She made us play chess. Smitty, playing white, the good guys, the offence, the army with the statistical edge, managed a dreary scientific campaign of mathematical precision that narrowly triumphed over my brilliant, intuitive, yet untutored and eventually beleaguered, defense of wondrous complexity.

"I believe that's Fool's Mate," he said quietly, smugly, and would I like to play another?

We were both Librans, fellow seekers of harmony and fair play, and likewise long-time sufferers of female Geminiian whims provided in profusion by Susan and her ilk. Smitty and I became friends instantly. How he handled the John Smith thing before becoming Doctor Smith was to be John N. Smith, as in Norton. Yet he is the only John Smith I have ever known, and if you were to tell me, "Some guy phoned, said his name was John Smith. Yeah, right," I would know it was Smitty.

"You should have cheated Jéfé. Why didn't you cheat?" asked José, when I told him about meeting Smitty.

"You can't cheat at chess, José. It isn't possible. Besides, what would be the point?"

"To win, Jéfé, the point is to win," he said with some incredulity. I was reminded of one of Steinbeck's *Cannery Row* characters, Mac probably, who was almost personally affronted by the fact that you couldn't cheat at chess. José took a similar tack and he explained that where he grew up cheating was a normal part of childhood games. If you didn't get caught red handed, in the act, it just meant you were more accomplished at whatever game you were playing. There was no stigma attached.

"Cheaters never prosper is what we were taught." And José just shook his head.

"Okay, Jéfé, whatever you say. Let's talk about that Volkswagen, then."

This was a car that had been parked in the alley beneath our office windows for over a month. Each of us saw an abandoned — and therefore free — car. We both wanted it, argued about who had seen it first, whose need was greater and who, rightly, should have it. A gambling man would have put his money on José. The only thing keeping me in the game is that my Latin friend wanted me to officially approve the deal — in writing — so that if there was heat it would come my way. It was also a way we had of playing.

José A. Garcia — Antonio — is likewise the only José Garcia I know. We both agreed the A could stand for "Annie's Lover." Although he didn't know any Annies at the time, it would do as a generic term for all women. In Taj Mahal's song, Annie's lover was a big old African man who had a farm with goats and chickens. "He sat on a hillside, playin' his guitar, watchin' it all come down in Har - Mo - Nee - e - e - e - e - e - e - e." This is allegory since José is not particularly musical as I recall. Indeed, he could hardly keep a beat drumming on a desktop, which he often insisted on doing anyway, mercifully only for short riffs. But he was a much-loved man, lady-wise and otherwise, and oddly, but definitely, harmonious.

I had come to work one morning and the new cardboard sign on the door next to the maintenance office read: BLACK LIBERATION FRONT, in hand-blocked letters. I speculated for days as to whom the new neighbour would most emulate — Huey Newton, Stokely Carmichael, Angela Davis (with any luck), or Malcolm X — and which of my fellow administrators was asinine enough to encourage extra heat when we could barely handle what was coming our way. I would also have to find a new venue for our upcoming Friday night poker game.

Enter José. He appeared in my doorway one afternoon. He was somewhat stocky, a solid five foot ten or eleven with a benign, cherubic face, looking more like the laid back Caribbean Latino he was than the angry black guy I had been expecting.

"Are you Ralph?" he asked, only a slight accent.

"Yeah," I replied, a bit what's-it-to-you-ish.

"I'm José. Can you get me a key for that office?"

"Ah, Black Liberation Front," I said, squinting and pointing my finger like a pistol at him.

"Yes," he said, taking my tone and pointing his finger right back at me. "Is that okay with you?" he asked, omitting the word "asshole" which I nevertheless heard — and deserved.

"Well," I said, somewhat contritely, "I was hoping for Angela Davis."

At that he burst out laughing and, nodding his head up and down, said, "Me too, man, me too." I came out from behind the desk and we shook hands.

The way I see it, the Black Liberation Front was generated as a device for José and I to meet. All that ever seemed to happen was that José would show up regularly, mess around in his office for a bit and then come in and shoot the shit with me. The only other guy I ever saw in there was Peter Robinson, who did look the part of the angry black man but in reality was an extremely intelligent, humorous Trinidadian banker taking a short course in advanced economics. I had come to know José as a perfect mix of tireless social advocate and effervescent entrepreneur. He was genuine about all his causes, ferocious even, but, while not expecting any of them to pay his way, he hoped one or two of them might. He was surviving. He set his lines as a trapper would, with the BLF being one that perhaps didn't work out.

The first time José came up to my room I invited him to smoke some hash. He refused. Where he came from only the low-lifes smoked pot. I explained that the same was true for Canada; only here people volunteered to become socially unacceptable just to get at the good stuff. In fact, there were so many of us that we were given this building just so we wouldn't contaminate the general public. I continued to elaborate on this theme until José put his hands up in resignation.

"Well, I can see it sure helps you pile up the bullshit, Jéfé. Maybe I will try a little of that stuff."

And yet another had succumbed to the intoxicating pleasures of the humble sativa. As with everyone else who abandoned all hope and entered, he had wanted to do it all along.

Standing in front of you, both feet on the ground, radiating a warmth and solidity that can only be faintly remembered from childhood, and engendering a sense of safety and well-being, José is BROTHER writ large. You are in good hands with this man. He will do what he can to protect you and never cause you harm. Leave your children with him, your house, your pets. They will flourish and thrive. If, however, José is going camping and doesn't have a Coleman stove or a tent and you do, either become very hard of heart or kiss your equipment goodbye. This is called sharing resources. After all, they are just things. The corollary is: if you need a stove for camping, José will find one and give it to you. No strings — except you might want to repay the favour some time. Or trade for it. What have you got? The fact that it might be my stove he gave you has no relevance. Obviously I could spare it.

José knew Che Guevara. They had fought together side by side but I could never find out where or when. He would just change the subject, sorry that he had let it slip in the first place. As to José's country of origin I had narrowed it down to Columbia, the Dominican Republic, or Aruba. Today I know. Then I didn't. Given the times and the Che posters plastered up everywhere, it was a story that José could have dined out on forever — and he was a guy who always had an eye out for dinner — but I never once saw him play the revolutionary card.

With the BLF taking up the last empty office, our first Friday night poker game was held in my office on the second floor. There was me, Jim Newell, Norris Eisenbrey, Bob Nasmith and a fifth guy who, if he reads this, will be pissed that I didn't remember he was there. It could have been any number of guys who subsequently played on Friday nights — Barney Frayne, Ken East, or even Jim Garrard. It wasn't Clay Ruby, not that time, because even though it was a memorable evening there was no talk of legal action vis-à-vis a bounced cheque as a method of paying off losses. Nor was anybody accompanied to their room to get the aforementioned cheque. That was another time.

Jim Newell was a little shit — and I say this with affection — who seemed to enjoy being called a rat. He had shortish hair plastered to his skull, beady eyes, and a wispy, thin moustache hovering above a small mouth from which protruded two tiny rat teeth poised above his receding chin. He was a paraplegic and had to be watched at all times — for your health, not his. Cards had a way of disappearing and reappearing in the folds of his wheelchair. Legion were the ways he had of using his unique angle of vision to get a peek at your hand. He won often — too often, as I saw it — and would cackle gleefully while raking in the pot with his stumpy little paws. Cries of, "Newell, you fucking little rat, you saw my hand!" were frequent enough to constitute a litany. He loved it and gloated constantly. His affectation was to be avaricious and generally unpleasant in manner on or off the field. Yet we would scarcely have a game without him. You need a guy like that. Poker is a tough sport.

Then there was Norris Henderson Eisenbrey from mainline Philadelphia, the Pennsylvania equivalent of Rosedale or Westmount. Had I met Norris in medieval times, an era in which I'm certain he would have thrived, he would doubtless have been known as Norris-the-Strange. He was one of the few who tore themselves away from Rochdale long enough to go to Woodstock.

A mere six foot eight or nine in cowboy boots — nearly always worn with hiking shorts — Norris had an athletic build, albeit one that was slightly stoop shouldered, developed, no doubt, from peering myopically at the world. At a period when we were all starting to let our hair grow out, his was just a bit longer than the rest of us. Proof, at least to Norris, that he might be a tad groovier. When he removed his thick, industrial strength glasses — which he could only afford to do for brief periods to rub his eyes or pinch the bridge of his nose — Norris-the-Nearsighted was a handsome man with fine, almost delicate, features — Prince Valiant without the bangs. Yet his constant, odd, fleeting, bemused smile betrayed him for the secretive, garage-dwelling loner he must have been as a kid, off in a darkened corner conducting strange experiments with insects while the rest of us were cycling to the beach. But, Norris was a true seeker and I suspect is still at it today, while many of us beach-goers have fallen by the wayside.

Norris was a New York pal of Ochshorn's but by extrapolation became a member of the Regina crowd, a sinister group it was said, who had designs on taking over Rochdale. Norrie, as Ochshorn called him, was able to confirm that our Bob was every bit as larger than life in the Big Apple as he had been here.

Unlike most of us, Norris actually had a trade — big time — as a cameraman in Hollywood. He did the camera work on the Robert Downey movie *Putney Swope* and is duly listed in the credits. Clint, who lived and breathed movies, explained to me how significant and great that was. It became almost too much to bear when I also discovered that Norris had a black belt, or its equivalent, in one of the more arcane martial arts. He was an enigma that I didn't really want to solve, and taking him at face value was almost too difficult to endure.

Nevertheless, Norris was always gentlemanly, if saucy, in a very courtly way. And never, despite his size and prowess, did he project even the slightest air of physical menace. A Great Dane who wagged his tail and acted coy so you wouldn't be afraid. You had to like the guy. And maybe, I thought, he's lousy at poker.

It should be said that there's a bit of history between me and Bob Nasmith. Matters came to a head, so to speak, post-Rochdale, at the old Embassy Pool Hall at Bloor and Bellair. (Now Harry Rosen's.) I was lying spread-eagled on a snooker table, with my shins barking on the end rail, using a short rake to sink the money ball. Nasmith came bounding up the stairs and, seeing me vulnerable to attack from the rear, jumped in behind me, buried his face in my ass, and gave me the raspberry just as I was taking the shot which, of course, missed. I jumped down from the table and swung my cue like a bat in an attempt to remove Nasmith's head from his body. This at least had the effect of strangling the laughter from the guys. I was beyond pissed off. I felt violated, not the least because Nasmith had exhibited in name, if not in deed, tendencies towards ambiguous sexuality. Perhaps ambitious sexuality would be more accurate. He would remove his clothes on the slightest pretext and had a seeming fondness for appearing at meetings in the nude — not just showing up, but striking poses and strutting about in a way that brought to mind porn flicks rather than freedom of expression. And in a way that was somehow an assault. There was always an air of seediness that attached itself to Nasmith, one that couldn't be scrubbed off. Still, I'm glad I missed.

Nasmith, however, is a good guy, a man's man, one of the boys. He goes fishing. For a time in his teens he was an apprentice pool shark, which gives him a bit of cachet in certain smoky rooms. He has an odd, flat-palmed style that looks amateurish — as if he couldn't form a proper bridge — until you're handing him your eye teeth. At about five foot eight he's also a little guy — the same way that pit bulls are small dogs. Being diminutive in stature myself, and one of the yappier breeds, I admired Bobby's ability to thump out the bigger boys; particularly since he worked it so they were always the aggressors and he was finally, reluctantly, just defending himself. This is a technique he probably honed and polished while he was a Canadian lad in the U.S. marines.

Now I'm thinking it wasn't Jim Newell at this particular poker game. It might have been Jay Boldizsar, Rochdale's accountant. The fact is it doesn't matter because the game was short and the night belonged to Norris and Nasmith. Whoever said: "If you would know a man, you must first play him at cards" didn't have dying cats in mind.

We were just nicely into the game, about an hour or so. The room was appropriately smoky so the door was open as was the second-floor rear patio door, a short distance away. The sound of quarters being anted up, cards slapping, and the usual banter was interrupted by a weird, high-pitched wail like a muffled two-second siren burst. This was followed immediately by a thud and a strangled cry of pain coming from the patio. Norris, who had folded, got up and checked it out.

"Oh, Jesus," I heard him say, and I was alarmed by the quaver in his voice. "Come here, there's a cat . . . Jesus. . . ." And we walked out to see a white cat lying at an odd angle on the concrete. A small blossom of blood was seeping out and matting in its fur. It had to have fallen from a long way up — from somewhere in the east wing. Pushed or thrown, more likely, by some bit of pond scum masquerading as a flower child.

The cat wasn't dead. It lay there breathing heavily, emitting a low-throated moaning. Its eyes were looking up inside its head, the whites glittering with each tremble of the lids. There was agony in every breath it took. Something had to be done. There was consensus that a vet was out of the question. The cat was smashed and broken far beyond the abilities of medical technology to mend.

Norris reluctantly took charge. Removing a small penknife from his pocket, he knelt beside the suffering creature. He grasped its neck — you could see he was trying to be gentle — and tried to cut its throat. The remaining spark of life in the cat moved it to resist the knife that was far too small for the job. Norris was in anguish, moaning, "Oh no, oh no, hold still," over and over. It was a moment of heart-break.

Nasmith suddenly took off to the far end of the patio and came back carrying a concrete block. "Stand back, Norris," he said grimly, and when Norris moved Bobby raised the block chest high and brought it down in full force, a two-hander onto the cat's skull. It twitched once and died, delivering us all from its pain. Nasmith then picked up the block and the cat and took them to the garbage.

Later, sitting in the soft-lighted warmth and comfort of my room I thought about Bobby bleakly taking care of business, and of Norris, kneeling in distress, providing balance, atoning for a vicious act of cruelty.

Some time after that incident Nasmith was in my office. I had gotten to know him a little better. José walked by and waved. I knew a lot more about him by then as well. I said to Bobby, "Hang on a sec, I want to introduce you to someone. I went next door to get José.

The United States had invaded the Dominican Republic in 1966, during one of their periodic political adjustments to Latin America. Bob Nasmith was one of the marines that landed. José, along with a group of his friends, had been there to greet them.

"I thought you two should meet," I said, getting right down to it. I told them why.

"Were you in Santo Domingo?" José asked Nasmith.

"Yep," said Bob, with a what-can-I-say expression.

"At the bridge?"

"Yep," said Bob, alert, wondering where this was going.

"Lotta shooting going on there, man." José was grinning.

"There sure as fuck was," said Bobby, smiling back.

"Well," said José, as he moved across the room. "I'm glad we both made it outta there."

"Me too," agreed Nasmith. And they embraced solidly, slapping each other on the back.

The Many-Splendoured Thing

A vision appeared in the murky gloom of a dusk-lit hallway. Glowing, in a circle of light, she looked like a ghost from a Spanish mission in Old Mexico, perhaps even Guadeloupe herself. She was tiny and dark, her hair divided into two braids that hung in front, plaited like the thick bell rope that summoned the faithful to prayer. Her dress was a white shift of rough cotton that appeared to ripple and shimmer like heat waves above a bean field. She wore flat leather sandals with a simple loop for the toe. An exquisitely beautiful face, with high cheekbones and liquid brown eyes, needed no adornment and, indeed, she wore none, as if innocent of any artifice.

She had been bent forward listening and nodding in silent assent to another girl when she caught me staring in awe like an idiot. Quite likely my jaw had dropped. Her head tilted to the side and, with puzzled, slightly raised eyebrows, she looked right at me and smiled. Beams of light shot from her mouth, radiating innocence and the love of small animals. I began to levitate, nearly rising out of my shoes. Beauty is everywhere, but this one had depth enough to drown in.

Her presence was humbling. I would have bet a million pesos that she had just arrived from Latin America somewhere, a refugee from the latest atrocity perpetrated by the colonels. I would have lost every centavo.

The familiarity of the other girl's short, dirty blonde hair, sporting a cowlick, finally registered. It was Miranda. Drawn by the lovely apparition's bewilderment, she turned and, sizing up my predicament in an instant, smiled widely. How had I not seen Miranda?

"Ralphie!" she cried. "Just who we were looking for. This is my friend Linda from San José. She's just arrived in Canada, and she needs a job."

"Costa Rica?" I ventured hopefully, perhaps scoring a point with my knowledge of geography.

"California," Miranda laughed. "Outside of San Francisco."

"Oh, that San José. I know the way." They laughed.

"Linda, this is Ralph."

"Hello."

From that one word it was evident that she had perfect diction, practically British, and musical. Was it too late to affect at least a moderate amount of cool? Probably, but I really didn't care. I helloed back and hung on to her extended hand a beat or two too long. It was warm and smooth.

You can't miss Miranda. She stood out like a Don Martin caricature in *Mad Magazine*, high rump in the air, her heels together and pointed south while her feet splayed out, pointing northeast and northwest respectively. You could spot her from blocks away by her walk, halfway between a classically trained ballet dancer and a duck. Miranda, never seeming to hurry, was an oasis of teetering calm with people rushing past her, either to or fro.

As she got closer, your focus would probably shift to an outsized pair of heavy cat's-eye glasses of the sort a suburban mom might wear to Las Vegas. Miranda's mouth was nearly always set in a crooked grin, a wavy line like a cartoonist's rendition of a state of inebriation. Yet her face was delicate, with almost translucent skin, embroidered by a faint network of royal blue veins. And, if she removed her spectacles — a rare event in public — her cornflower eyes were startling, far more like a cat than her eyewear. She couldn't see, perhaps, but she could pounce.

Miranda was a second-look girl whom you might scarcely

notice on the first glance. Later, though, she would knock you out. She could thicken her soft, southern U.S. accent at will. She was a bad girl. She was fun. And she was very, very sexy. What, then, was this waif doing, bobbing along in Miranda's wake? Well, I was never very sharp when bedazzled.

Our fearless leader, John P. Bradford, had been spending a lot of time with Miranda of late, making her First Lady. Of course we could find something for Linda. In the meantime, could someone perhaps show her around? No? Another time, then.

In the evening, the day having delivered more than the usual assortment of wonders, I sat, finally, suffused by a glorious melancholy. Ah, me. The last guest had gone. Clint, who rarely toked up, perennially broke, had returned from the movie I had sent him to see, having given him the three bucks. I knew it would produce in him a state not unlike the stone from very good hash. We could therefore converse. He was only mildly interested in my babble about the Mexican girl, having heard, and, indeed, been the author of similar eulogies. Nor could I tell him this one was different, having worn that out eight or nine declarations ago. But she was, and I knew it.

Clint made a final attempt to draw me down to stray babe patrol on the front patio, then left me to my dreams. I turned on the radio, a wood-cabinet Grundig, with a turntable affixed to it, permanently tuned to CHUM FM. The soothing voice of David Marsden boomed out between songs, nearly all of which were destined to become classics. Aside from Sammy Davis Jr.'s rendition of "Candy Man," and a few other clunkers, were there any bad songs? It seemed there were not. The list would carry on for pages.

Months later a girl would phone in; Marsden sympathized with her on the air. Jimi Hendrix had died, and she spoke of trying to reach him in some sort of séance that involved an ordinary pack of playing cards. She told the story well, and when, "honest to God," the Jack of Clubs (Hendrix) exploded from the deck and burst into flames in mid-air, it gave me a shiver.

Procul Harem's "Whiter Shade of Pale" played, followed by "Rocky Racoon." It reminded me of a girl from Pennsylvania, one that got away, fortunately. I remember chasing her around during the first couple of weeks at Rochdale. Somehow, and against my better judgement, I ended up dropping acid at her place, grooving on *The White Album* until a biker named Mike showed up. Things felt worse and worse until I split and returned to the refuge of my room.

When I was fourteen, I had met a girl at the beach, and we danced to the jukebox in the canteen. As I walked her home, I asked her to think of me exactly at eleven that evening and whisper "Secretly," the song we had listened to all afternoon. She looked at me as if I was nuts and may have even been a bit frightened by my intensity, causing her to agree readily. I never saw her again, but it was weeks before I gave up whispering "secretly" at eleven, straining for some sort of reciprocal sign from the cosmos, like praying. The thing is, down deep, I didn't feel as if my romantic self had made all that much headway since then. Perhaps I could play the game better, be cool, but underneath it all was the same needy child: vulnerable and not at all self-possessed. Nor had I learned much, really. Nor had I given up trying.

The many-splendoured thing, encouraged as it is by story after story and song after song, has much to answer for. I realize now that my first addiction was love, particularly the soaring high part — although I must have gotten a good deal out of the lows, wallowing around in them as I did. Nothing in my life was as capable of delivering me from the squalor I inhabited to the gates of paradise as the hope of romance. If it went well, I eventually got restless, needing another fix. If it went poorly, I tipped the balance into obsession and self-abasement, until it seemed as if misery was really where I wanted to be. I wanted to change this, the low parts at least. I was resolved.

Linda got a job with Troyer, who had somehow managed to add restaurant manager to his portfolio. Whether it was his experience with lawn mowers or the McBee system that identified him as the one to run the restaurant wasn't clear. Midlevel management, no stranger to Rochdale council committees, is only too happy to hand off the things they don't understand. With the restaurant being closed for inventory, Troyer reasoned correctly that it would be weeks before he was found out. Linda began counting sacks of potatoes and canned goods, which tended, unlike the furniture, to at least stay in one place — midnight munchie raids led by Troyer notwithstanding. She should work very, very slowly, I advised.

After a while I stopped even pretending that I had a reason to be in the storeroom. I had not worried about rejection or being cool. There was something about her that made me unafraid.

"Linda, I'm drawn to you. There has to be something to it. Let's go out and see what happens. How about after work?"

She looked me in the eye and said, "You'd better not get involved with me."

I could tell she meant that, and in a kind way. By then I had discovered she was an actress, and I had been warned about actresses, which made no sense to me at all. Dancers, perhaps. It was too bad, but I wasn't crushed. What would have done me in was not having at least tried.

"Okay," I said, staring her boldly in the eye.

She burst out laughing. And so did I. Laughing at the same things is a good sign.

"I'll be ready by seven," she said. "I'm staying with Miranda. And don't say I didn't warn you."

Well, why not? After three months in Toronto, the world had changed. I had found an alternate reality in which I was accommodated like I had never been before. It was a world in which I had influence, in which I had become successful, in which I was not lonely, in which I did get the girl. Hell, I was even two inches taller.

She was quiet when I called for her, teetering on the cusp of begging off. She wore a print dress that fell just above her knees. I had come to expect her beauty, even as it threatened to overwhelm me again. I waited for the bluebirds to stop circling my head and the warbling to die down.

"You'll need a sweater," I said. This created just enough curiosity for her to continue. She had been thinking too much. I knew all about that. It felt as if I had known her for a long time.

"Really?" It was not quite muggy, but hot.

"You'll see."

Clint had shown me the way to Centre Island, and I meant to take Linda there. Not knowing one ferry from another, we boarded an open-decked craft, much smaller than I had remembered, and ended up on Ward's Island. Lost, I forged ahead like I knew what I was doing. It could not have been more perfect. We followed the shore and passed some tiny cottages, obviously the ones I had read about. I explained how they were under siege and likely would be bulldozed soon. We turned our backs to the city skyline, heading inland, and soon found a little path that led to a small beach looking out over nothing but water. Just like that, we were in the country.

There's a magic quality to the light just before sunset, bathing everything in a rosy glow, smoothing lines, softening skin. We sat on a blanket-sized piece of beach, surrounded on three sides by reeds, facing the water. In this private world, tiny, wind-ruffled wavelets expired on a narrow strip of glistening, red-gold sand. The breeze played with her hair and, in reaching to smooth it down, I could not believe how soft it was. Seeing it for what it was, a perfect Harlequin moment, we followed the script without irony and kissed. It was surprising how easily it had come together.

I remember the last time we had sex, but not the first. It was probably the next night, the night we went to Grossman's. I do know that nobody had any claim on the other because of it. For whatever reason, it seemed to work between us. I made no assumptions that we were now an item, even though my feelings for her were becoming overpowering, threatening to throw me to the ground from a great height, and dash me to pieces.

Grossman's Tavern sits a few blocks south of College on the east side of Spadina. It's still a happening place. In the late summer of 1969, if you felt like sharing a pitcher of beer and listening to some fine music, there wasn't a better venue in the city. A young harmonica player, Donnie Walsh, was there most nights, a white boy playing the blues. Half the room was black, and they didn't seem to mind. Donnie's group was the nucleus of what became the legendary Downchild Blues Band — or perhaps they had already formed, not yet a legend.

Toronto was not quite as multicultural then, although the seeds had been sown. The freedom marches in the U.S. South weren't exactly ancient history. The fight was still going on. Race riots had spread from the Watts neighbourhood in LA to Boston. Nearer to home, Detroit had been trashed and burned in 1967, and several cities in Pennsylvania had been rocked by arson and shooting.

Just after Martin Luther King had been assassinated in 1968, I sat around a kitchen table in Regina talking to a black draft dodger from Tennessee. He had joined a group of us who had just come from the public library where a standing-room-only crowd of students and radicals of all ages had expressed solidarity with the students and workers who were rioting in Paris. Whenever anyone asked this guy a question or talked to him directly, he stared hard at the floor and gave an embarrassed sort of titter before answering. It was mildly irritating. I asked him why he did that. He looked at me, only briefly, and then explained.

"Back home, a black man don't need to be looking at a white man. You got to be looking the other way, man. I know it's different up here in Canada. It's supposed to be different back home now, but it ain't. I'm gonna do better but it's hard for me to change. And I guess I'm laughing 'cause it's a little embarrassing for me to be talking to a room full of white men. I'm not used to it, is all. I know y'all are on my side and I feel so good about that it makes me want to laugh, too. But I'm still a little shy."

He laughed again, raised his head, and looked hastily around a room that had gone silent. I had a lump in my throat the size of a walnut. It was right to not want to be part of a world like that.

At Grossman's you could be black, white, Asian, straight, hippie, whatever, and nobody gave you a second look — not on that account anyway. It was about long tables where you squeezed in where you could, it was about a cool pitcher on a hot night and digging the music. But when I walked into the room with Linda, between sets, there was a noticeable hush and it seemed as if everyone was looking at her. A heartbeat later, the din of the jukebox and loud talk resumed. She had the white dress on again.

This was the night that James Cotton, who was in town headlining at the Ex, dropped in between sets. With hardly any protest, he agreed to do a few numbers. Since his sidemen were with him, the Downchild crew gave way gracefully. Blues from the big time filled the room and, after a short set and an encore, Cotton abruptly left. Donnie and the boys (Jane Vasey had not been there) didn't play after that. It was a smart, professional move — no compare, no despair. Besides, it had gotten louder by then, and the jukebox was wailing out south side Chicago blues — "Snatch It Back and Hold It" with Junior Wells doing harp and vocals and Buddy Guy on guitar. The evening had taken on a magical momentum.

The place was packed. Linda, having been gone a while, came back from the washroom looking, if not glum, at least reflective. She squeezed back into the chair I had had to constantly lay claim to while she had been downstairs. I might have consumed three glasses of draft, which left me with little restraint. I leaned over and told her, out loud for a change, how absolutely beautiful she looked.

"Really?" She said, scrutinizing me closely to see if I was shining her, finally believing. "I was just looking in the mirror downstairs, thinking I looked like a hag."

Was she serious? Apparently, being as human as the rest of us, she was.

We walked back to my room, hand in hand, arm in arm, my arm around her shoulders, hers around my waist, sometimes apart, stopping now and again, in the dark between street lights, to embrace. I recall, also, much laughter. We hadn't bothered turning the light on when we got home and, for two cerebral people, everything fell together in a remarkably untroubled way. By morning everything had changed. I wasn't sure how, just that it had.

The true nature of my attraction, the depth of it, had more to do with a kind of empathy we shared, and her quickness of mind, than her looks. We had both been born below stairs and had not wished for that to be etched in stone. At first glance she had been some kind of fantasy, a Third World innocent with a come-hither, back-to-the-land appeal. Shy, naïve, and in danger from the urban jungle, surely she would need protection, for which she would be grateful, loving, and constant. (We had been raised to think of women as delicate creatures in need of protection.) Fortunately, I had held that view for little more than a minute.

Erlinda Segura — Linda — had grown up in a Mexican-American community in San José, a California girl. I'm not sure she ever realized how similar my working-class background was to hers. Her dad had been a boxer. My dad, if you count the alley outside the Legion Hall, had had a bout or two himself. She acquitted herself well in high school, took drama, and got a job at a bank. This period of her life seemed to amuse her.

"I'd get ready for work and head out in the morning in my yellow dress. I'd hold my purse just so, marching down the street, my little heels clicking and clacking. Every now and again I'd pass someone sitting on the steps or in their front yard and, mostly in fun, they'd call out, 'Hey, Gringa, Gringa Salada.' I'd just laugh. 'Gringa salada,' 'salty gringa,' means someone is putting on airs, trying to act superior. I was being teased."

First impressions aside, I tended to forget that Linda was a visible minority, or even Hispanic. Linda was Linda. She was beautiful. She was smart. She was American. I had bought a small, second-hand motorcycle, a 125cc Yamaha, for a buck per cc. After the requisite number of accidents to purchase experience in the alley behind Rochdale, we went riding on the 401. I wore ordinary glasses, discovering, through the blur of teary, wind-scoured eyes, why goggles are necessary and, again, that love makes us brave. We survived the ride, the bond between angels and fools having been strengthened. On the way home we came to a sign that said SQUEEZE LEFT. I reached down and gave the appropriate thigh a squeeze, and she laughed right away. I had read her mind. The next day I sold the bike.

One afternoon she called her mother from my place just to say everything was okay and not to worry. It was the usual stuff. Yes, she was eating well, and she had a line on an acting job, and so on. I was half listening until, "Well, we had some trouble getting across the border into Canada. . . . I don't know, Ma, I think they maybe have a prejudice against Indians." The reality of what she had just said hit me between the eyes. She had said it so calmly, so matter-of-factly, like it was automatic, a given, an indelible part of her reality, who she was. In comparing our similarities, it hadn't even occurred to me. We had read the same books, listened to the same music, laughed at the same jokes, and seen the same movies. It was tough for me to get around the fact that people would judge her for her looks. The irony, of course, totally escaped me.

Although Rochdale was now drawing most of the heat, Yorkville Avenue was still ground zero. In 1967 it had been the Canadian equivalent of Haight-Ashbury. It was where the hippies gathered, and where the police came to put a stop to it all. Television across the country broadcast the conflict, identifying where it was at, man. Kids streamed in from everywhere. Traffic on the one-way street crawled along, almost at a standstill. Nobody was in a hurry, they were too busy gawking at the hippies, at the long-haired freaks in buckskins, bell-bottoms, tie-dyed T-shirts; at boys in headbands, at girls who wore no bras. They looked on young people as a different species, one that threatened the order of things and the good life. It had not occurred to them that they were looking at their own children, their neighbours' children, that, essentially they were looking at themselves. This appears to be hardwired into the human psyche, the sense of "other," the "us" and "them" thing, duality. The costumery represented perhaps an attempt to examine that.

Midweek, on a warm night in late September, Yorkville had died down to a dull roar. On weekends and throughout the summer it was a zoo. That's when all the kids would come down from the suburbs and hippie out, doubling the crowd. You could opt out of the adult world completely, the infrastructure having been formed during the previous years of protest. All you had to do was hit the streets. Free clinics, set up at Rochdale and elsewhere, like Digger House, ended up treating, for the most part, these suburban kids and absorbing costs that would have normally gone to the city. Unlike a visit to the family doctor, questions were not asked regarding the why of things. Birth control was distributed freely, without censure. Every summer there were a few more who didn't make it home to Willowdale or Scarborough.

There would still be a crowd on a warm night in Yorkville, but manageable and more laid back with fewer gawkers. You could get a decent sense of the feel of it today by spending a summer's eve walking between the various restaurant patios of College St. between Crawford and Manning in Little Italy. Essentially, it would be that of a coterie of like-minded people admiring themselves. Replace the cellphones with bongs, ditch Armani for denim, put vans where the beemers sit locked and armed, and you're there.

The Grab Bag — a legendary convenience store where six different kinds of cigarette papers shared shelf space with gumballs, liquorice, copper screens, and the pipes to go with them, as well as bread and milk — hung on for a while during the gentrification of Yorkville but eventually foundered. There was always a crowd of freaks inside the store, spilling out onto the street. You met people there, left messages on scraps of paper. Further down the street, past The Riverboat and The Penny Farthing, was the other street-gathering spot, the old folks' home. Behind the iron picket fence sat the elderly in placid defiance, while on the street the hippies lounged, often leaning back against the fence, their only visible means of support according to some of the elder wags. It was not uncommon for remarks to be made on both sides of the divide. It was also not out of the ordinary to see joints pass back and forth between the generations.

This was where Pops did his stroll. He looked eighty at least, always dressed nicely in a blazer. He often sported a beret studded with pins atop his snowy white hair and a sash to denote he got the costume thing. Pops walked around, a courtly little man, always smiling, and the kids would give him a big hello to which he would respond in kind. He thought they were all right, and there was a lot of sense to be made by making love instead of war. Pops was demonstrating that the capacity for joy knew no boundaries, certainly not that of age. As for the Age of Aquarius, you could count him in.

Today, there's an exclusive (well, pricey) French restaurant where Mike's Mexican Cantina stood the night Linda, Miranda, and I decided to stop before catching Jerry Jeff Walker at The Riverboat.

"Hey, what's this guacamole stuff that comes with everything?" Linda rolled her eyes.

I enjoyed my sinchronizado (sic) which was a tortilla stuffed with ham and Swiss cheese. Miranda played with a plate of nachos, Linda ordered nothing and, two months later, Mike's was gone. It had been a great patio, however. Delicious creatures of all sexes paraded by in a dream of beauty.

Jerry Jeff, as Miranda avowed, had written "Mr. Bojangles," along with a billion other songs and, as it turned out, she really did know him. We sat as close to the stage as we could get, with Miranda at the point of the wedge, beaming at the headliner like an auntie watching her favourite nephew. At the end of the set I realized that we had been strategically positioned between the stage and the dressing room as Jerry Jeff bounded off the stage and proceeded to walk past us. "Jerry Jeff," cried Miranda, joy in her voice. He acknowledged her as he would any table of adoring fans with a "Hi, there. How y'all doin'?" and kept going.

"Jerry Jeff, now you just hold on," she said with a mixture of familiarity and honeyed rebuke, perhaps Becky Thatcher giving Tom Sawyer what for. "It's me. Miranda."

At that, he stopped and focused on this wildly bespectacled creature. "Shee-it, Miranda Smith, what are y'all doin' here?" Then they was a-back-slappin' and a-huggin'.

I love that good ol' boy vernacular. In fact, envy would not be too strong a word to put to it under certain circumstances. Peyton Brian, of the cleaning crew, and his pregnant and saucy roommate, Jennifer — and they were just roommates — would entertain for hours with their Tennessee drawl. Jennifer had the ability to elicit a deep blush and have you squirming when she got to flirtin', even though you knew she was just having sport. I was less enamoured of the Texas Troubadour eyeballing Linda while he was hugging Miranda. Nevertheless, we were a jolly group as we hopped into a cab. I was behind the driver with Linda on my lap while Miranda sat in the middle between me and Jerry Jeff. Turns out he had indeed heard of Rochdale and wouldn't say no to having his mind expanded.

At first, I thought, well, that's show biz, I guess, and isn't it free and easy, what with Jerry Jeff fondling the back of my neck on the cab ride to Rochdale. He was kissing Miranda and playing with the base of my hair at the same time. I decided to err on the side of cosmic, genderless affection and said nothing. We parked in the alley behind the building, and he stayed in the cab with the two women while I ran upstairs. I had had to move my neck, of course, to exit the back seat. That he was startled confirmed my second opinion — he thought he had been stroking Linda's neck. I looked over at him before closing the cab door and gave him a stage wink. Man, did he laugh. It had really caught him off guard.

We toked up in a secure spot on Yorkville across from The Riverboat with a portable pipe carved from soapstone. The ride back had been uneventful. Linda and I took in a few songs from the next set and then abandoned Miranda, who seemed not to mind at all. Jerry Jeff winked at me from the stage when we got up to go, or perhaps it had been for Linda. My turn to laugh.

"I just wish John Peter wasn't so selfish in bed," Miranda volunteered, not quite out of the blue.

The red light in my brain was flashing "danger." It had been fine when she was talking about me and Linda, saying that Linda appeared to be happy with the way things were going, particularly the sex. I hadn't solicited any information, but when isn't that good to hear? I gathered that had not always been the case, and neither Linda nor I had exchanged much information about our past loves. So I was eating Miranda's comments up, but it seemed as if the bill was now due and I didn't want to pay. I got the feeling that she was going to share a confidence, that I might be expected to pass on to Bradford, of a type that no guy would willingly broach with another. Moreover, he would have to kill me. Better not to hear it.

Fortunately, Bradford appeared earlier than expected, extricating me from a difficult situation. He showed up with a huge, black Great Dane whom he introduced as Olive. Up until then I hadn't seen his affectionate side. "Hey, Bradford, Miranda wants me to talk to you about matters pertaining to the bedroom. Sure, bring the dog." I don't think so. Besides, I would be the last guy to be giving pointers.

Linda was moody. When her body was present, often her mind was not. She was chewing away at something, quietly. She didn't lay a trip out with it. One night just sitting around she wrote a poem and gave it to me. I had been staring out the window thinking about one of Dunc's cosmic axes that he would every now and again grind: animus and anima. I don't know from which body of work this originated, there were so many. It was a great time to be a philosopher, people were buying almost anything, particularly those doctrines that emphasized permission instead of prohibition. To Dunc,

animus and anima boiled down to there being for everyone, somewhere in the world, a perfect mate. That would explain a lot,
particularly about the times in which the doctrine of free love
seemed to enable a faster processing, and a larger number, of appli-
cations. I was comfortable just sitting there, not doing much. It was
okay that she was occasionally morose. It didn't have to be happy
all the time.

The poem was only four or five lines long. I can't remember
them any more than I can remember much of what I had written
back then. What she was saying — not that I understood — was
that sooner or later all this playing would have to stop and that I'd
expect her to enter the adult world, and that she wasn't about to do
that, now or ever. She was a year younger. In me, for sure, she had
the wrong guy and I suspect she was talking about someone else —
Dennis, perhaps, whose name kept coming up. "Whaddya mean?" I
asked, goofing around, going for total immaturity. She capitulated
soon enough, but not before saying ominously, "You'll find out."

I had come to realize by then that I hadn't really had a complete
childhood. I had been too worried. The way to health and whole-
ness, I concluded during one of my habitual ruminations, consisted
of revisiting that and doing it right. Then I could be all that I could
be. It was crackpot theory number three, of many. There was never
a more perfect environment than Rochdale to encourage this line of
thinking, to encourage play before adopting the terminally serious
proclivities of being grown up. A free range of behaviour, providing
it was social and not harming anybody, was not only condoned but
encouraged. Having looked around and seen the cost, nobody
wanted to assume the role of adult — not in this society.

Linda could be happy, too. In fact, the balance had been tipped
that way — according to my point of view. Who knows how she saw
it? I was in love, possibly blind. How would I like to do some acid
with her? Sure, let's do it. When I agreed, I knew it was a risky
proposition. The absolute truth would come out or leave you shivering in fear, if you denied it in any way. I even brought this up, but

she said it wasn't that kind of acid. Surely, there's only one kind? I think it's some kind of hybrid. Miranda thinks it's good.

It was not like any acid I had tried although I did get very stoned. I hadn't gotten weighed down with introspection at the beginning, or struggled through much of anything to achieve liftoff. It could have been the company I was keeping. More likely than not, it was MDA, also known as the "love drug," and not acid at all. Or, it may have been a little of both. I will never know. I prepared myself for it to be acid, knowing to never take it lightly.

We dropped it in my room around ten in the evening, a shared act of faith. You never knew what you would find, which is the payoff and the danger — times two in our case. Stan Bevington had come in and gone straight to his room, as usual, and from which he wouldn't stir until morning. The outer door was locked, the phone disabled, the inner door shut, the night was ours. We fussed, trying to settle in.

Linda had changed into a patterned robe, mostly red with smaller bits of blue on a white background. Sometimes it was roses and blueberries on snow, or it could appear to be a series of ancient Egyptians lined up in rows of hieroglyphs, or there were other symbols I couldn't translate — if only they'd stop moving around.

I had put the South American flute album on the turntable. Stately, above all other creatures, the great bird soared, riding the updrafts through the Andes. El condor pasa, gliding toward Aconcagua. He would rather feel the air beneath his wings, yes he would, he surely would. I lay back on the bed, awaiting whatever might come. After a while, having been lost somewhere in her head on her own personal journey, Linda crawled in beside me. Time passed.

At what point had we become naked?

I remember feeling complete as she lay there quietly looking at me. I was on my side, propped up on one elbow. Our eyes held. Smiles welled up, unafraid and secure. I ran a hand along her body and slid between the smoothness of her legs that simply unfolded as I got near.

My fingers were anointed as they slipped easily into the warmth. I had been given a great gift. It was all so simple, really, and I was just as ready, sure and stable. Accepted and enveloped, I was almost over-whelmed by a golden sense of welcome. What else is love?

It was amazing how naturally we had mated. We were not the most likely candidates, both being more self-conscious than carnal. Our sensitivity to one another was at least attuned to the point of being able to recognize that whatever was happening was mutual. It was as if a fog, comprised of past experience, prohibition, shame, and prurience, had lifted to give us a glimpse of what things might be like in a more perfect world. It was as if we were animus and anima.

I have known you a thousand years, a thousand times a thou-sand. Welcome home, my love.

Somewhere between the second and third consecration of the harmony that is bedrock to the cosmos, we developed a powerful thirst. In one of the many feats of magic performed that evening we found ourselves standing by the running tap in the kitchen, still naked as Adam and Eve might have been beside a gushing spring.

We drank from the tap, the backs of our hands becoming nap-kins, until we were full. My cheeks ballooned out with a final prodigious gulp, and I happened to catch her eye — or to be caught up by her eye — just as I was about to swallow. It's a silly thing to be puffed out like that. Drawn to the occasion, she had a mischie-vous look that said "Don't you dare" before I had even formulated the thought. It was almost an encouraging look, playful. I took the dare. The spray turned into a cascade of diamonds, each one pre-cious and reflecting a rainbow, adorning her perfect face, trailing down her body, and shaken off into a halo by her laughter. After I had been similarly baptized, we reappeared in bed, dressed gaudily by our antics at the spring.

There are persuasive reasons to drop at night. For one thing, there are fewer distractions, and it's quieter. And a twelve-hour journey through the dark depletes energy. It can be a little bumpy coming down. One minute you're striding about the heavens, and the next you've stubbed a toe. The colours fade and your step may falter so it's best to take your revelations into the brightness of day. You can smoke a little hash to smooth out the bumps, but there's an energy cost to that as well. Somehow it's more hopeful to snooze through the light.

Morning came up absolutely clear. We took turns wandering to the window, watching the dawn display simple turns of resonant pastels. She looked out over the lake into the distance. I watched the rooftops below, seeing pigeons take their morning stretch in flight. We were two solitudes again, having been one. This is as it should be, even so early and so soon.

Linda had put on her robe. I call it a robe hastily, and only because the sleeves were much wider at the wrist than the shoulder, and bias cut. But really it was a dress, an empire-waisted thing, loose, and floor length, a dress whose pattern still shimmered and danced. It continued to suggest an archetypal, runic message that went well past the time my people covered their bodies in blue clay and followed the warrior queen

The sun had almost fully risen. Linda stood, framed in the window by that soft and early, most hopeful, blue. In a gesture that would have done the Egyptian goddess of nature proud, she, as Isis, lifted her face on high and slowly raised her arms in embrace of Horus, god of the sky, her son, our son. As Osiris, I sat on the bed in the shade, my back against the cool wall, and admired her. My domain, the underworld, had worked its magic of creative force. Life would prevail. Was not our offspring proof of that?

Perhaps I should not have, but I was moved to speak. Words are imperfect and create distance. Isis, Osiris, and Horus were too much. Egypt was too far away, as were the Woads of Britain. I transposed an image closer to home, where there were also pyramids and an ancient language to decipher.

Thinking her so fine and beautiful, I couldn't help but say, "Standing there like that, you look like an Aztec princess." Never mind I didn't have it right. It should have been "Mayan," and it should have been "goddess," or at the very least, "queen." They were only words after all, and ones of admiration.

Her arms fell to her sides, and she bowed her head. When she turned to face me, her smile glittered as if reflecting off a piece of tin, bright but not golden.

"Do I indeed?"

"Indeed you do," I insisted, sensing, perhaps too late, she was not in the mood for compliments.

"I have to go."

"Now?"

"I need to sleep. It's too bright here."

"I'll pull the curtains."

"I want my own bed."

"Shall I come with you?"

"No."

She gathered her things and left. Nothing was left behind as an excuse to return. I groped for the difference between reality and illusion. Perhaps it was all a dream. I had envisioned her coming back to bed where we would hold one another in sleep and awaken joined at the hip. I was stunned, with no clue as to what had happened, where she had gone in her head. Had I ever felt closer to anyone? Had she not been right there beside me? It had all rung true. I could still feel her warmth and hear her laughter. Okay, it had to have been a reaction to the drug. She slipped into a dark place not of her choosing, she would sleep, all would be well.

My own fatigue put it to rest. I placed my face on the dent in the pillow her head had made. Breathing in her essence, I fell into an old wringer-washer of dreams, an agitator is what they used to call the twisty part in the middle. I awoke bleary eyed and hungry, late in the day. I looked for her on the way to the Varsity for eggs and tried her room again on the way back. Since we weren't in the habit of accounting for our time — which took quite some effort on my part — days could go by without our seeing one another. I told myself to relax, everything was back to normal.

She was at home the following afternoon. Miranda let me in. Linda was in the act of pulling a nail from an old wooden pallet and only briefly glanced my way, offering a tight "hello." Apparently, the pulling of this nail was of grave importance. She had it three-quarters of the way out and, having abandoned the concept of leverage, was just tugging ferociously on the handle. In my experience, that was Fat Lip City waiting to happen. So I reached for the hammer to show her how to put a block under the head to make the last bit easy.

I hadn't said, "May I?"

She swung the hammer away from me in an alarmingly forceful way. Miranda and I took a step back.

"I was only trying to help."

"I didn't ask for any help."

"Okay. Sorry. I just came by to see how you are."

"I'm fine."

"Maybe I'll see you later?"

"I don't know. Maybe."

I looked at Miranda since Linda was again fully engaged by her labours. Her gestures said she didn't know what was going on either.

"I guess I'll go, then."

Miranda nodded affirmatively and patted my shoulder on the way out. Linda had said, "Bye."

What the fuck was that all about? Ah, Jesus. A kind of despair settled in, more like a relative that you could do with seeing much less of, than it was an old friend. Twisting aimlessly on hope and denial, I drifted through the gloom.

Obviously there was some sort of flaw in me that I couldn't see. I tried to get at it, spending a couple of weeks in a circular inner debate that seemed to be the precursor of the eight-track loop. Not knowing at the time, or even having heard of, the stages of grief, I pretty much moved to a sad acceptance of the facts right away. Troyer, being a bandage-ripper with an instinct for pain, was the hardest thing I had to deal with. "Whatever happened to Linda, I thought you two were quite close?" He'd watch closely to see if I twitched. I'd talk about some beautiful blonde and how this was the sixties and how frustrating it must be for "you married guys." It worked well enough.

Some of it made sense. I remember thinking that I hated that Linda and I were both fucked up, that we couldn't really be normal. It's all fine in the beginning, but sooner or later the issues would creep out. She often hinted at that. I hated that we hadn't come from health, that we hadn't come from a tribal situation where there was enough extended family to provide us with all the love we needed as we grew. I had no doubt that the fit between us was so good that, given the right circumstances, we could have been together forever. We could have weathered the pain, the tragedies that crop up in the way of things. As it stood, we were bound to founder on the first rock. I knew all that going in — as did she — but in we went.

There had been so much shit to wade through in the past few years that I didn't want to wade through any more. I didn't want to be down. I wanted to feel good. I had begun to feel good before I met Linda — great, in fact. I want that feeling back, I told myself, repeating it in my head one evening as I went to answer the door.

She stood there with her face framed by a tempest of soft dark hair, bound in a cocoon of wool cardigan over a cotton dress, propped up by tiny feet in cheap tennis shoes, wrapped in an aura of hope and confusion, and reticence overcome by bravery. Guadeloupe! She was as the first time I had ever seen her, except more comforting, like the earth, and more beautiful than ever. Her arms were crossed, hugging herself, retaining warmth. She looked at me openly and there was sadness in her eyes, but I was welcome to it and all the other things.

In that half sleep before darkness, I had called for her every night for weeks. She would come, then steal away. How many times would I lose her? How many times a day had I forced myself to think of anything else? And yet for solace I would deliberately call up the hot, dusty day we skinny-dipped in the quarry deep in the woods. My mind would revel in the eternal beauty of her emerging naked and shining from the water, her hair in braids, her feet silently treading the bright green moss. Now she was right here in front of me. Her name was no longer an echo.

"Hello."

As ever, her voice was music. Such a tiny girl, really. I was so relieved to see her. I was *so* relieved to see her.

What came in the flood, however, what had been held back, was fear. We would be happy now for a year, a month, until the next time? Where was the guy for whom a moment would be enough? He ran away, frightened by a bit of sunlight flashing off an old can. This can't be right. My body blocked the doorway.

"Well, well, what brings you here?"

She had known I would perhaps be a little hurt. She had expected that. But she had trusted in that last night we had been together. She knew what had gone on, and so she trusted me.

"I wanted to see you. I'm feeling kind of down, and I really need to be held."

Do I have any regrets in life? No, I'm fond of saying, and I mean it. On occasion, however, my capacity to be an asshole astounds even me, and I have behaved in ways I would rather have not. Add a dash of cowardice and childhood resentment, of being angry with mummy, and a moment is created one wishes could be taken back at almost any price.

"So? You think you can just wander up and see me any time you feel like it? Forget it."

The most powerful scene in *Zorba the Greek*, for me, had been when the darkly beautiful Irene Pappas had openly invited Alan Bates to her bed, and he turned her down. He had portrayed the coward so well, the scene had affected me deeply. Bates's performance had been so good that I loathed the man in every subsequent movie in which he appeared. I could scarce look at him. Anthony Quinn as Zorba told him, "When a woman invites you to her bed, you must never turn her down. It is a sin." I could relate to that, being at the time in an unhappy marriage where nearly every attempt to invite myself to her bed was rebuffed. I thought Bates to be quite the fool.

Linda looked at me to see if perhaps I might be just joking in poor taste. She must have seen something prim and self-righteous. In her face I saw disbelief, confusion and, because she had trusted me to be there, hurt. You have no idea what I've gone through to come to your door, her eyes said. And I will never come here again.

Whatever it was she had to say, because she had also come to tell me something, was forever left unsaid. She turned without speaking, her arms still folded across her chest, and walked slowly down the hallway. Then and there I wanted to scream, "Wait, come back. I love you. I didn't mean it, please come back." The words stuck in my throat. I wanted to run after her, which wouldn't have taken much, she was walking that slowly.

Please, I didn't mean it.

She didn't look back. The doorway at the end of the hall swallowed her up.

To the crime of being cruel to protect myself, I can only plead the desperation of the wounded.

I lived with it. I didn't try to contact her again. She was in a play at Theatre Passe Muraille that Clint and I went to see. It was a silly, experimental thing where she, although one of the chorus, had a few lines to herself while they all paddled an imaginary canoe. She was great, I thought, and I hung around after the show to tell her that. I got a flinty, hard-eyed, over-the-shoulder "thanks" and ended up staring familiarly at her back.

The last time I saw Linda was a couple of months later at the corner of Bloor and St. George by the Shell station, now an architectural monstrosity called the Bata Shoe Museum that dominates the corner, moving you right along. It was sunny and quite warm for winter and again I was with Clint and Linda was with Miranda. They were bundled up in coats. We talked, at least, while Clint chatted with Miranda. Linda said she had been sick for a while, and she had missed her mother then because nobody brought her beans and rice, which is what you do in her community sometimes when a woman is sick.

"I would have brought you beans and rice if I had known," I said. Trying.

"Oh yeah?" she replied, pleasantly enough, as if to say, "that's nice."

Then I told Clint we had to be going. I didn't want to see her walk away again. Something nagged at me. In my haste to get away, before I was reduced to begging, I felt as if I had missed an important cue. No doubt it was wishful thinking.

That last night with Linda, obviously forgotten in the euphoria of new love or the black depression of yet another loss, ghosted along in the back of my mind for years. It would surface at times, odd times really, long after its importance had diminished. It had become a curiosity that I had more or less wrapped in tattered grief and put where the unsolved mysteries go. Gradually, the neurons would die and not be replaced and I would have no recollection at all.

The night she had come for comfort, the moment I had dreamed of and strangled in my own confusion, had been an unfinished encounter. Gone forever was my chance to ask her what the hell had happened ? Why had she suddenly turned on me?

During a spell of daydreaming, not all that long ago, when I was blocking out some of the things I might want to address in a memoir, I shot bolt upright as they say. I hadn't even been aware of thinking about it, but suddenly I had the answer. It was simple enough. "Aztec Princess" had far different connotations for her than for me. Believe me, when I saw Linda, I saw only Linda, beautiful in an exotic dress. Perhaps in school, during studies on Meso-America, she had been teased. She had heard something I had neither felt nor intended, a kind of insult. I had called her an Indian.

Alice

When I first came to town, it was fascinating going around to various TV studios with Eddie and Clint. Youth, having been discovered in the fifties, was being molded into a culture and all sorts of programs were being made to reflect that. I was meeting the sons and daughters of nationally famous people: Brent (a.k.a. Barney) Frayne, son of Trent (a.k.a. Bill) Frayne and June Callwood; Suzanne DePoe, daughter of Norman and sister of David, who had gotten a lot of press due to his leadership role in the Yorkville riots in 1967; and Paul Saltzman, son of Percy. The offspring, Clint, and Ed were all heavily involved in redefining the boundaries of a medium that was just switching to colour.

In their own way, these people were pioneers, just as their parents had been. It couldn't have been easy following such icons. The shows were mostly of a format that involved bright, attractive young persons discussing issues relevant to "today's youth," a form that has survived in infinite permutations.

It was a Toronto-as-centre-of-the-universe kind of thing. One minute you're in the frigid nether regions of the country, the next you're on a vaguely familiar set as a background, non-speaking youth and exchanging stage winks with one of the female producers. If Ed was to be believed, the studio was the same one that had been used by Go Go '66 (and the not-quite-as-good Go Go '67). He knew I'd be impressed. Everybody had watched Go Go '66 in which two girls were hoisted above the stage in separate cages and danced to the latest tunes in shiny miniskirts and boots over the heads of the band and the cheering studio audience.

To older people it was a scandalous show, generating controversy, and to the hip it was pure camp, like Batman. But, across Canada, little girls as young as five and six donned their white plastic go-go boots (with stylized flowers that resembled asterisks on the sides) and climbed up on coffee tables to dance their hearts out; imagining, if not in fact, their hair was long and flowing like the miniskirted terpsichores in the cage. For a generation of females for whom liberation was to be more of a given than an issue, their first declaration might well have been, "No more pixie cuts for me. I'm gonna let it grow."

I had picked up a habit in Regina — begun out of irony and seeming to persist and grow of its own accord — of saying "far out" far too often. And so I became, in what was later to be demonstrated to me, all about what I'm not. Anything new or unusual or beautiful pointed out to me (about every fifteen seconds in the Toronto of 1969) would receive the utterance "far out." Eventually, "no way," or "wow," or "fuuck" said softly with two *u*s, or "too much" provided vocabularic relief. To my credit, I had never sunk to using "Far out, man" except in obvious parody. However, like certain adopted malapropisms that become so ingrained ("the mind biggles," "one never know, do one?") that other people may feel as though they've just seen through your rather thin veneer, the thing persisted until I became known in some circles as "Far Out Ralph." This had the effect of being both embarrassing and amusing in equal measure. But it was "far out" this and "far out" that as Clint and Ed revealed to me wonder after wonder.

In the late fall, firmly ensconced in Rochdale, by now overcome with counter-cultural passion, walking the walk, talking the talk, and becoming more hirsute by the hour, I was invited, as "Far Out Ralph," to appear live on the local television show, *Perry's Probe*. The half-hour format consisted of having a panel of three guests with different areas of expertise being interviewed by the host, Norm Perry. After the interviews, the phone lines were opened and people could call in and ask questions. These were fielded off camera, written down, and handed like bits of ticker tape to Norm who would direct the queries to the appropriate expert.

That I agreed to do it at all was a triumph of vanity over experience. As a spokesperson for our free school in Regina, I had gone down to the local studio to do an item that would be aired at a later date. I thought I was ready, but when I was suddenly blinded by the headlights of a DC-9 while standing in the middle of the runway, I froze completely. Then I knew how it must feel for my ungulate woodland brethren an hour or so before they're gutted, flayed, and hanging upside down in some thug's garage. Like Leacock's errant financier, who had withdrawn his money in fifties and sixes and promptly walked into the safe, I heard howls of laughter from the reporter and cameraman as I closed the door on the way out.

This time I did okay. First, we went to the Frayne household, and I was introduced to June, and Trent, and Barney's siblings. It was Saturday or Sunday and there was an important CFL game on the tube. Everybody was watching it, and I remember thinking that was a good thing. Whoever drove me to the studio, Ed or Barney, sat with me in the green room and helped prevent my mild panic from turning into outright terror. It helped to be one of three pigeons. And I didn't need to be earnest, thanks to the Beatles' paradigm of being irreverent and un-serious to the media. I could say pretty much whatever popped into my head in selling the product of disaffected youth — no script, no axe to grind, just go out there and irritate as many "straight" people as I could. Far out.

Being bearded, I required only a touch of makeup, the concept of which I found very amusing. My fellow guests, one a coin collector and the other, I think, a fireman, were also teetering between self-mockery and what we hoped looked like nonchalance. Witty asides were exchanged, the stuff of gallows humour. Norm Perry, whose unassuming appearance was not intimidating, looked each of us in the eye as he outlined the plan. You suddenly knew why it was his show. We were in good hands.

It helped that we sat behind a long table. It's always good to have a place to duck under; even better, I was on the end in case all was discovered. The coin collector sat in the middle. The moment the lights came on, I realized that the Irish fisherman's sweater hadn't been my best wardrobe choice after all. I began to sweat immediately and profusely, reinforcing what was certainly my image to most of the viewers, that of a barely disguised felon. I should have gone with the suede bomber that could have at least been unzipped.

My turn to be interviewed came last. I have no idea what I said, just that I was drenched while I said it. Passion was involved. We were in a generational war, and there had been casualties. I had been escorted deep into enemy territory to plead our cause. The members of my constituency had been banished or gone AWOL from homes all over the country. Many of these wanderers would follow the beacon and find their way to Rochdale, broke, hungry, and some of them wired on one drug or another. We would be the ones to deal with them for the most part. During a time of budget surpluses and economic health in the community at large, our resources were strained. We needed help.

During the break, I removed my sweater and towelled off. The other panellists quietly uttered their support in a genuine way, as did the TV crew. Apparently I had made an effective plea for understanding. I felt a lot better as we waited for the part where people phoned in with their questions.

It was a deluge.

"I have a fifty-cent piece from 1920. Is it worth anything?"

"Is it the 1936 penny with the dot that's the most valuable Canadian coin?"

"What can you tell me about 'shinplasters,' and how much could I get for one in good condition?"

"I have a 1943 nickel, but it's brown. Was that because of the war?"

The man in the middle was getting all the questions. Finally, the fireman fielded a query, leaving only one bookend. During a minibreak, one of the staffers approached. "It isn't that you aren't getting questions," she said. "It's just that they . . . well, you look." And she handed me a scrap of paper that said, "Why do you sit there and shake your stupid long hair like a horse's head?" There were other questions that she didn't want to show me.

"What is the silver content now of quarters and dimes?" was the lead-off question of the final segment, followed by another about coin vintages.

"I have a question, Norm, if I may be permitted?" I asked, having first put my hand in the air, like school.

Norm brightened visibly, partially in relief and also maybe sensing a ratings moment.

"Of course, of course," he said.

"I have a 1951 girl, previously uncirculated, but found wandering the streets. Her parents, who emigrated from eastern Europe, have disowned this girl after discovering her in the company of a long-haired boy whom they suspect of being the devil. Why else would she want to take a year off before university? After assuring them of her innocent behaviour and that she hadn't taken drugs, she refused to kneel publicly on the front steps of her house and beg her father's forgiveness. She never made it back into the house. She was an excellent student and, despite being bounced around lately, is still in good condition. Can anybody tell me what she is worth?"

Coin guy, the fireman, the crew, and Norm himself issued a comforting mutter of approval. The point had been made just before the show ended. Good. Not everybody was against us. Back at the Frayne household, the group had apparently tuned in to the show and had approved. It had gone far better than I had expected. Words of praise came from June which, considering her already impressive track record of social activism, were humbly received. Trent added to my ashtray collection, giving me a dark glass one from the Woodbine Jockey Club. I still have it.

Alice had already moved on, by the time I had done the show. She had been my guest for a few days. One day, on alert in my office, I saw her standing very still beside the elevators, looking out the narrow window facing west. I had been watching out for Michael A. I had met his cousins from Regina (through Fossum) and, years earlier, had bought a guitar from his older brother who was apparently incarcerated in a facility for the criminally insane, having attempted to strangle his wife. They were both large, pleasant men but, for reasons I couldn't quite grasp, suffered from delicate mental health.

After recognizing the family name, I had extricated Michael from a hassle with Rochdale Security. As a form of gratitude, he had taken to hiding behind a pillar or flattening himself against the wall just outside my office door and jumping out to hug me when I exited. Michael was well over six feet and, regardless of the weather, always wore a thick wool coat. He'd leap from the blue, landing solidly on both feet in front of me with his arms outstretched. I'd be engulfed and then we would both thump each other vigorously and grin, after which he'd bow and then leave. It was like having my own bear. The first time, I was nearly moved to incontinence, and I never quite got used to it. But, in truth, I encouraged the behaviour by occasionally sneaking up from behind and ambushing him. Fair's fair. I had no idea what he was playing at. It stopped after a few weeks.

The game had made me somewhat wary, and I had taken to looking out the office door frequently in the late afternoon. This is how I knew that Alice hadn't moved in a very long time. She just stood there. She was attired in what seemed to be several dresses, voluminous, layered, and entirely in black, crowned by a lacy mantilla. From the rear she resembled a giant cone of incense, or a big nun, or, possibly, a Mennonite widow. Beside her was a cluster of twine-handled, brown, paper shopping bags stuffed with what mostly looked like normal clothing. Her hands were clasped tightly together under her chin, surely in prayer. No one had spoken to her. If she was on acid or otherwise in rapture, she was more or less keeping it to herself. I later found out that Alice didn't do drugs.

It was easier for me to become involved than not. The urge of my people, the swarming Samaritans, to answer calls of distress dies hard. In walking past her for a closer look, I saw the tears quietly coursing down downy cheeks. Pale blue eyes, a blonde wisp of hair attempting escape from the scarf of doom, a Slavic bump on the bridge of a nose not yet substantial. Bulky old lady clothes hid her young body in an accommodation of instinct.

"Are you all right?" I asked.

"It's the sky," she said.

"What's wrong with it?"

"It's just so beautiful today, don't you think?"

I had found it dull, but on second look, I could see it was torn with ragged holes, shot with sunrays. It was a good call.

"You're right. So everything's okay, then?"

"Oh, yes. Thank you."

There's a hollow feeling of need that sometimes reveals itself when, unbidden, your offer of help to a stranger is declined. You feel foolish because charity is often conditional upon the donor's need to feel superior. Being found out can give rise to indignation. Sure that I had seen at least one sign of distress, I turned to walk away, feeling somewhat let down.

"Wait," she said, and reached into a pocket and handed me an oval brown pebble, flint, I think. "This is for you. I found it yesterday."

"Thanks." A gift to restore balance.

"It warms up quickly, and it's so smooth."

"Yeah, it's a beauty all right."

"Yes, it is." She laughed. Then she stared at me for a moment before asking, "Do you know where I could get a bath?"

"Yes, I do."

Several conditions of short duration exist, brought about by trauma. If they persist, these states are considered by certain communities to be treatable, and by others, divine. It's all about perception. Let's just say that Alice was surviving by finding her new world a place salted with beauty. She was gifted like a savant, seeing spun gold in the trees. And you don't have to pin it to a board and name it "butterfly" to enjoy the dizzy ride.

She stayed with me for a few days. Certain things were made clear before the covers on the bed were turned down by a sweeter-smelling girl, totally blonde like an angel, dressed in oversized cotton night things. There would be no sex, although angels didn't put it quite that bluntly.

"There was a boy I liked, and we found a mattress like this in an old shed. We couldn't make love. I couldn't. Want to see my vials?"

"I beg your pardon?"

She laughed.

"Wait," she said. "I'll show you."

Alice rummaged in one of her paper valises. She had reconfig-ured the room, putting the mattress in the middle of the floor with her things at the head behind the pillows. The clink of small, glass objects could be heard. Her hand emerged with four, clear, thimble-like items arranged, one on each finger in order of size, from the smallest, on the pinkie, to the largest on her index digit. She wig-gled them playfully.

"See? I got them from a doctor at the clinic. He said I was too tight. He couldn't examine me properly. I'm supposed to enlarge myself, starting with the small one for a while and then work my way up to the largest."

I just stared at her, not knowing what to say, wondering if she was putting me on. It was funny in a "How stupid is that?" kind of way. Was it for real? Was this considered a legitimate therapy? Was there even a doctor? Could this be Alice's way of avoiding unwanted attention? It was almost too farfetched — like the rest of her, come to think of it. Not that I had had any plans anyway, beyond being lonesome for company.

When she got up to turn the overhead light out, it was like a rising pup tent with a head and arms sticking out. Who makes stuff like that? Before closing the door, she was backlit for a moment from the glaring fixture in the hall. Not only did that create a halo effect around her golden curls, it also flashed a silhouette of her slender, beautifully formed body. That might explain her strategies. Alice was a knockout. I wished I hadn't seen that.

The sweetness seemed a reaction to whatever had traumatized her. There was more to her story than she was talking about. Probably there had not been much strife in her life until it had all blown up. She seemed to live in an hallucination in which the perpetual discovery of small delights played a large role. A Saturday walk down Spadina to Kensington Market might involve a number of stops with Alice — again, dressed as Victoria mourning Albert — gasping and clutching your arm to point out the newest wonder: a late-blooming flower here, a pigeon nesting in an Edwardian cubbyhole there. I can never get enough of the balance provided by delight — mine or somebody else's — however it may come.

A glimpse of what equilibrium requires appeared on Monday afternoon after the slack tide of a too-quiet Sunday where welcome was wearing thin. I entered my room to find Alice seated at one open window and, my desk having been moved, some guy I had never seen before sitting by the other window, also open. It was chilly. He was handsome, or would have been had it not been for the black cloud and rumbling thunder that I could feel raging beneath his forehead. Alice, who had at least looked at me when I walked in, appeared almost as troubled.

Nothing was explained. I had been told by one of the crew, and had not believed what I was now witnessing. Alice and her silent friend sat facing one another, each holding a large box of wooden matches. Slowly, mechanically, they were lighting matches one by one and launching them out the windows. There was no rhythm to it, no choreography; first one, then the other, perhaps attempting simultaneity but just off a bit. Some matches were allowed to blossom and settle, some were thrown out in mid-explosion. Fewer still survived the eighteen storeys to land fully lit, crying for attention, succeeding.

I watched them for a moment.

"Alice?" I was asking if anyone was home. She looked up. "He'll have to go."

"I know."

"And you have to stop this match thing."

"Yes."

As it turned out, she was just on her way. She and her silent friend were heading West. Then they were going to go to the East Coast. They had plans.

"I want to see the great Bay of Fundy," she said, referring to a yarn I had spun. She smiled broadly then, like the old Alice, the Alice of a few days ago.

"Good luck with that," I said.

Dreamtime

One evening, having run out of anything to smoke except tobacco, I decided to clean and reorganize my room, and indulge in the whim of sobriety rather than continuing the attempt to track something down. An hour into the task, and almost finished, my sweeping dislodged a large brown lump from the baseboard behind the mattress on the floor. Hello, what's this? Closer inspection proved it to be a chunk of Lebanese that had obviously gone astray but had never been missed. The beginnings of a parable? A metaphor, possibly; just another brick to pave the road to hell.

A rounded cube where its corners had been lopped off, it was a lovely piece, and healthy, softening readily between my fingers, fragrant and alluring. I sniffed its ass for a while like a happy little doggie before reaching for the wooden-handled Ex-acto knife fitted with the forty-five-degree angled blade. The empty, circular spot on the cedar plank desk where I had begun to carve (vandalize?) a compensatory star with said knife was, at first, glumly noted. Then, I had to laugh. Christmas was approaching, and surely I was staring at an askew parody of "The Gift of the Magi."

One of my treasures had been a cleverly wrought, cherry-wood container, roughly the dimensions of a cold cream jar, that had a threaded lid. It was simple and of indeterminate provenance (meaning I had conveniently forgotten whether it was a gift to me or I had filched it), acquired during my peripatetic ramblings with Hoffer in Montréal. It had held stamps, coins, coloured rocks, and pipe tobacco respectively until it finally found perfect employment as a storage receptacle for hashish. It threw itself into the role, taking on a reliquary air, and was much admired. I had come to believe it somehow had a curative affect on the produce stored within, rendering its effects clearer and more profound.

Everyone has their own way of performing the daily necessities. A pack of cigarettes is opened the same way today as it was yesterday and shall be tomorrow; the tea is stirred and the spoon is tapped twice on the rim to be placed face up in the saucer, or face down on a napkin; an apple is peeled in one long spiral. Likewise, my sharing of hashish, the dispensation of the sacrament, had developed its own liturgy. It was more a ceremony of the altar, of a mutual hope, than the solitary rituals of habituation.

The little cherry jar was held in the left hand, the lid was unscrewed by the right and placed to the side; the container was sniffed like a legendary vintage, the hash removed. A cut was made, always an approximate amount, never the same dimensions. The piece was placed in a shallow, disposable spoon fashioned from aluminum foil whose bottom blackened from the applied flame. A thin plume of smoke signified its readiness to be crumbled into the perforated foil bowl.

It was by no means canonical law, but after the mixture was lighted — on one edge so it would burn evenly across — the pipe was passed to the left unless there was only one other supplicant. It seemed more appropriate in bestowing or receiving to use both hands. But that was just how I did it. There is no prescribed procedure for such a diverse and impromptu communion. One hand or two, left or right, an accompaniment of mumbo jumbo or no, makes no difference. You are only ringing the bell to the gates of perception and expressing a willingness to share.

The joke? In a clumsy bit of karma, I had traded, in a roundabout way, the ark for the covenant. I had lost faith in one of the cardinal tenets of a new creed I was embracing: *Everything comes to you when you need it*. Yes. It not only begs to be true, it is true. This beguiling lump that had appeared out of nowhere served as a prime example. This miraculous provision renewed a belief that has since been occasionally shaken, sometimes forgotten, but never renounced. Everything does come to you when you need it. That I never found a suitable replacement only served as a reminder each time I reached for the pipe.

My supply had been getting low until, the night before cleaning day, it had run out. Several large busts had created a temporary drought. Nobody had dope. I continued to share, more often than usual. Jim Neff popped in. Jim was a guy who could spot a treasure when he saw one. He admired my cherry-wood jar with the right degree of reverence as we shared a puff. He was from, I think, a tribe of transplanted Russians in BC's southern interior. Lean as a fence post, prone to wearing denim overalls that hung loosely by one strap, and long-bearded like those old illustrations of the Karamazov boys, Jim was of the sort who would one day inherit the earth. He would rather have been down on the commune than having to come to town to scrounge up the wherewithal for another bucolic episode.

He had a line on some smoke. This surprised me as Jim was not the first guy anybody would approach if they were about to resupply a needy community. He wouldn't have the money for starters which, sure enough, he didn't quite. But he was a sweet man, and a truthful man, and I was approaching, well, not panic so much as a sense of impatience with the marketplace.

I blame D. Stanley Troyer. He actually had some hash, and he was finally able to get rid of it, given market conditions. It was reputedly from India and, in appearance, not at all like the Middle Eastern varieties. Instead of a cotton-wrapped salami squashed to a one-inch thickness, this stuff was thin, hard, dark, and flat, like a charred piece of McIntosh toffee. Cutting into it — virtually impossible without a heated blade — revealed an olive green interior. You couldn't shave it into fine enough pieces to keep it lit. Heating it in foil took forever and even then it would only crumble into a coarse particulate resembling bits of vulcanized rubber. It certainly tasted like old tires and only produced a more marginal buzz than a second-hand retread. You could get high on it, but only after smoking a ton, the preparation of which made you feel as if you'd just put in a shift at the Goodyear plant.

Of course, I shared these observations with a none-too-pleased Troyer (who had bought in quantity) and declined to support his entrepreneurial venture. He had, apparently, been quite miffed. D. Stanley was forever coming up with "blends," mixing this grass with that — the inferior with the slightly better, I called it — and giving each batch a name (e.g., "Moonburn") more glorious than the product. These habits were a source of contention between us. During one of his "quitting cigarettes" periods, he rolled twenty joints per day, which I suspect he had further adulterated with tobacco, and smoked them instead. As a result, we always smoked my stuff because, with his, you could never be sure of what you were getting.

On the whole, Troyer was not a reliable source but "pickin's" were thin. So, when at last I approached him, he, with his twitchy little lips puckered primly, refused to sell me a chunk of India rubber. "It's moving quite briskly without your help," he said. "Besides, I wouldn't want to be guilty of abetting you in lowering your considerable standards." Getting into the spirit, I returned to my room and wrote a conciliatory ditty, which I duly performed for him on my return. The bastard still refused, saying I would no doubt thank him later.

As for Jim Neff, he had raised enough for two ounces, but the guy was only dealing quarter-pounds. Jim needed a hundred and twenty dollars — a suspiciously low figure — for the two remaining oh zees, sixty apiece. Would I front it to him? He had seen the stuff, Nepalese, according to the gold seal. The flashing lights and sirens told me, "No fucking way." It wasn't Jim, but who might prey upon him that had me concerned. But he looked so hopeful, as if this might be his chance to return to the country for a while. Combined with a frisson of doubt regarding my recently acquired philosophies, this proved more than a match for my resolve. I gave him the money.

We couldn't figure out what it was. The gold from the partial seal rubbed off on our fingers. It wouldn't heat, couldn't be crumbled, and was impossible to shave. My guess was baked or dehydrated shoe polish. Jim felt very bad. He ran to get our money back, returning with the air of a much-kicked dog. You would have been hard pressed to find a sorrier looking chap. He was sorry about my money and sorrier about his, which hadn't really been his, not all of it anyway. Jim was sorry, sorry, sorry, deeply sorry; a gloomy, bushy-bearded Russian with moist eyes, and getting sorrier by the minute.

"Jesus, Jim, take it easy," I consoled, refraining, but only just, from putting my arm around his shoulders. "It's only money. Fuck it."

"But I owe you . . . ," and then he couldn't speak.

"You don't owe me anything, man. We tried, that's all. Let the bad karma be on the other guy."

Given his commitment to the barter system and simple living, there is no way Jim could have ever come up with the money. His bank account would be the stone from which blood could not be squeezed. What would be the point in making him feel worse? Then, I suppose to compound my loss and, in the way of double negatives cancelling one another, hoping for perhaps a reversal of fortune, I gave Jim the cherry-wood jar, the ark, the talismanic container, the holy relic. Be happy, Jim. You fucking well had better.

From then on, at odd times, at intervals of no particular length, a soft knock at the door would produce Jim Neff. "Here, this is for you" or "I thought you might like this," he'd say, gifting me. Once, it was an old balance beam in a wooden box; another time, a very decent bud of gold Columbian. Sometimes things come to you even when you don't need them. I never asked, but doubtless my cherry-wood jar had long since been traded. My cherry-wood jar? Well, nothing is really yours until you give it away.

As I cleaned and re-foiled my pipe to fulfil the destiny of the serendipitous lump, the phone rang. The voice on the other end, my usual source, pronounced the dry spell as being over, did I want my quarter delivered tonight, and would I like it cut into four one-ounce portions, to which I replied, "far out," "why not," and "yes."

He showed up within the hour. I gave him two hundred and fifty dollars, two hundred and forty of which had been fronted to me in three separate eighty-dollar transactions for whenever something became available. My ounce had cost me ten dollars, and the other three had cost their purchasers ten dollars less than the current market price of ninety dollars per ounce. The seller had probably gotten a pound for eight hundred dollars or fifty dollars an ounce. So, after I made three phone calls, at least five people were happy. The math was righteous.

Most days, on jukeboxes and radios, you would hear Crosby, Stills, Nash, and Young sing, "The dream never dies, just the dreamer." And it was a dream. A pipe dream, perhaps, but a fantastic one, a dream of love, a dream of community, a dream of peace. You could see the dream in other faces, and those dreamers could see it in yours. Could love, community, and peace be possible? Why not? Everything was possible.

The news footage circa 1967 of the girl placing a daisy in the soldier's gun barrel had seemed amusing, if a trifle optimistic. (We would see, twenty-two years later, a similar and even braver act in Tiananmen Square as a lone student faced down a tank, bringing it to a halt.) Then, toward the end of 1969, with the sort of timing that has ever been a plague, I jumped right in and abandoned myself to the religion of enlightenment. Pass the flowers and show me where the guns are. It was a leap of faith from which I have never quite recovered.

During the seminars in my room, the dream was mostly funny, downright hilarious at times. We did examine serious matters, or at least we began to until their more comic aspects would set us off. If you want to be serious, you shouldn't smoke dope. Instead, as our artistic French brethren had, a century or more before, we mused on angels dancing on the heads of pins too, only ours wore minis. We discussed the dream and the nature of the dream and whether we existed at all. What is the true nature of reality? Reality is how you feel at any given moment. Laughter is a pretty decent reality.

During quiet periods after Elevator Al, the Otis repairman, had worked his short-term magic, I would glide slowly past each floor on my way down or up in a functioning car, and picture in my mind the activities of all the residents, level by level, as I passed by, as if the floors were made of glass. The accumulated visions added up to an inner view of the Tower of Babel as seen by a surrealist. This was a recurring fantasy when I was stoned in a particular way, one I apparently shared with a number of people who saw it the same way.

Meanwhile, a remote, jungle-bound tribe in South America ingested a local psychedelic then sat back as a group and hallucinated a performance by the New York Philharmonic Orchestra. "It really happened, man." "Yeah?" "No shit. And none of them had ever seen television, movies, magazines, or an orchestra." "Fuuck." The things you hear on an elevator. What we wanted to know was how could we get hold of some of that stuff? Maybe we could conjure up a return trip and watch them dance around a fire in the Upper Orinoco Basin. After all, we are all connected. "Toke, man?" "Thanks, man." "That'd be some shit, wouldn't it?" "Whoa."

Bloor St. ran past the building like a great river. It was ours between Bathurst and Avenue Rd., along with all the tributaries of the Annex that flowed into it. Heads and freaks and beautiful chicks, draft dodgers and deserters, speeders, panthers, professors in headbands, goddesses in beads, the newly arrived Czech kids in red plaid flares and platform shoes strode up and down both banks, crossing from side to side at the bridges of intersections. The streets were alive and sinuous, a gigantic courting ritual thronged with prime specimens of both sexes glowing with colourful auras and driven half mad by the perfumed haze of pheromones that only the cloying overlay of patchouli could blot out. Out of streetside windows, and doorways, and parks and alleys, tiny wisps of smoke from joints and hash pipes, underlined with incense, would join and mingle with the musk.

The new cry for "spare change" and the mooching Hari Krishnas appeared only as balance to the grand parade of beauty. What was beautiful was the hope, the earnestness, the desire, to come together and make a better world. Mammon *would* take a back seat to virtue. You need never be ashamed of wanting that. You need never be ashamed of thinking, for however long, that love was the answer, that love is all you need, that love is all there is.

As for the dream of the perfect mate, it fell into a rhythm. You'd meet someone, become entranced, become un-entranced, and figure out a way to end it. You'd wonder what happened to all the beauties who were beckoning when you were trapped; you'd finally forget and get sandbagged again. Six-week cycles seemed to be the norm, unless you were seized by an anomaly. The reasons for moving on had seemed so right. There were literally hundreds of members of the opposite sex who had, you thought, smiled at you in a beguiling way. Chicks bopped down the street in twos and threes. Come hither, their look said. Dudes were trucking along, snapping their heads left and right. So, things hadn't worked out between you and whoever. Bummer, man, but ya gotta keep on keepin' on. You join the parade and suddenly the looks aren't coming your way. Could you be too ready? Oh no, she hooked up with that asshole. There's no going back.

I was standing outside the building with Clint when Flanagan came along. He was holding hands with a big girl, six feet tall, a brunette with her hair tied back loosely. Flanagan is not tall. He was holding her hand and grinning. He gave Clint a big hi ho on the way by. Barely looked at me, a curt nod, still mad I saw. Love had made him happy. She didn't look our way, deliberately, I thought.

"Isn't that the girl I saw you with a couple of weeks ago?" I asked Clint.

"Yeah."

"Thought you were in love."

"It wasn't happening. She doesn't like the cinema."

"Looks like she likes poetry."

"Yes, it does."

"Tall girl, even for you."

"She's nice."

"The way they're holding hands there, it looks like Flanagan is going shopping with his mommy."

"He'll forgive you eventually," Clint said when he was finished laughing.

"I finally said hello to the redheaded lady."

"Which one? Wow, did you see that? Now there's a redhead."

"She's not a redhead."

"Spiritually, she is. Look at that walk. Oh, baby, I am in love."

"She's one of the Coach House people."

"You know her?"

"Not her, the redhead. You know, the one with the wicker baby carriage that walks by the office every day."

She had ignored me at first, despite my being obvious. Her hair was short, a pale red, and she had freckles. She wore a green coat, a plaid tam that was mostly green, and pushed an enormous old-fashioned conveyance, also green but fading, with large wheels. It held a moon-faced baby adorned with a knitted cap tied under her chin. The baby, a girl as it turned out, with wispy red hair, had round blue eyes. Baby had made friends with her mucous and smiled constantly through the muck. I would never meet a more sweet-tempered child.

Lynn deigned to talk with me — she was a poet, and serious, not given to suffering hippies (as compared to real artists) gladly — because I had said, as she wheeled out of the elevator, "That's quite the perambulator you have there." It was the word, she confessed later. "Pram" might have done it, but "perambulator" clinched the deal. It is a good word, all you really need to render poets helpless to your charms. That I lived with Grand Master Bevington impressed her even more. Matters proceeded apace.

By mid-January, we were having people to dinner. This would be a stretch for my room, but it was just David and Leslie who hadn't met Lynn. I told her he was a writer as well as having been a janitor on the crew. She took this dinner business seriously, deciding on sauerbrauten, which requires marinating a roast in beer for twenty-four hours. All I had to do was clear the desk and make it into a table, for Christ's sake. Could I do that, at least? Yes, I could. I'd have to borrow a couple of chairs, some cutlery, and maybe the wine glasses but no problem.

The guests arrived, and Lynn brought the main course up from her apartment. It smelled pretty good. But as the lid was lifted, Leslie took one whiff and nearly passed out. She recovered enough to be sick in the bathroom. David fussed over her. They left, Leslie apologizing with a wan smile. Although I had known Leslie for a few years, never once did I realize that she was one of the early vegetarians. The chef ate in silent fury at our table for two, apparently immune to praise for a dish that perhaps tasted better than it smelled. There was not going to be a word precious enough to get me out of this one. For years afterwards, I would always eat a late cheeseburger before dining at Leslie's.

It was during the next six-week period of being available that I got elected to Rochdale Council. Even though I was now one of my own bosses, nothing much changed. I had gone to all the council meetings anyway, as much out of amusement as anything. Bradford and Evitts were out, having tried to sell Rochdale to retire the debt and move to smaller premises more in keeping with the original intent. A new executive was needed. A moratorium on mortgage payments had been negotiated with CMHC, mostly due to Wilf Pelletier and Ian McKenzie, who were trusted in Ottawa.

The first in-camera council meeting was held in Peter Turner's room a day or so after the election. Peter, who I didn't know well, claimed to be a draft dodger. He was a little, red-haired guy with a bushy moustache, kind of small to be drafted, standing about five two or three, but who knows? He took over the meeting right away and, in that American style, talked to everybody else as if we were in a huddle and he was the quarterback. Obviously, he had worked out a few things with some of the other council members prior to the meeting, as politicians will, a fact I became vaguely aware of after the meeting was over. Rochdale isn't about politics, is it?

It was like a circus in his room. Peter sat in an enormous black vinyl office chair that towered a foot above his head, making him appear even smaller. It had come from his mother's office; she was a corporate lawyer in New York. Behind him, on a separate desk, was a mangy monkey in a cage, doing what monkeys do when they have a lot of spare time on their hands and nothing to eat. Peter's girl-friend, taller than he and much better looking, a babe, in fact, sat off to the side. Not everybody was there — Wilf was missing, for example — but we had a quorum.

The little quarterback had a plan. To ensure fairness until we got to know one another as a legislative body, he proposed that we have a rotating presidency. That nobody goofed around by turning in their chairs or invoking dervishes was a bad sign. And, he went on, since so-and-so (I forget who) had served as interim president after Bradford had resigned then he, The Right Honourable Peter Turner, would be happy to serve as head of council for the first wee while. Were there any objections? Nope. President Turner, allowing as how there would be a bigger council meeting in a few days where new business could be tackled, moved for adjournment; it was sec-onded and carried.

As proof that behind every door in Rochdale there lurked adventure, an older woman entered the room carrying a tray. She was solidly built, about five six or seven, with short, sandy hair and bangs of the style preferred by Emily Carr or Gertrude Lawrence.

She wore a flower print muumuu draped over her powerful shoulders, as a fullback might on Halloween, which suggested she would be more comfortable in pants. "Oh goody, cookies," Peter exclaimed, clapping his hands together in delight. Remembering his manners, he introduced us to his mother. She would become somewhat of a fixture on weekends, an eminence rouge. She was not one to trifle with.

How to become president without really having been elected as such, was a lesson in politics never forgotten. Americans, as recent history has proven, seem to be good at that sort of thing. There were large numbers of dodgers and deserters, as well as U.S. students, residing in Rochdale at the time. You hardly ever knew about it, save for the giveaway of a Texas twang or Tennessee drawl here and there. We were mostly on the same page, of the same culture, and what was the border anyway except an arbitrary line? In fact, one of the first things I learned from my Indian friends is that the continent divided peoples into a north/south arrangement culturally and linguistically, rather than east/west. But as with the San Diego crowd in Regina a few years earlier, in any group of Americans there will be a vociferous minority who think that the only thing wrong with Canadians is that we don't know how to do politics right. It appears to be the God-given duty of these folks to set us straight.

Peter, of course, never relinquished the presidency until, many months later, he felt compelled to resign. Nor could I ever bring myself to take him at all seriously despite the cost. I just couldn't huddle and plan attacks or play the us-versus-them role like he and his cohorts. I could play politics a bit. I learned how to get folks to vote for my resolutions by compromising and agreeing to support theirs. But the absolute solemnity with which the inner circle conducted clandestine meetings, hatching schemes, creating, and destroying opponents was ridiculous to me. I remembered rainy Saturday afternoons in the geeky kid's garage who got to make all the rules because it was his board game, and I'd laugh out loud. I was wrong, I know, because the deadly serious are deadly and serious, seeking power and wielding it. How very fucking dreary. As far as I'm concerned, everything fell apart and took a turn for the worse during Peter's watch, part of which was my watch too. His chair appeared to get bigger and bigger.

I spent a lot of time talking to Wilf about the new council — he was a member, too — and to Ted Poole whenever he came to town. Initially, their comments were a challenge, and I went after each one like, I suppose, a fish at a lure.

"I'm really pissed off at Peter Turner," I said to Wilf.

"That's too bad," he'd say. "All that means, see, is you're really mad at yourself." That was the one that hooked me. I thought about it for days and finally concluded he was right.

"People who know what to do — and I'm not talking here about fixing engines or gutting a fish or baking the best pie, because the top guys in those kind of things are a pleasure to watch — I'm talking about people who know what's best for you and me, who know the kinds of organizations we should have, and the way things should be run, these people are dangerous. The more convinced they are of being right, the more dangerous they become. There are tons of guys like this in politics, almost all of them, but they're everywhere: the church, schools, corporations, the armed forces, and so on. See, nobody knows what to do, not really. Down deep, we all sort of know that about ourselves, that we don't really know what to do.

"Somebody comes along and says: 'This is a mess,' or, 'that's a problem, but I know how to fix it.' And some of us are relieved. I mean, at last, here's someone who knows what to do. So we throw ourselves behind this person, give them our vote or our support and stand back. That's how people who know what to do accumulate power. Maybe someone else sees that and decides 'I'm better than that guy, why should he have all that power? Besides, he's got it all wrong, this is what we need to do.' And the people who were getting sick of the first guy, or who were never completely convinced by him, are relieved. And another guy comes along saying the first two have it all wrong, and so on. What's forgotten is maybe none of these guys really know what to do, and maybe they don't even care except that they have power."

Wilfred then started in on the type of culture that seemed to run the show, not just in North America but pretty much everywhere. "It's an adversarial culture," he said, echoing Ted Poole. It seemed obvious after they had pointed it out, but I hadn't really thought much about it until then. "We're in a state of constant warfare, we're fighting everything all the time. We fight for rights: minority rights, women's rights, animal rights, equal pay for equal work, welfare rights, the right to vote. We fight against crime, poverty, illiteracy, traffic, and weeds. We fight cancer by inventing better drugs; we also have a war on drugs. We fight fire with fire. Coming home in the evening, we fight stress; during the day, we fight fatigue. All that fighting just wears us out."

No doubt everybody in the world knew this, but it was a perspective I hadn't considered. I spent many an evening sharing this and getting other people's views in the seminary known as my room. Also considered and debated was the "problem industry." This is one of the main tools of the people who know what to do. Something is identified as a problem and the identifier of that problem just happens to have the solution; or, there is no solution just yet, but one is needed, and he or she is just the person to chair a committee to deal with it. These so-called problems are always skewed toward the status quo. "Absenteeism" at work, for example, will nearly always be attacked by offering some sort of incentive to overcome this bad habit rather than looking at the work itself and finding it wanting.

Neewin Publishing Company, formed by Wilf, Ted, and two silent partners, was created to publish a little chapbook entitled *Two Articles*, written by Wilfred Pelletier. In twenty-six pages of text, these two articles, "Childhood in an Indian Village" (which first appeared in the Spring 1969 edition of *This Magazine Is About*

Schools) and "Some Thoughts About Organization and Leadership" (a paper presented to the Manitoba Indian Brotherhood in 1967), essentially talk about differences between First Nations and Western cultures, between a culture of cooperation and acceptance and one of aggression and competition. Despite being a self-published text, *Two Articles* received, unsolicited, a rave review in the *New York Times Review of Books*. It's brilliant, as was its author.

What it did for me was to expose the myth that the culture from which I had sprung was somehow absolute. Religion had never been absolute for me, being a sort of religious half-breed. The social values I held were under revision. I had no home, other than where I happened to be. I had no family, other than a scattered few, and a select company of surrogates. I had no god, save a vague comprehension of the meaning of everything, still to acquire definition. All in all, I figured I was in pretty good shape for a new beginning. I had hope.

Ian Argue, a tousle-haired, skinny, blonde kid from Belleville was the rentals manager. Since the November mortgage payment default, we had all been scheming for ways to raise money. Ian's idea was simple. In early March, Share-the-Wealth-with-Rochdale-Week was born. A group of us were to each pick an area of the country and visit university campuses to sell two-day tickets to stay at Rochdale for ten dollars. We would also offer to exchange our newly minted Rochdollars for Canadian dollars. I drew Calgary.

The newsmaker, however, was our decision to sell degrees and non-degrees. Rochdale College, although not accredited, was, due to some sleight-of-hand by Campus Co-op and bureaucratic slumber on behalf of the appropriate government body, actually empowered to dispense degrees. When the Ontario Department of University Affairs looked into it, they eventually determined there was nothing to be done.

Twenty-five dollars bought you a BA, an MA cost fifty and, for a hundred dollars, you could get a PhD. The degrees were issued in whatever discipline you chose (or chose to make up) and printed, with a border of marijuana leaves, by Coach House Press. They sold like hotcakes. In keeping with the times, a large proportion of them were Doctorates of Divinity in newly declared religions where the word "cosmic" appeared in many different combinations. In fact, BA and MA sales were dismal, being out performed by doctorates on a scale of nine to one. There were cases of fraud — at least one person practised medicine with a Rochdale degree, and there were several psychotherapists — but to a group that believed all university degrees were more or less fraudulent, nobody much cared. As for me, I realized that it was probably my only chance to become a doctor — of what was the only thing to be decided. I let it percolate.

On a Wednesday I found myself on a stretched DC-8 to Calgary with only two other passengers. We each had our own flight attendant. After a first-class meal on real china, I settled back and smoked luxuriously before catching some sleep, lolling across three seats. Heather Wagg, who now has a real PhD, picked me up at the airport. I had met Heather on a train, the one I had taken to visit Leonard Cohen in Montréal; the one she was taking to enter her second year at McGill. She still looked like she was twelve. We walked, seemingly in the middle of town, along the Bow River. I had almost forgotten what stars looked like in a clear night sky. The clean, bracing air reminded me of all the things I loved about the northern edge of the Great Plains.

Surprisingly, there was quite a turnout at the Calgary campus of The University of Alberta. We talked — no speeches — for an hour or so. They expressed solidarity by making a sizeable donation to Rochdale. They had not only heard of us, they were with us, having conducted a bottle drive to raise the money. The other fundraisers had had similar experiences, and we marvelled over that in a humble way upon our return. This was still a time when you flashed the V sign to people who at least appeared to be of similar persuasion.

On the way back, I stopped in Regina for an overnight visit. I had to see Tauno, now five, a very important age. He was matter-of-fact, not indifferent, not aloof, but somewhat reserved at first, soon happy enough with the attention. His mother had found someone, a tall, soft-spoken ceramic artist named Mel Bolen. He seemed a decent guy. He treated me well, and I was glad of that, and to have him around for Tauno.

Tauno, at one point, crawled onto Mel's lap and looked very comfortable there. It was a declaration of sorts. He had to move on, I know. He had to survive, which required having two dads, the other of whom was at least a good guy. Tauno's life had requirements, too. I knew all that. Yet seeing him climb so easily into his new dad's lap was one of the most difficult moments I had ever endured. I felt almost disembowelled. I sat there with a shit-eating grin, carrying on a light conversation as if nothing at all were out of the usual, silently whimpering underneath it all. My boy, lost.

In the middle of the night, I got up and pissed off the back step rather than go upstairs. Dobra, the golden lab that had just wandered in and adopted the family after my time, had just come down, which meant that Tauno was asleep for sure. Her job as sleep nanny completed, she joined me and Curly Jetfood in the guest bedroom, which, during regular hours, was the dining room. Curly, easily the largest German shepherd I had ever seen, was just visiting as well but seemed pretty relaxed about the arrangement. The old studio couch had me on top, Curly stretched out the length of it, and Dobesy curled up under the round, teak table top placed on a concrete pipe that I had fashioned myself two years or so before. The moon shining through the window was so bright you could have tap-danced on the spot. The beast within me howled.

Wilf, in town on an unrelated matter, was on the same flight back to Toronto. He dropped by early, and I introduced him all around. Tauno was curious. He and Wilf got into it almost right away. They were challenging each other, each upping the ante. Finally, Wilf said to Tauno, after asking him who he thought was the toughest guy, for which Tauno had nominated Batman.

"Oh, yeah? Well, suppose I told you that I could beat up Batman?"

"You can't beat Batman," said Tauno, snorting in disbelief at such a ridiculous assertion. Wilfred's stock had just gone down a bit.

"Well, then, suppose I just take the moon and stars away from you?"

"Ha, you can't do that either." There was almost pity in Tauno's eyes.

"Why can't I?"

Then Tauno said something that was obviously nothing he had ever been taught. He didn't even have to think about it. He just knew, with the certainty of a scholar, why that could never happen.

"Look, Wulf," he began, with his own pronunciation, to explain patiently and in a matter-of-fact manner how these things work. "You can't take the moon and stars because everything like that is some of yours, but it's part of everybody else's."

Wilfred roared with laughter, as blown away as the rest of us. He admitted defeat, graciously received by Tauno, who had edged closer and closer until he was leaning on "Wulf's" knee, showing him what he had been drawing while they had sparred. He gave the drawing to Wilf, who accepted it with great solemnity.

Children, rather than being empty vessels that need to be filled with knowledge, are born knowing everything they need to know, according to Poole. Life is just a process of forgetting. Discoveries are, essentially, rediscoveries of things you already knew. You can't formulate a question unless you know the answer.

The redoubtable black steamer trunk I had paid five dollars for in Montréal followed me everywhere, arriving late, like a faithful old retainer laden with nonessential comforts, travelling slowboat while I pushed on ahead. There was never a key; a certain trick with a screwdriver popped the lock. It was a decorator piece: footstool, coffee table, headboard, and settee. Within, along with books, perfumed letters, and treasures like the departed cherrywood relic, lay the entire output of my writing. The early poems were there, written in fountain pen with blue-black ink. The novel written at

Hoffer's in black ballpoint was in a paper bag. My sewer poems, typed first on an old Underwood and later with a portable Olympia, sat in a folder, loosely bound. Stories and fragments of stories bulked up the collection. I used to write to a mythical woman named Rose and ask her questions, tell her things. Where are you now, Rose?

The hero of my current work, an epic narrative poem of indeterminate length, was an Anglo-Saxon boy named Birt racing civilization through the centuries in an effort to find the switch marked "off." His spirit guide was a white-haired Druid elder with young features of whom he was occasionally uncertain. As research I read translations of Old English poems. For a while, I'd get stoned in the late afternoon, wait half an hour to settle down, and read the poetry from a compendium of English literature, an old 101 text, to see which of the poets from Donne to Eliot really knew what it was all about. Blake stood out, a towering giant. I retired the text and bought his collected works.

Later, Poole, who had delighted me by saying that he thought civilization was a passing fancy like the hula hoop, gave me *The Way of Life* by Lao Tzu. There are many different translations of *The Way of Life*, some better than others. The one Poole gave me, by the poet Witter Bynner, is by far the best; it is simple and profound. In the eighty-one sayings, you can find whatever you need by way of comfort or insight. I thought about Bynner, delving into these things before I was born, realizing there's always been a small few to ponder isness, being, the meaning of existence, and the importance of having at least some of us do that.

That would explain Ted Poole. Poole was human in that he was stuck in a body and inhabited the earth. Otherwise — and although I'm speaking from thirty years of knowing him — I knew then he was like nobody I had ever or would ever meet; he was in an entirely different league than the rest of us, one in which very few ever get to play, in earthly guise, at least. They're out there, these few, probably in every culture, more or less the remnants of our medicine people from a time when we lived in interdependence as a whole, more in harmony with the earth. Some are poets. Fashions change, mores change, languages change, civilizations come and go. Existence and the right way to live does not. Bynner was onto that, and so was Poole.

Ted Poole believed in the evolution of mankind, in the absolute necessity of it. He told me that, by the early fifties, he had feared that it was over for us, that some sort of limit had been reached where feeling no longer had coin, only intellect. I wasn't quite sure what he meant by that except that art would be seated even further back from engineering and economics. Today, I have a real good idea of what he was talking about . . . and as great a fear. The cowboys are winning.

Ted was delighted with the revolutionary spirit of the sixties. To him, it was a step forward to have a significant portion of the younger generation question the idea of jobs, degrees, titles, marriage, and war, to name but a few. He saw the movement toward communal living as being especially hopeful and believed that the most successful way to live was tribally.

LSD was a sacrament to him, as was anything that gave you an assist toward a glimpse of enlightenment. All of the early researchers into its effects ended up in this camp, and it's a great pity that LSD was made illegal, cutting off legitimate experimentation. As a culture, then and now, we need all the help we can get. It's a powerful drug, and has the potential for great benefit or great harm — not as much harm as the educational system perhaps or alcohol, but enough to be significant. "Just say no," my ass.

Wilf grew up tribally, in Wikwemikong on Manitoulin Island. He was Odawa. Almost everything I have learned about Indian culture, I have learned from him. In one sense, it saved me. It was a culture of the dispossessed, and I was dispossessed. Being dispossessed, it was a culture of poverty, and I had grown up in poverty. We shared the same gallows humour. Baloney — never Balogna — is Indian steak just as much as it is round steak or New Brunswick steak. It is a culture of resilience. It is a respectful, spiritual, human culture that springs from that part of the earth with which I am most familiar. I have always had a difficult time relating to that gang from the Sea of Gallilee and all the smiting and smoting that went with it.

The cosmic entity formerly known as Ted Poole passed away a few years ago. "Passed through," he would have said, through the portal into a new adventure where his body, and his ego, would no longer be holding him back. Whenever I observe truly daft human behaviour, I think of Ted. The slapstick of a Rosedale matron chasing her Pomeranian through the park, waving a plastic bag at the clump of doo stuck to its ass, provokes a "Poole would have loved to see that." He had a wicked laugh. He regarded the human condition, in all its glory and not, to be a never-ending delight. Likewise, when the patch is more thorn than rose, I also think of Ted and ask myself what he would have said or done. He dwells within my consciousness, the chief of less than a handful of advisors whose silent counsel I have come to trust.

I do not mourn him. He had a decent kick at the can. If there's mourning to be done, I mourn for me — if memory-provoked laughter can be construed as grief. The same goes for Wilfred Pelletier who likewise abandoned himself to the light a year and a bit after Ted. Wilf's name in Odawa translates loosely as He-Who-Walks-About. He's able to do that now, free from the ravages of cancer. I suspect his presence anywhere that immoderate laughter has erupted. If the world is evil, it is also good. The universe is as much about laughter as anything.

I saw a group of bureaucrats from Ottawa cavort around Wilf and Ted, undoing their ties, ready to play, willing to be silly. They had met the dynamic cosmic duo before, at one of the many cross-cultural workshops the two had conducted, and were clearly delighted. Becoming sensitive to another culture frees you from the petty tyrannies of your own, enough to gain some insights. It wasn't just the young who were impressed by Wilf and Ted. They had conducted workshops with the clergy, police, federal mandarins, and educators. In fact, Wilf's role as advisor at Rochdale had gone a long way toward securing the co-operation from CMHC that enabled it to keep going. They couldn't get enough of him.

As a god, Ted would belong in the same northern European model as the cunning Troyer — only as a balance and a superior force by far — resolute, stern perhaps, but guided by love and forbearance. Wilfred, however, would be closer to Nannebush, the trickster, an all-too-human deity fond of tricking the animals and being tricked in return. His creation tales would be rollicking, memorable jests like the time the chickadees, to get even for one of Nannebush's tricks, somehow got him to throw his eyeballs into the air and stole them. Being unable to see, Nannebush burned his ass in the fire, shreds of which stuck to the bushes as he ran to the lake, thus creating mosquitoes. These stories were prized by young and old alike and awaited with much anticipation and delight, much as Wilfred was awaited. He was so human, accessible, and loved. Activity had a way of surrounding him, like a halo.

In another world, another time, Wilf might have been king, or chief, or first minister. He had a brilliant mind for politics. As a scholar, he had completed grade six. Wilf's enduring success was as a healer, often in the guise of a clown, and no matter what involved him he would automatically default to that. It was his nature. He'd be the one in times of privation to have everybody in stitches while slicing up the last potato, trying to make it stretch eight ways. But, in any room in which you found him, regardless of who was present, there was never a doubt as to where the power lay. This, of course, can create envy in lesser men.

We all want heroes, especially the young. Examples are needed who stand out, whose existence says: "Yes, you can;" who stand there fully realized — not in a box — and represent clarity of purpose, the fulfilment of ideals. We all need teachers whose word we believe, whose encouragement that we should find our own solutions rings true. We need rock-solid examples in which to have faith, and shelter in their lee, taking solace from the refuge to encourage our own faltering steps. We all need guidance in the area that should come most naturally, being human. Ours is a world that does not yield easily this simple thing.

Before I met Wilf and Ted I only had suspicions that something had gone horribly wrong with the world. Perhaps not everything was my fault. They helped me put a voice to those innermost thoughts that one keeps to oneself lest people think one is mad. Gratitude was unnecessary and unwelcome. As they would be the first to point out, they had both a duty and a need to perform that duty. I hadn't yet failed enough to appreciate how difficult that must have been at times. Anyway, I know what I know now, and though I became so bedazzled by them that I got lost in the message for a while, I am so very, very thankful to them both.

The religion of enlightenment, particularly through use of herbal agents, has not only been brutally suppressed through killings and incarceration, but has been debased through lack of information. Drugs are dangerous. So are lawn darts, apparently, having also been banned by legislation. We have so lost faith in ourselves that endless hours are taken up to legislate against our own stupidity. Then, we are made more stupid enabling more legislation which, in the arcane formulae we embrace, nearly always results in employment of the "Big Brother Is Watching!" kind. For some, it's a career choice.

As Lao Tzu would say: *"Act after act prohibits everything but poverty. Law after law creates a multitude of criminals."*

Two little criminals slept, having to be awakened by the intruders. It was just after nine . . . early, like dawn in Rochdale terms. They must have been criminals since they were part of security's "volunteer" force, crashers maybe or a minor deal had gone wrong. I had seen them before, a baby-faced couple that you had to view from the front to determine which one was the boy. They were cute; had they not had torn and dirty flares, bare feet, and tie-dyes they could have passed as a pair of Bobbseys. Their shift bound them to the entrance where they would pass the night in an old, stuffed armchair, intertwined and wrapped in a ratty sleeping bag, ensuring, when not totally lost in sleep, that all who entered had a right to be there. More like guard birds than guard dogs, they were to squawk to security if anything seemed greatly amiss.

The boy ran up to the second floor, where I had just gotten off a very tricky elevator on the way to my new office. He was wild eyed. "Narcs," he blurted. "They're after Rosie." I followed him down the stairs to the first floor. From what little I knew of Rosie Rowbotham, except that the Turner crew was sucking up to him, I had a good mind to do nothing. He was a big dealer, one of several who were moving in and operating out of Rochdale. Most of council was prepared to live with this arrangement and perhaps exploit it. I was one of the dissenters. The dealers mouthed all the right sentiments: they were dealing "soft" drugs, it should be legal, they were obeying the will of the people, they were fighting "the Man," they were financing the revolution, fuck the pigs. Their mission, however, from what I could see was more entrepreneurial than revolutionary. It was a great advantage to deal out of a building that was essentially a fortress and had become so to protect a fledgling culture rather than act as a front for large trafficking operations. Grass for the building, sure. Enough to supply half the city? Count me out. Whatever these guys said, and they were all of the same stripe, they were in it for the money, the big score, the claim to be top dog in the pissing contest. They were cowboys. Love was not the answer here, it was something you could share in a hot tub with three chicks while the fourth opened the Champagne.

This was a situation one step removed from harbouring bikers. And we had fought bikers, literally from the fortress, bolting the gates, pouring hot oil over the ramparts. Encouraging the dealers would be the end of Rochdale was my most successful prophecy. That it took until 1975 was the only surprise. However, as much as I was opposed to what Rosie represented, he was still a Rochdalian and the three guys standing by the elevators were plain clothes cops, clearly the enemy. I turned to the kid and, sotto voce, told him to take the stairs to the seventh floor and warn Rosie.

We had negotiated an arrangement with the Metro police. If they had warrants and business to attend to, they would call and we would provide an escort. This was to curb the habit of building residents throwing debris of all sorts out the windows every time they saw more than one cop car parked outside. A small task force had been formed, dubbed "The Mod Squad," to act as a liaison between the forces of order and those of chaos. So I knew the three agitated types rapidly punching the elevator buttons had to be RCMP.

"Excuse me, gentlemen, but what are you doing?" I asked.

They whirled around to face me. Their leader was a middle-aged, balding guy with dark hair on the sides and a moustache. I knew he was the leader because the youngest-looking of the trio came at me like a snarling dog until the leader raised his hand. The third guy was short, beefy, and nondescript, and hadn't moved.

"That's none of your business, son," their leader said, flashing a badge.

"I'm afraid it is, *Dad*, and I need to see two more badges and a warrant."

Dog-boy cursed and took another lunge at me. This time the beefy guy restrained him.

"Who are you, then?" their leader asked.

"I'm the general manager of Rochdale," I trumped. I had just been appointed a few days before and, in truth, I could feel myself puffing up a little importantly when I said it.

I was shown two more badges and a writ of assistance, meaning, amongst other things, I had to assist their efforts; the name, Robert Rowbotham, was on it. Surely, I thought the kid had made it to Rosie's room by now, so I took them up to the seventh floor. Just to be on the safe side, I led them to the elevator most likely to fuck up. It had been shooting down to the subbasement lately before going anywhere else. This time it performed like a normal conveyance.

We stood outside one of the bedroom doors in the seventh-floor ashram. The kid was nowhere in sight. I had the key, *the* key, the grand master, but I knocked on the door.

"Don't knock, asshole, just open the fucking door," Dog-boy snarled.

After fumbling loudly, I opened the door. The trio pushed me aside and rushed into the room, no manners at all. I entered discreetly behind them. A young guy, barely able to produce the wispy hair above his lip, lay shirtless and fast asleep on a bare mattress. He was awakened roughly. "Robert Rowbotham, blah, blah, blah." Rosie just sat there trying to blink himself awake, not that he wasn't totally aware of what was happening.

At this point, and it was very bright in the room, I took a closer look at Dog-boy, who had tried to push me back outside until the leader said I could stay — so I couldn't round up a posse. He wasn't much more than thirty, if that, and already he was a wasted human being. His face had a greyish pallor that served as an appropriate backdrop to a thin-lipped sneer and small, red eyes. Give him a pair of tusks and a foaming snout and you'd be there. I suppose paramilitary organizations need a few guys like this, but they should be confined to the real battlefield, not set loose among the people. I thought about narcs and how their job is to infiltrate, befriend, and betray. What sort of value system permits duplicity to be used for the common good?

Rosie sat on the bed while they tossed the room, having been lightly tossed around himself. Dog-boy produced a stiletto whose long blade flicked out at the press of a button. Everybody standing stepped back. He laughed, and after waving it under my nose, he used it to unscrew the light-switch plate. As he had with the people in the room, including his colleagues, he had shown a lack of respect for the knife as a tool. A total lack of respect, his problem and his fuel, lay behind the sickness that radiated from him in almost tangible waves. At least four of us in that room knew who among us should perhaps be in a cage.

They found nothing. After telling Rosie they'd get him — Dog-boy emphasized their statements with a cuff — they left. I made sure they got on the elevator then took the stairs. Rosie, not having the faintest idea as to who I was, had said, "Thanks for staying, man." Sure, man. Thanks for bringing the OK Corral into the building with you.

The urge to sample strange plants, to chew on a blade of grass, or a twig, or to have dreams that this or that bit of flora has curative powers, goes back a long way, past this current hiccup in human evolution we call "recorded history." The mammalian urge to alter our state of consciousness by ingesting a mushroom or eating fermented fruit seems to be hardwired. It is likely a part of an evolutionary process begun before we were scraping our knuckles on the ground as we learned how to stand up straight — a necessary part. It is natural behaviour.

The world was in serious trouble at the end of the sixties and beginning of the seventies; it's in bigger trouble now. It was clear that traditional methods of solving problems weren't working; we needed to open the floor to all suggestions, all avenues of exploration; we needed new ways of seeing; we needed new ways of behaving. People who are really, really serious are a fearful bunch, prone to being in control. For the most part, they run around espousing the tried and true, accommodating any shortcomings by saying we just need to screw it tighter. Conducting, managing, and controlling, they make life tough for everyone. Perhaps they are necessary in terms of managing traffic patterns, but who put them in charge of the whole machine?

These types, and the leader-cowboys who can't afford to relax for a moment lest someone piss higher up the tree or steal something off their pile, have a huge stake in maintaining the status quo. If you can't relax and you come across something that works because it relaxes you, and fighting it only gives you a bad time, you have a bad experience. Therefore it's harmful and dangerous. For them, alas, the harm has already been done. Their tendencies have not been softened by wisdom so much as having been encouraged as a desirable model we all should aspire to. Who put these guys in charge? Who made this rule? Sure, we need guys like this sometime. Should they be running the show?

Wilfred talked about leadership on occasion. There wasn't just one chief above all. There were maybe several in a loosely defined way. In times of war, they would have a guy who knew how to fight take charge. When the war was over, he'd step back and relinquish control. The best hunter might lead a hunting party.

I was smoking a joint with Ted Poole. Mushroom season was coming up on Vancouver Island and he was laughing about our ancestors and how we made out for medicines and what an adventure certain discoveries must have been.

"Think of a guy just walking through the woods and he spies a little mushroom of a kind he hadn't seen before. He turns to his buddies and says, 'Hmm, I wonder what that one's like?' So he picks it and eats it. After a while, he grabs his stomach, writhes around, and drops dead. 'Wow,' the survivors say, 'We've got to warn the tribe about that one.' One of them, however, sees another mushroom just like the one his friend had eaten. He picks it, looks at the others, and says, 'I wonder what'll happen if I only eat half?'"

Helpless

Being asked to leave the room while those who stay behind are going to talk about you is not an easy thing, especially since I had realized that the outcome meant more to me than I had led myself to believe. I wanted to be general manager of Rochdale; in fact I now needed to be general manager simply because I had agreed to stand. So I paced up and down the corridor while Ian Argue, the other name proposed, stood calmly by. Jack Jones delivered the news. I was the new general manager, just as Wilf had predicted. Ian seemed relieved; he had told me that he didn't particularly want the job in the first place.

Kathy Keachie was not pleased. She smelled a rat, and when Kathy smelled a rat you could bet there were rodent droppings somewhere nearby. She was smart, responsible, hard working, committed to the revolution, and tougher than the rest of us combined. She was a fighter. All of five feet tall, she, too, was a wearer of clogs. Kathy was a babe, although one would never dare suggest that to her. She was also very sure of her opinions. Kathy and I had been bickering, not very seriously I had thought, a disagreement between friends and colleagues. Kathy, along with Ian, was in charge of rentals.

Shortly after the meeting, Kathy confronted me. "You knew," she said. "You knew all the time that you were going to get the job, didn't you, you bastard?" She was right to the extent that I had been told the job would go to me but, pacing the carpet, I really didn't know how it would turn out. People say all kinds of things. I also couldn't figure out why it mattered so much to her. I told her I had no idea what she was talking about.

Kathy called a staff meeting to cut me down to size. It was held midafternoon to ensure a good turnout. I was learning about power, particularly that bit: "Uneasy lies the head that wears the crown." Although I knew all the faces and had felt loved and wanted, there appeared to be no relationship between the mob in the room and me. Maintenance was there, and to me, they looked as surprised as I was when the accusations came rolling in. What was going on? Originally, Wilf, who had been filling in as general manager, had told me that I would be the one to succeed him. I hadn't even realized that there was anything particularly wrong or underhanded about this. I had been asked to keep it to myself.

What was happening at this meeting was an entirely different matter. I was being accused of many wrongdoings, things I had never heard of. For a while I thought it was a put on and at any minute someone was going to wheel in a cake. People got up to voice their concerns that I had done this or that and had said this and that. It was amazing. I sat on a bench, leaning against the wall, and listened to my accusers one by one. As Wilf had suggested, I did not speak, leaving my defense up to him.

As the accusations got wilder and wilder, I almost began to enjoy myself, wondering what I had done next. I could see what a great tactic it was to remain silent. Wilf sat beside me during the onslaught, every now and again looking sadly down at the floor and shaking his head. He, too, remained silent. People I had never met — all meetings like this were open to anyone who wanted to attend — were accusing me of stuff that had even Kathy rolling her eyes. The room had become downright silly.

Kathy's interest, I finally learned, was that she thought a dispute between rentals and maintenance (i.e., her and me) was going to be resolved by me getting promoted and firing her. As for my stake in the dispute, I didn't dare admit to her that not only did I not care as to the substance of the quarrel but that I had started scrapping with her mainly because she was so damned feisty. It was fun that had gotten way out of hand and, because she was so serious most of the time, I couldn't own up to my frivolity. That she could ever think I would power trip over her to resolve anything showed she neither knew nor trusted me. That rankled; hence this meeting.

The litany of accusations petered out and, becoming tired, doubled back into repeats of the same old stuff. Things livened up a bit when some guy nobody had ever seen, who had just wandered in off the street, started heckling me and Wilf. Joe Palumbo told him to shut up. The stranger, six foot plus and looking like the kind of heavy that enjoyed hippie baiting, looked at five eight Joe, and his angelic roman bust of a face replete with curly golden hair, and smirked. He pointed to Joe, then himself, and gestured with his thumb, suggesting they step outside to resolve the matter. The poor bastard. Under his loose-fitting sweater, Joe was built like a Bulgarian weightlifter. Truly, Joe was (and no doubt still is) one of the sweetest men on the planet, a soft-spoken scholar with the looks of a choirboy. Unfortunately, like Ferdinand the bull and bees, Joe, a Leo with Taurus rising, could be stung into action if the cause was just. He had sworn off this type of physicality after Jack Jones had criticized him in a column in the *Rochdaily* for pushing Lionel Douglas at a council meeting. We shouldn't malign the dead, but Lionel, who thought people and the world were like a motorcycle engine that just needed a tune-up, was nearly always obnoxious at meetings, and at this particular one he had it coming. There were cheers, as I recall. Joe only took on people who deserved it. So there were no catcalls as Joe, with a grim face, got up to lead the guy outside. At this point, Wilf cleared his throat and spoke.

"Well, I've been hearing a lot of things said about Ralph this afternoon. A lot of accusations have been made. To me, none of it sounds like Ralph at all, and I'm just wondering if anybody here in this room has asked Ralph, has gone to Ralph and asked him did he do any of these things?" The room fell still, and Wilf continued. "I mean, the guy is sitting here and listening to you people accuse him, but I haven't seen anybody turn to Ralph and ask him if any of it is true."

Kathy wasn't the first to speak, but someone from the floor said, "Okay, Ralph, did you (I don't remember the substance of any of these accusations) do such and such?"

"No," I said, simply and quietly.

It was my moment, and I understood the game just by watching Wilf. And to all the other questions I said just a plain "no." The murmurs told me everything. Finally, Kathy asked, "You mean you didn't get together with your cronies and plan to have me fired?" She posed the question incredulously. It was an absurd suggestion, and I told her so. It was the only time I had ever seen her bewildered, and I suspected someone with a different agenda had been feeding this bullshit to her. "Oh," she said and sat down. If she had asked had I known in advance I was going to be general manager — and, I still didn't get how this mattered — I don't know what I would have said. Well, I do know. I would have used sophistry, like all politicians, and declaimed, "What do any of us know really? Just because a thing is said do any of us know . . . ?" or some such bullshit. I'm glad I didn't have to do that.

Kathy was a true-blue straight shooter; combative and funny and competent and honest and a better choice to be general manager than any of us except she could not be managed, nor could she be bought, as all men, in any position of power whatsoever, can. Her métier was advocacy.

The meeting dissolved. I was patted on the back, as if to heal the stab wounds. Somewhere, I had an enemy, or several. I had survived the first week, not only exonerated but firmly ensconced. Kathy came up to me, and as we talked, I told her I would never use power in that way. She could see that I meant it. "Okay, maybe I was wrong about you, but I still think there was something funny going on." She had been wrong about me, and she was right about there being something going on. There was an agenda that I was not fully aware of. I always meant to ask Wilf if he knew where some of the more ridiculous rumors had started.

Kathy and I had made up, and we all headed for the lobby where Joe was just applying the finishing touches to the heckler with a triple Nelson or some such move he had learned on the wrestling team. Showing mercy on the guy, we had security rescue him and toss him out. Joe, hardly winded and looking perky, looked at me and asked, "Who won?"

I said, "Why, you did, Joe, clearly."

"Not that. What about the meeting?"

"Not guilty, Joe, but you knew that." I felt great.

A question formed as I sat in my office the next morning: now what? Robert Holmes and Michael Mitchell, who had joined the maintenance crew some months before, were jointly running maintenance far better than I had. So there was no going back. In fact, those two worthies had stood and saluted when I passed by their office in the morning. Bastards. I didn't like the new office, being in the east wing, cut off from the swirl of activity that surrounded the elevators, next door to accounting. *Whenever you don't know what to do, step off the stage, don't do anything.* Was it Wilf or Ted who had said that? Sounds good, I thought. Armed with that, and Wilf's assertion that nobody knows what to do, I formulated a plan.

During Wilfred's temporary stewardship, I had learned that things seemed to run better when the G.M.'s office was empty, which it frequently was. All the department heads knew what their jobs were and did them to the extent the building allowed. No amount of interfacing was going to improve that. The most important thing Wilf had done in terms of reducing anxiety was to sign the paycheques every week. As long as that happened, everything seemed to function in the mode that passed for normal. Lao Tzu cinched the deal. "*A leader is best when people barely know that he exists, not so good when people obey and acclaim him, worst when they despise him. 'Fail to honor people, they fail to honor you;' but of a good leader, who talks little, when his work is done, his aim fulfilled, they will all say, 'We did this ourselves.'*" Okay.

In my first and only meeting with department heads, I told everybody that they knew their jobs better than I did. If they had a hassle that I could help with, fine. Otherwise, I had nothing to add. It took about ten minutes. I was to go on and sign cheques every week for six months. This was a record, far exceeding the average of two months for the position. During that time, Rochdale ran like a counter-cultural top, humming with *the even tenor of a well-run state*.

The secret of my success was — and, although I use that term loosely, those who manage would do well to heed this — I didn't pretend I knew what to do. Instinctively, I knew not to get in the way of something that was already working. Other than that, I didn't know anything at all about being a general manager or being any type of administrator in a bureaucracy. I hadn't a clue. But I didn't see where anyone else was more clued in and, most importantly, I didn't have to work for anyone who pretended they knew which way was up. So I laid low, signed the cheques on time, and tried to have as good a time as possible while doing it.

There were lessons. Rochdale, as a government, regardless of rhetoric and expressed ideals, resembled a cross between a banana republic and a medieval fiefdom. As one of the satraps, I had known everything: the rumours, the hassles, the plots, and who the plotters were. I was courted; attempts were made to manoeuvre me to take one position or another; I had power; I was a force to be reckoned with. As governor, I was out of the loop. Nobody told me anything anymore; I was the last guy to find out; the office had power, but I had none. The head guy never knows what's going on; he's an imbecile, really. It was, fortunately, a very small part of what I cared about.

The office had a chair, a desk, two visitors' chairs, and a window onto the mighty Rue Bloor, a dozen feet below me. There were possibilities to be explored with that. Alas, the young Tanya Roberts — *that* Tanya Roberts, who went on to become the beast tamer, a Bond girl, Charlie's last angel and, Donna's mother, Midge — was no longer around. She had lived briefly with Colin Parks (of Bloor and Yonge earring-selling-for-years-and-years-before-he-died-too-young fame) who, being a Regina boy, did a stint on the crew. When Colin showed up for work, late as usual, looking exercised, it was a signal to rush to an east-wing window. Tanya, fresh from the shower, perhaps not fully dry, soaking through the T-shirt a bit, would bounce beautifully across the street to Zumburger's for her morning coffee. The north face of the east wing looked like a giant Whack-a-Mole game at the Ex; gophers were popping out everywhere.

Gone, too, was the speeder who plied passersby with a tune that resembled the screech from a switching yard for almost forty-eight hours on a six-string, then five, three, and finally down to a one-string guitar. It took eight cops to haul him away without having to kill him; not one thing was thrown at them, a sizeable endorsement. He had left behind a cloth cap with a little over a dollar in hush money that survived as some sort of memorial until someone finally cashed it in.

Occasionally, like a shut-in making his own fun, I would slide the window open and have conversations — at first, with people I knew. Later, following an episode of "today is the first day in the rest of your life" being shouted up to the window, shouting "happy birthday" back, and having three people turn around, I moved down to the street to wish every passerby a happy birthday until that wore thin. For a while, I was "Happy Birthday Ralph." Every tenth or eleventh time, someone would look astonished and ask, "How did you know?"

There were ceremonial functions. First, I went on Bruno Gerussi's CBC morning show, the predecessor to *This Country in the Morning*, and presented Bruno with a Rochdale doctorate. He was a great guy: funny but not mocking, serious and sympathetic about the issues regarding kids on the street, and a consummate, gentlemanly host. I also presented Elwood Glover with a degree on his noon-hour television show, which was still local. It proved to be a bit of fun as well.

Pierre Berton, at his suggestion, came by to see what could be done, what he could do to help Rochdale. He was no doubt put up to it by his daughter, Pam, a committed Rochdalian, a mover and shaker around the building. In the meeting, it was tough to get past the fact that this was Pierre Berton, a Canadian icon; he behaved just as he did on TV. We couldn't come up with anything concrete and were failures in terms of utilizing this formidable resource.

June Callwood, meanwhile, was in the trenches doing what she could to help kids on the street: kids fucked up on drugs, kids who needed shelter, kids who needed to be forgiven and returned to their homes, kids who needed support to stay away. Digger House was just one of her achievements. There were a lot of people from our parents' generation who cheered us on, which was more important than we realized, but none so famous as June, nor as tireless, as genuine, as gracious, or as compassionate. Trent Frayne backed her up, as good men will, and wrote a sweet article for the *Toronto Star*. It featured me, but only as a vehicle to say some positive things about Rochdale. These were wise people. Let youth be young and optimistic, you never know, they might be on to something. Love your kids, back them up.

Delegations made appointments to visit. The LeDain Commission was a lot more fun than I thought it would be. What stands out, though, was a group of high school teachers from Nova Scotia, all of whom were guidance counsellors. Clearly, they wanted to understand, and to do a good job. Of the half that did understand, they realized that the current system was going to have to change a great deal. I gave them all As.

One guy stayed behind. There was a phenomenon developing — the confessional — a flip side of the good folks who gave hippies the finger or shouted at us from car windows. Straight people would approach some of us as if we were priests and allow as how they'd be right there with us if it weren't for this or that. Mostly, they wanted to talk about freedom, about kicking off the traces, and about drugs. This guy wanted to talk about sex. He confessed about an obsession he had with one of his students, a thirteen-year-old girl. How young was too young? Were all kids today into free love? I just looked at him. To his credit, he got a little sheepish; he really was in trouble with this and looking for help. But the way he was talking, especially about the girl, made me think of him as being perhaps dangerous. I asked him how he ever got into counselling. He said he taught in a small town and had taken a summer school course in Halifax. We both agreed he wasn't suited to the work, but he said the extra money was hard to pass up. "You need to stop doing this, man. And you need to be making an appointment to talk to somebody." He said, "I know." We both knew he wouldn't. He hadn't mentioned his name or the town.

A lady showed up from the Dutch government, a delegation of one. Her card indicated she was an assistant-deputy, mandarin class, in the ministry that was responsible for youth. She was on a six-month tour of the United States as an observer of hippie culture, the drug scene, the politics of youth; her particular area of expertise was street clinics. She was a plainly dressed woman, mid-thirties, with thick glasses who, at first, appeared rather serious. She had made no attempt whatsoever to assimilate into the culture by apparel, language, or demeanour. She was who she was, and she was asking questions, accepting the answers without judgement, being thorough before moving on to the next question. Rochdale had been an unscheduled stop on the way to England. She had been to New York, the southern states, the Midwest, and had just come from California where she had heard about us.

As you might expect, she was very bright and insightful, but also quite funny. I was amazed that any government would put its resources into a project so obviously pro-youth, let alone put policy-makers on the road. She had come to investigate ideas and programs that could be of service in her country. Then she would go back to Holland and make them happen. It put our governments to shame. Even more humbling, to those of us we thought were cutting edge, she had run across very little that the Dutch authorities hadn't done already. Toward the end of what had turned into a session to educate me, Wilfred burst through the door raving in gibberish and brandishing a giant cardboard tube from a carpet store. He threw it on my desk and left. He had taken to doing that every now and then, presumably to make sure I wasn't getting too serious. The Dutch lady hadn't blinked an eye. It came as no surprise, when I read in the paper a while later, that the Dutch army was allowing conscripts to wear their hair in any style and as long as they wanted.

Zip, Tuck, and Newfy Ed, the paid members of the Rochdale Security Force, stood in front of my desk, on the carpet for sure. Zip, the Reverend Peter Almasy, according to a mail-order degree whose pedigree stretched further back than those of Rochdale, was a small, dark man with shoulder-length hair and a Fu Manchu moustache. He was slight, making one wonder: how tough could he be? Zip was prone to riding around in a three-wheeled motorcycle as well as being a cartoonist whose caricatured progeny was known as Acidman. He was also Rochdale's official chaplain, and never seen, day or night, without mirrored sunglasses.

Tuck, as in Friar Tuck, was a beefy, freckled redhead of no great height, leaning more to girth than mirth. He might well have been a descendant of Falstaff, having, in the ensuing span of centuries, suffered some dilution of family intellect, but keeping the other appetites, predilections, and talent for mayhem intact. There was a certain native slyness about Tuck that was nearly always unravelling behind his attempts at being shrewd. He was a hard guy, save for one of the security volunteers or an unfortunate on the other end of a "sic 'em, Tuck," to take seriously.

The acknowledged leader of the trio was Newfy Ed, a self-professed military historian. I can't remember on which hand he was missing the top half of two or three fingers from the knuckle up. But, like carpenters of old, they had the effect of being a qualifying résumé for the job. Ed was the type of heavy that didn't need to prove it; his manner was mostly relaxed, with a constant smile that may or may not have been a smile. It was possible to have a conversation with him. The three wore black shirts that said Rochdale Security. Stormy, Ed's wife, was an ex officio member of the crew, and she wore a black shirt too. In all, they were an improvement over their predecessors, Clay and Stumpy.

The fire inspector had reamed me out for using our fire hoses and putting them back wet. You have to hang them in the stairwells until they dry; then you put them back. I was sharing this information with security because there had been no fire. Instead, it being unusually warm for early spring, the east wing had arisen like the flow of early sap, creating quite a stir at the back of the building. Freaks were leaning out their windows, hollering at one another in a joyful sort of way, throwing things back and forth. There was the inevitable droppage; security, having been victimized by some of that droppage in the form of a water condom, became involved. Tuck — and I knew it was he as the other two took a giant step away from him when the question was posed — initiated payback with the fire hoses. By all accounts, and they were still filtering in, it had been a decent battle of some duration. The cops had not become involved because all activity mysteriously stopped when the bright yellow patrol cars arrived, only to resume at their departure. It was probably them who ratted us out to the fire department. The next two days found security struggling with hoses while being supervised by R.E. Bruce Martin, fire marshal, until they threatened to make him into a soprano. They weren't all that happy with me either.

On the night of the long hoses, I had gone to a party with Clint somewhere in the Annex. It was a rare social excursion away from the building. We walked, having a laugh about another recent social event, also away from the building. Debbie was with Clark now, but on that night she had been with me. Again, Clint had been the social director since he was always in the know, particularly when it came to film community events as both of these had been. Debbie was seventeen which I only discovered after I had become interested in her, meaning I found reasons for that not to matter. She looked and behaved older. In tight hair with a bun and a kiss curl, she could have played a green-eyed Carmen. She had a shine in those eyes and a wry sense of humour that I found irresistible.

It was not responsible to take Troyer's Ford wagon, but I did. The three of us drove somewhere in the inner city along the streetcar line and climbed a flight of splintered wooden stairs. The room was packed, a strobe light flashed off to one side, emphasizing the effects of the mescaline I had taken, and slides of an organic nature were projected onto the crowd, the walls and the ceilings. People were dancing, people were huddled closely trying to talk, people were grouped around joints sharing tokes, and I was in that particular state of confusion that crowds seem to induce. There was an open window, and we made for that. It was like an old stable door with the top half open, Dutch style. The air was cool. Debbie stayed close, Clint wandered off.

The sound of small arms fire drew my eyes to a building across the alley. I saw a line of policemen, their backs to me in a series of windows, each holding a weapon like they did in the movies. They were shooting at something. Since one never knows for sure, I asked Debbie if she saw what I saw. A guy answered, "That's the firing range for the cops. Far out, huh?" Just then a buzz was circulating through the crowd. Clint appeared out of nowhere. "There's going to be a bust," he said. "Anybody under age will be scooped." What I had indulged as paranoia turned to panic. I grabbed Debbie, and we split, flying down the stairs out onto the street.

For a moment I thought we were too late. As in those fifties tabloids and noir films, flashbulbs started popping and I threw my arm up to shield us from the cameras, thinking, "That's it, we're fucked." There was a loud, grinding squeal and the softer sound of Debbie saying everything was okay. "It's the streetcar turning," she said. I looked up at the wires, the air was filled with moisture, and a spark would flash every time the connector hit a joint in the wire. There was more of that on the drive home. I was still strobing myself while I grappled with the lights from the oncoming traffic doing tricky things on the windshield. It was like driving in a blizzard past the odd muzzle flash of an artillery piece on an ocean liner every time a streetcar went by. As I had done in a blizzard once, I drove with my head out the side window, pulling it in to let the Queen Mary pass on the port side. It seemed to take hours of heading east to reach Bathurst St. and turn north. (I knew Spadina would have been too tricky.) I had not exceeded fifteen miles per hour, according to my passenger who had not ingested anything.

Back in my room, we had a small toke of hash and did what seemed the natural thing to do. It had seemed a bit awkward. After, she said, "Boy, my mom said just be sure you're with a decent guy; she never said it would hurt." I hadn't known. She must have seen a certain look on my face because she laughed. "Relax," she said. "You seem like a decent guy. And besides, I've been on the pill for six months." Somehow this was funny, and we laughed. I took a good, close look at her. She was brave.

Early afternoon the next day, Sunday, I drove her home to Willowdale. Clint was with us and we stopped for brunch at Fran's on St. Clair at Yonge. We got two steps in the door before a guy came at us, waving a menu like he was shooing flies. "No, you don't. We don't serve your kind in here." My confusion resolved itself into anger, and I went for the guy. "What the fuck do you mean, our kind?" I asked, being restrained by Clint for long enough to realize it was hopeless. Clint got in front of me and, to get even, pointed to Debbie and asked very loudly, "Are you kicking us out because she's Jewish?"

The guy was flabbergasted — as were Debbie and I — especially when a couple of burly guys in yarmulkes advanced toward him, demanding answers. In the ensuing mêlée, we fled. I had never been refused service before because of my appearance, and I was outraged. The phrase "the first time" came out, which Debbie greeted with a wink and a grin. Even so it took a moment for that to sink in before I burst out laughing.

"What even made you think of saying that?" I asked Clint, as we reminisced on our stroll through the Annex to the party.

"Brilliance, my dear chap. Sheer brilliance," he said. I supposed that he must be right.

The party was one of those under-attended affairs that never quite got rolling, where stray clusters of people knotted together by earnest conversation, inhabited the far corners of rooms they hoped would fill, giving them the best seats. Several sets of eyes were upon you each time you crossed a threshold. In the kitchen was a girl in a brown dress, a real dress, with a belt and of a length deemed decent. Her brown hair was parted in the middle and tied in back with a ribbon, too low to be a ponytail. She had high cheekbones and an overbite like Juliet Prowse, the actress. Her eyes, dark and lively, looked right at me, and communicated at once her disappointment that it had not been someone else that had come through the door. I smiled at her. She turned and resumed her conversation with the hostess.

Clint was off somewhere so I stood in the kitchen and eavesdropped. Some guy had come to the party with another woman, and this was an annoyance to the fair Juliet. It was a voice that exuded intelligence with an inflection somewhere up around the flared nostrils, indicating private-school breeding stock. As soon as she noticed I was listening, she shot me a dirty look and left the room. Was that a French phrase I had heard, spoken in a perfect accent? In no time, to her obvious exasperation, I had her cornered in an upstairs room. It took effort for her to converse politely; she was more interested in a couple in an adjoining room. She was thinking what a great dolt I was not to have divined her lack of interest. Her name was Frances, and Frances had not the slightest interest in me, Rochdale, or having a toke. It was convenient, however, to have someone there to provide cover. She pretended to talk to me while watching the other room.

Of course I knew what was going on — from the start. I had nevertheless become smitten, an occasionally perverse condition in which all attempts to rebuff said affliction are seen as encouragement. It was a slow night, and I was determined to make the best of it. I knew how irritating I must have been to her, the more so because I was necessary for a while. At eleven, she gave up and rose abruptly to leave. I insisted on walking her home, which, it being dark, and she, being from Montréal and not yet certain of the neighbourhood, was an offer that was accepted. By then, the familiarity of proximity, had loosened her up enough for her to be civil.

Frances was, if I must know, interested in movies. She had been pursuing interests in Toronto but would likely be returning to Montréal soon. "The guy in the next room, huh?" She stared at me, moving her head forward to take a closer look as if she were extremely nearsighted, and smiled for the first time — Mona Juliet. "Was I that obvious?" she asked, and when I said no, she looked me over again.

"We show movies at Rochdale."

"How nice."

"Tomorrow night it's *The King of Hearts*, Geneviève Bujold and Alan Bates."

"Geneviève," she said, pronouncing it correctly.

"Okay, Zhenna-vi-yev then. How about coming to see it with me?"

After a polite demurral, she relented. Something to eat prior to the movie would not be necessary, and we'll see how late it is before committing to coffee afterward, but we'll see the film together. I gathered that I had suggested a film that she thought might be interesting. Because Alan Bates was in it, I wasn't going to bother. Holmes and Clark, via some sort of arrangement with Reg Hartt, had been showing almost first-run movies, usually good ones, for some time in the space that used to be the second-floor cafeteria. I had a date, if she didn't back out.

Weekend cinema at Rochdale was my idea of a good time, the nearest thing to those beloved Saturday matinées. The seats were harder, chrome and plastic stackables, but they were portable, and you could bring your own treats. Since you could also smoke anything you wanted, and everyone did, there was usually an impressive assortment of munchies: hash brownies, chocolate chip cookies, cake, popcorn, and homemade candy. None of it was wrapped in noisy plastic. The barter system ensured a more or less even distribution of drugs and sweets. And there would be at least one cinemaphile so stoned on psychedelics that they were clearly watching a different movie than the rest of us, often providing an interesting perspective — laughing, for example, during a weepy moment, or offering encouragement ("go for it, man, it's a beautiful trip") throughout a death scene. It was the perfect venue for showings of *Reefer Madness*, a perennial favourite.

Frances was not only a Westmount girl, but of a family from which a major NHL trophy had been named. She indeed spoke French flawlessly and with the type of accent, vaguely Parisian, that only a wealthy Anglo could affect. Her carriage was erect; her grooming and manners were impeccable. I knew her neighbourhood very well. In my neighbourhood, it was wise to keep one's intellect to oneself, having the effect of solidifying certain speech patterns and a vernacular far from the parlour. So, to bridge any perceived gap she might have noted, and having found a tweed one an inch and a half wide at the bottom of my black trunk, I wore a tie with my suede bomber, flared Levi cords, and clogs. Elegant Ralph. (Unfortunately, I had been spotted and spent several weeks living that down, beginning with a cardboard box delivered to my door with a note: "Last night you wore a tie. Why?" The box was full of discarded neckties.) The first thing Frances did when I called for her was to suggest I must be uncomfortable in "that thing," and she removed it. Okay, but the paisley shirt stays.

About half way into *The King of Hearts* — on my all-time, top-ten movie list — I became aware of Frances looking at me. When I turned, she flashed me a very warm smile that I found, well, stirring. She could do that because the movie was half in French and she didn't need to see the subtitles to get the dialogue. Later, she told me it was the film that had revised her opinion of me significantly. Before that, she had been composing her regrets. But that wasn't the reason she had smiled.

As well as being a playing card, the king of hearts also means "the king of fools" in French. During the First World War, a small town in France sits between the German and English lines. The Germans have rigged the town to explode. Fearing that and an impending battle, all the townspeople have fled in such a panic that they escaped with only the clothes on their backs. Bates is sent on a scouting mission to look for booby traps prior to the British army moving in to occupy the town. He discovers an insane asylum whose inhabitants have been abandoned in haste, still locked behind bars. The remnants of a German patrol happen by, and Bates, to escape them, removes his uniform and joins the inmates. When called upon to explain who he is, he spots an upturned deck of cards and claims to be the card on top, the king of hearts, not aware of its double meaning. The inmates rejoice, their king is among them at last.

When Bates leaves the asylum to reconnoitre — still out of uniform in case the Germans are about — his loyal subjects follow. Thus begins the lovely heart of the film. The 'lunatics,' first creeping tentatively down the street in their white hospital gowns, slowly begin to inhabit the empty shops and houses in the town. Each adopts a persona partly according to whatever shop they happen upon, but clearly informed by their own dispositions. They select the attire, or costumes, of their chosen professions with a mixture of reverence and joy, holding various articles up to the light for admiration. One guy becomes the mayor, sash and all; another, previously a homicidal maniac, becomes the town butcher; one becomes, deliciously, a prostitute; Bujold becomes a ballerina. The people are radiant, appearing eminently suited to their professions. My personal favourite is the priest, barking mad, donning the robes of office piece by cherished piece. He gives blessings, swings the smoking censer on a chain, and performs the various duties of a holy man with pious conviction. But for the well-timed tics that occasionally reveal their recent origins, the inmates perform their roles with more authority than those whom they've replaced.

It's a lovely bit of cinematic magic. There's a plot, of course, and an anti-war message, but the beauty of the film is captured in those moments when the fools and their king play at being towns-folk. There was never a happier or better-run place. As a parable, *The King of Hearts* had particular relevance for the situation at Rochdale, let alone the world beyond.

It turned out that Frances had been in what she loved to call "the loony bin," having been, several years before at sixteen, com-mitted for being essentially unmanageable. She had been delighted by *Le Roi du Coeur*. She came upstairs after the movie. We exchanged histories in earnest.

Three hours into the trip, on a Saturday afternoon, I answered a knock at the door. I had to come back quite a long way to put that together. So I was in "handle it" mode when I opened the door. It was like treading water in the middle of the ocean while chatting with someone in a rowboat. I had to get to the bottom of this word *business*. Ross Prassky stood there in plain clothes. His lips moved and a beat later the words "may I come in" penetrated my con-sciousness. Ross, along with his partner, Dean Audley, headed up the "Mod Squad" for the Metro police. His vibe was not threatening in the least. I welcomed him.

It was getting on towards evening, the shadows were length-ening. I gave Ross a seat with his back to the north wall facing the window; I sat to his right on the west wall and watched him settle in. His eyes swept the room like a searchlight, like cartoon headlights, and I could see the twin spots move up the curtain, along the track, down the other curtain, onto the desk where they froze on my coffee can pipe, zoomed in, then continued, unhurried, around the room. It was methodical and thorough. He was well trained and probably could not enter a room without sizing it up. His eyes ended up on me, moving from the ground up, and he got a bit of a start when he found me looking calmly back at him. He held my gaze for a moment. We were both satisfied that everything was going to be all right.

Softly, I asked him if he wanted anything. No, he had pulled Saturday duty and thought he'd make a courtesy call. He was telling the truth. No, no coffee, thanks. We talked, at first about the building, what went on, how it functioned. He was aware, I think, that I was stoned, probably on hash, he didn't realize it was acid since I had my back to the light and he couldn't see my pupils dilated the size of saucers. It didn't seem to concern him.

We talked easily; it got darker. How did he like being a policeman? Was the liaison work with Rochdale considered a plum assignment or punishment? That got a grin; actually, it may prove to be fast track. I was very relaxed, and Ross, as people will, nestled into that. We chatted on and on. At a couple of points it swam into my focus that this was a cop and I should be careful. The reality is that he could arrest me, he had the power to place me in handcuffs, take me downtown and throw me into a cell. I decided to trust the vibe and get back into the trip. Meanwhile, behind it all, I was treading, treading.

We discovered, while taking the afternoon into twilight, that we were the same age, and were exchanging stories about our early experiences in school. Ross, clean-shaven, his chair balanced on two legs, was leaning back against the wall. I sat in the wicker basket chair with my knees under my chin. We were laughing. Then came a comfortable silence. A thought hit me. "What happened to us, Ross? How is it we could be in grade three together, playing happily, and grow up to be on opposite sides of the fence? I sense neither of us has changed much. What stands between us?"

It had not been the question to ask. Things could only go so far after all. Had I expected him to convert? After a heartbeat, his chair slammed abruptly onto all four legs. Officer Prassky stood up, not answering the question, and peered through the gloom at his watch. "Jeez, I'm supposed to be off shift. I've got to get to the station." Halfway out the door, he turned and extended his arm. We shook hands but it was too late. Grade three was a long time ago. I could feel his relief through the door, and I acknowledged mine.

Only after he had gone and I had fallen back on the bed to the comfort of my blue wool blanket did I realize that I was still pretty far out there. All the time I had been treading water and talking to the man in the boat, the real stuff was happening beneath an ocean that was deep and vast. I submerged into the depths and snagged a ride on the Gulf Stream, wending my way above the peaks and valleys of the ocean floor, swirling, tumbling, soaring with arms outstretched, on occasion, like Superman.

At one point, I had turned on the lamps and opened the door to the corridor, although I was still on the bed. I had felt the need for comfort. The sounds of my neighbours bounced through the door and off the walls. If we were not indisposed, we left our doors open in the evening, wandering freely into each other's apartments. For some reason, my hearing had become acute in the extreme. I could hear Stan and Rose Marie preparing dinner. Next door, beside them, Marty Wall was fooling around on his new harpsichord. Shelley said something to him, he stopped playing and talked to her for a minute. I heard the lobby door open and close and Linda poked her head in to say hello to Stan and Rose Marie before unlocking her door. She left it open. I was amazed by my newly found aural acuity.

Normally, you could hear shouts in the hallway and snatches of music if you were standing in your own doorway. I sat on my bed and heard Troyer word for word tell Rose Marie that he was thinking of building a shelf in the storage closet. Their apartment was the furthest from mine. Rose Marie asked him if he had remembered to get the wine. They might as well have been standing in my kitchen. I covered my good ear to shut the sounds out, like I cover it at night to get to sleep — being deaf in one ear is advantageous at times. I could still hear them. Obviously, I had not done it correctly. This time, I made sure my finger was on the flap above the lobe and I pressed it as hard as I could into the ear canal. With only my deaf ear exposed, I heard Linda join them for dinner. Rick won't be home until ten. I could hear in my deaf ear. I don't believe in stuff like this. My left ear is stone-cold deaf, period. I cannot hear anything in that ear. But for two hours or so it appeared as if I could. D. Stanley even wandered down after dinner, and I gave him a demonstration. I told him what Rose Marie had just said. He couldn't hear her at all. He ran back to check. He's still wondering what the trick is. Me too. It could be there's a lot we don't know about our abilities, inherent in everyone. It never happened again, nor do I expect it ever will.

Some days it would be all there. Some days it was like there was some kind of code just beyond my reach that, if I could grasp it and crack it, everything would fall into place. An elevator door opened and a big girl stood there, eyes shut, swaying. She pitched forward and I caught her, she was dead weight and almost took me down with her. She was moaning, her eyes rolled up so you could see the whites. The clinic was closed temporarily. The hospitals had been turning people away of late. They were sick, as it were, of ODs. I sat with her a while and then took her to Wilf and Dorrie on the seventh floor. They nursed her for two days. Suddenly she was gone. I ran into her again, she was high on something and had no idea who I was.

The problem with words, see, is they are abstract. Naming a thing, say, "flower," puts one word between you and that object. "Pretty flower" is two words, and so on. The more you talk about it, the further away you get from the actual experience of that flower. Sure, we use words to communicate, and they do a pretty good job. We can describe that flower: its colour, the number of petals, maybe even its Latin name. We can describe everything about that flower except our relationship to it, how we feel the first moment we lay eyes on it, the reality of our encounter. We try to describe our feelings, but words are never accurate enough.

I began to think that words were getting in the way of me realizing who I was. It's a little more complex than that, but words — and I had so many by then — figured to be a large part of the problem. I began to think that if I could reduce my vocabulary (and the only way I could do this, I thought, was through atrophy, refusing to use polysyllables) I would get closer to reality. The closer I got to reality, the closer I would get to me. I knew it would be a work in progress, and results would likely be gradual.

It was a scheme not well thought out. Reading was impossible to stop, it could perhaps be managed. I resolved not to read too much fiction and to look for simpler narratives. Lao Tzu would be fine, poetry okay, and, for some reason, anthropology (which I read like dime store novels) could stay. If I ran across a new word in my limited readings I wouldn't look it up — which I often didn't anyway, hoping the meaning would settle on me whilst rushing on. Giving up the *New Yorker* would assist this cause immensely. Then I realized that it had been a good long while since I had seen a *New Yorker*. And, I had always preferred a simple narrative, being a simpleton. Fine. I would stop looking up words, even the ones I had seen before whose meaning might be a little rusty. My dictionary was toast, or at least destined for the bottommost reaches of my trunk.

What was easier to resolve was writing. I would stop.

Not forever. But I think the heart of what this was about was that whenever I wrote *seriously* I would eventually become overwhelmed by the fact that I didn't know anything, or much of anything. I thought writing should be about TRUTH in capital letters and I didn't really know the truth — and what little I did know, I was too afraid to put it down on the page, naked. The books I had read and loved were great things to me. Even not-so-good books were great in a way. A book, I thought, should have something to say. Before I had anything to say, I would need to learn more — a good deal more. (Or, get to a point where what you know is pretty much topped up, and if writing is still an option, you had better get to it.) From reading Henry Miller, I knew I had to find a voice before the words would flow. I believed Henry and knew I wasn't there.

It took three trips to gather every bit of writing I had stored in my trunk and throw it down the garbage chute. The Anglo-Saxon boy joined the last load. I didn't feel liberated, just sad. It may not have been very good writing, but it was personal, and I had been attached to every word. However, in that moment, before I had any time to think about it, I had been resolved. This must have been a Friday, because on Monday Peyton told me that the garbage chutes had been plugged all weekend. Oh joy. I ran, first up to my floor, then seventeen, then sixteen, and so on until I realized he had left out the part where they had dealt with it. There was nothing on top of the bin either, it had been emptied and the refuse carted away. Sometimes the bridge collapses behind us; then we are committed.

Of course, the next thing that happened is somebody gave me a book, *Seven Arrows* by Hyemeyohsts Storm. It is fictionalized anthropology and a great bit of storytelling. The "seven arrows," or stories, each represent a generation of a tribe of Indians, from the first contact with a white man up to the 1960s. There is continuity from one story to the next over the two hundred years the tale encompasses. The fall of paradise is catalogued in a very moving way. It had a lot to say to me.

The back to the land movement had its attractions. Rochdale had ties to a community in Killaloe, Ontario. Several of my fellow communards had land outside of Orangeville, on the Grand River. Everyone knew someone who had gone rural and couldn't, at times, wait to join them. I agreed with the concept and had visited a few places, but the homespun granola ethic and macrobiotic diet thing resembled poverty a little too closely to settle on me with any degree of comfort. As with the Marxists, these were predominantly middle-class kids who were most enamoured of the lifestyle. I had grown up on a macaronibiotic diet at times, which meant there was no money for meat. But blessings to those who gave it a shot, especially the very few who made it work for them.

What was becoming plain to me is I lived in a culture that was almost totally cut off from any meaningful relationship to the earth. The phrases, "man versus nature," or, "once again, man is on a collision course with nature," are still current, supposing that man and

nature are two separate things. Our animal nature was either something to be ashamed of, or something to overcome.

> Bountiful life, letting anyone attend,
> Making no distinction between left or right,
> Feeding everyone, refusing no one,
> Has not provided this bounty to show how much it owns,
> Has not fed and clad its guests with any thought of claim;
> And, because it lacks the twist
> Of mind or body in what it has done,
> The guile of head or hands,
> Is not always respected by a guest.
> Others appreciate welcome from the perfect host
> Who, barely appearing to exist,
> Exists the most.

Today, I could walk down Bloor St., turn south at Huron St., go east
through the alley behind the building now known as The Senator
David A. Croll Apartments — formerly Rochdale College — and
south onto bp nichol Lane, walk into the old coach house, and find
Stan Bevington, much as I could have done thirty-five years ago. I
have not done this yet, but I accept as an article of faith that Stan,
should I visit Coach House Press, would be there. In the twenty-two
months I shared apartment 1825 with him, I never knew him to
miss a day of work.

Every now and again, I'd reflect on what a pain in the ass it
must have been for Stan to share that space with me. For at least
eighty per cent of the time, the place was a magnet for activity.
There was a constant parade of people to my room at all hours.
There was music, loud talk, laughter, rattling in the kitchen,
flushing toilets, and shouts down the hall. Throughout it all, Stan
would leave in the morning before I was up and about, and come
home late in the evening and go straight to his room. On occasion,
I was able to intercept him and talk him into having a toke and join

whatever was going on, but he would never stay for long.

Stan, a redhead, had a long, Karamazov-style beard like Jim Neff's, a bird's nest of thinning hair on his head, and round, rimless glasses that accentuated a slightly wild look. He dressed in dark jeans with suspenders over a khaki shirt rolled up at the sleeves, his forearms and neck covered by an undershirt. He would not have looked out of place in a mechanic's garage in northern Alberta, the kind that fixes everything, or a daguerreotype of nineteenth-century frontiersmen. And Stan didn't talk much. One day, I managed to intercept him outside the door to his room, and I asked him how his day was going. "Well," he said, "I'm having trouble with yellow." We both let it go at that. A few years later, another printer explained to me that, of the four colours used in printing, yellow could be very difficult to work with. Once, I asked Stan if all the activity and noise coming from my room bothered him. He stopped a minute and really thought about it, and then said, "Nope."

So we didn't converse much, or cross paths all that often, but I was always aware of him and found comfort in his presence. I admired him; he was a true leader. The Coach House people, and there were many of them, were an elite subgroup of Rochdalians, whether they lived in the building or not. There was not a fragile ego in the bunch, and yet they made art harmoniously. They learned how to print on old-fashioned equipment, setting type by hand, and they learned state-of-the-art, and they published in both. Stan presided over all this activity yet I'm sure that almost everyone there would be in a position to say, " I did this myself." I may have aspired to that, but to Stan it was the real thing. It was very Zen.

One evening, I sat at my cedar desk. In this incarnation of my room, the mattress was up by the window so I could look out and see nothing but sky. The desk sat facing the open doorway at the back of the room. I faced the doorway from behind the desk. There was a single lamp on. I was tripping on acid and I was grinding my teeth a bit. I don't remember what the problem was. There was a blockage somewhere, and it was creating a bother. I had taken out a terra cotta, pre-Columbian artefact roughly two inches in diameter, a small head in a headdress, that had been broken off at the neck from a larger figure. I held it in both hands, occasionally transferring it to one and using the other to run my fingers over its features.

Michael Mitchell had given me that head. It was over eight hundred years old. Mitchell, co-head of maintenance with Holmes, was a French 100 class shy of a doctorate in archaeology, and this had come from a bag of odds and ends he had brought back from a dig in Mexico. He was in the process of leaving archaeology behind to take up photography — that turned out to be a great career move for him, and for Holmes, who joined him at Ryerson. Mitchell was the first guy in Toronto to tote a shoulder bag. It was a leather cylinder about nine inches in diameter and two feet long with a single strap. He had curly dark hair and a set of mutton chop whiskers to further distinguish him from the crowd, as if an IQ past genius didn't. He was also one of the few Rochdalians who had actually been born in Toronto.

The head was a comfort, and I would often look at it, trying to throw my mind back to a North America before the Europeans claimed discovery of a land that the Indians say was never lost. Who made it? What kind of life had they lived? I suppose it was closer in pedigree to the stuff sold at souvenir shops than to art, but it had survived almost a millennium and therefore had a certain primitive purity.

Stan Bevington walked in and said "Hullo" as he passed the doorway. I responded brightly, I thought, despite a troubled head on my shoulders and an ancient clay one in my hands. At once, Stan — and you could hear him do a U-turn — was standing in front of my desk. His was a look of concern as he asked, "Are you okay?" And I was amazed that he had picked up such a faint distress signal while sailing past at such a fast clip. It indicated the sensitive nature of someone also used to tripping. I was grateful; his reaching out had touched me, and it's always good while plying the heavens to have some human contact on the way down. It's one of the more affirming things in a quiet, undramatic way.

"I'm fine, but thank you for asking."

"You sure?"

"Yes."

He pointed to the object in my hands, and I passed it to him. He looked at it for a while, turning it over, and then handing it back. "Nice," he said.

Stan returned to his room. I put the second lamp on and softly played a record that José had given me. It was a release by the Mexican Folklore Society of indigenous folk songs in beautiful, slightly off-key harmonies, some, hauntingly a cappella. The Mexican government had included it in handout packages for the 1968 Olympics in Mexico City, the one with the iconic "black power" salute. I fired up a bit of hash to smooth the transition. For some reason, I felt much better after Stan's visit.

The first rumour — that the phone company, a.k.a. Ma Bell, was already in charge of everything or, if not, very close — was taken with a grain of salt. That we might be scooped off the streets at any moment and whisked away to 999 Queen St. to be declared insane and held indefinitely had more resonance. After all, most of us knew somebody who knew somebody where that had already happened to someone they knew; and, if so-and-so hadn't gone looking for them, man, they'd still be with the man, man. After Woodstock, some of the alternative newspapers were quite certain that the U.S. government was going to host a free rock concert, out west somewhere, in the mountains, where you could get in but you wouldn't be able to leave. The site or sites, basically remote concentration camps, were being secretly prepared right now, people. This was entertained as a possibility, however remote, if the government could pull it off, which was doubtful.

So, these little bits of folkloric paranoia bounced around the back brain to be brought up at appropriate steam-letting moments like campfire tales. To know these things was part of being hip and streetwise. It was part of flipping the finger at cabinet ministers who wanted to gather you up in butterfly nets. It was part of flashing the V-sign at folks in a vw van going the other way on Highway 17 a few miles east of Sudbury while they were flashing it to you. Peace, brother. It was part of linking arms together in front of a row of mounted police, singing, "We shall not, we shall not be moved." And maybe our bodies would be moved by the charging horses, but not our spirits. In the U.S. especially, it was part of being against the war, the draft, recruiting on campus by chemical companies, or whatever else was selling on an early spring day when the sap was rising. Think of it as a form of innocence.

The sixties did not truly die until May 4, 1970 when a protest at Kent State University in Ohio went very wrong. What was the issue again? Does it, or will it ever, really matter? Two groups of mostly young people faced one another, having long since been separated. One group wore uniforms and helmets and shouldered rifles; the other carried books and held hands. It had all happened hundreds of times before. Indeed, it was almost over when a new kind of panic set in. The records show that four people were killed that morning, shot by their brothers, by their neighbours, who were just playing at being Ohio National Guardsmen.

What also died was a kind of hope — not just in the States, but in Canada and much of the rest of the world. It was no longer a struggle in which the truth would eventually prevail; in which you might be roughed up a little and spend a night in the slammer. Shit, no, and besides, that might help your chances with the long-haired babe that sang like Baez. It wasn't like you could fight the fight for a while in mostly a good-natured fashion and, when you got tired, your kid brother could take over, and so on, until good sense finally triumphs. It wasn't innocent anymore. We were, and remained, peaceful people. Those fuckers were willing to kill us anyway.

Little Big Horn

Don Black and I had mutual friends. As a fellow council member, I liked how he behaved at meetings. He was honest, a little more serious than I was, but a fellow seeker of truth. He had, like me, decided on a spur-of-the-moment adventure to drive to Montana. The prospect of attending a gathering of medicine men and women from indigenous peoples all over North and South America was irresistible. We were from Rochdale and therefore had kinship, but we were still looking for other areas of commonality on that first day's drive, somewhere in Michigan.

A car full of our elders, three blue-haired suburbanite ladies and a couple of old gents, passed our International Travelall — one of the early suvs, where you sat up high, in full view. Everybody but the driver turned to stare, poking each other and pointing at us as if we weren't there. By Rochdale standards, we were conservative dressers — jeans, T-shirts, full beards, and long hair. These folks, however, were staring at us and seeing circus freaks or cartoons come to life. I don't think it occurred to them that we were any more real than animals at the zoo.

Simultaneously and unscriptedly, without even so much as looking at one another, Don and I raised our right hands slowly, and in unison, with the middle-finger salute. It was a manoeuvre so perfectly executed that it might have been choreographed by Balanchine. The effect was stunning. The jaws in our small audience dropped, one, two, three, like a Martha Graham improv. Then they clamped shut, their faces reddening and turning grim as they sped off. Don and I, still in sync and having, in a moment, become closer, burst out laughing. It was the best. This is what the finger was for, a tool to communicate with people who didn't get it any other way.

Somewhere west of Ann Arbor on I-94, I told Don about Jim Garrard's visit to my room and why I had resigned as general manager and from council. It was Don's turn to drive. I settled back with one foot on the dash of Wilfred's Travellall that had more or less become mine. The pall of gloom surrounding me had been left behind at the border. Both of us were surprised at how trouble-free our entry to the States had been. The guy just waved us through as if hippies were yesterday's news.

Since Don knew Jim and had seen him operate, I didn't have to explain how intrigue and plotting behind closed doors seems to almost be a necessity for some. Jim was my neighbour. He lived directly across the hall between Marty and Shelley and Jack Dimond. Jack's door was never left open — that he had been assaulted by bikers in the first month or so of Rochdale had a lot to do with it — and I don't recall Jim's door being open more than once or twice in almost two years. Then, Jim wore his hair and beard long, bearing an uncanny resemblance to John Barrymore in *Svengali*, an effect I suspected he took pains to achieve. Jim, of course, was an actor and founder or cofounder, of Theatre Passe Muraille, which survived its early years in part through financial assistance from Rochdale. It was a pittance, really, although Jim was, like any fundraiser, always looking for more.

One of my uncles on my mother's side was forever saying things that were so outrageous and mean that you weren't sure if he was kidding or not, but you had to decide he was kidding because the alternative was too horrible to contemplate. If it was humour, it was the kind that punched you in the stomach to provoke a reaction. I was reminded of that when Jim introduced me to his wife, Susan, who worked as a schoolteacher as, once upon a time, had Jim. He said some nasty things about her that she didn't seem to register at all. Okay, he likes to kid around.

Several months later, I attended a gathering of mostly actors at Jim and Susan's. He shot a quip at me, one of those quasi-humorous things designed to show rank. I retorted, he answered back, I shot another volley back, eventually winning the point, all to the amusement of our little improv's audience. Moments later he guided me to the kitchen and said if I ever, ever talked like that to him again in front of people he'd have me drawn and quartered, or some such dramatic thing. We had been playing, I thought, were we still? We must be. Actors, they're always "on." Entering into the spirit of the thing, I just laughed and asked if he might be taking on such drastic action all by himself. He replied: "I'll get you for that, you little prick." He had to be joking, just affecting that tremble of contained fury.

Don told me how Jim and his cronies, a few months before I had arrived, had declared Rochdale a monarchy and himself as King James the First. They held meetings behind closed doors catered by the cafeteria. Jim's rent was subsidized, Passe Muraille was given space. I hadn't known any of that. Men who would be king, even in play, should be closely watched. It seemed as if Jim had it in for Wilfred and the Indian Institute, and Ian McKenzie. They were getting way more money than Passe Muraille or him. It was as simple as that, I believe. That CMHC might not have given Rochdale a mortgage without Wilf and Ian's involvement, and would not have entertained a moratorium on payments, was not discussed.

Funding for Passe Muraille had been cut off in May. Then Wilf and Ian both resigned from council. A smaller quorum would be needed to carry motions. I was part of Wilf's crowd. Peter Turner, whose chair had gotten enormous, dwarfing the room, was one of Jim's old pals. I hadn't known that either. Don and I were as one regarding the involvement of dealers in Rochdale. We were against it. Peter wanted them to have a seat or two on council, claiming it was a necessary evil. Dealing at Rochdale was like hiding behind your mother's skirt and sticking your tongue out at the cops.

Council meetings had become, for me, a huge drag. At one point there was a drive led by the Marxists to unionize the staff, which would have been a disaster — we couldn't even pay the rent. A proposal was entertained to run the building by a committee: comprised of the general manager, department heads, and one member of council. I pointed out that the department heads would lose all their power and their departments most of the efficiencies they had developed. Finally, it was becoming more and more difficult to determine whether security worked for Rochdale or for its resident population of dealers. All of this was really eating into my enlightenment time. I guess Lao Tzu and I just made it look so easy to run the building. When Jim came to my room in late July, to sound me out on whether I would resign as general manager on behalf of Peter and his group — which now seemed to include the larger-than-life Rosie Rowbotham — I only needed a second or two to reply in the affirmative. He was surprised. At that point I could have still made it very difficult for them, but I was sick of the bullshit. "As a matter of fact," I told him, "I'm going to resign from council as well." Jim, looking a bit puzzled — this wasn't how you played the game — said, "Jeez, you really are a nice guy, aren't you?" I asked him to leave.

So, I may not be a reliable narrator when it comes to Jim Garrard or Peter Turner. I think I am, although I would never consider myself a "nice guy." As a matter of fact, I owe Jim a debt of gratitude for helping me keep one streak alive. A couple of days after I had officially resigned, I told Jim I had forgotten to get my Rochdale degree so I would like it now, having decided upon a doctorate in cosmology. He looked at me like a cat with yellow feathers around its mouth. "I'll see what I can do," he said, "but you'll have to give me five dollars for the printing costs." Although I told him to shove it up his ass, I couldn't help, later, when I had calmed down, laughing at the joke. I had even failed, despite having been in charge of the business that had dispensed them, to get a degree at Rochdale.

Two guys get to Montana from Toronto by taking turns driving and sleeping until you're there. The International had a huge V-8 engine that seemed to invoke awe at just about every gas station we stopped at. There was no seat belt law, and the vehicle had a manual throttle so that during the long, straight stretches you could pull it way out to approximate a primitive cruise control and drive with one or both feet up on the dash. Plowing through the black, pungent Iowa night, a snippet of poem came to me, the first in a while. It was the click of the high beams on the floor. That was the chorus. *Comes a car. Tip toe. Whoosh, gone. Tip toe. One more time. Tip toe. Gone, too. Tip toe. Come again. Tip toe. Beam too high, tiptoe, tiptoe. Low beam good, tip toe. Whoosh, gone, tip toe. Tiptoe, tiptoe, tip toe.*

Give me a warm wind rushing through the window and a thousand miles of highway in front of me any time. You can feel the shit roll off your back. Between A and B, you're free. Nowhere, my favourite place.

Just outside Sturgis, South Dakota, we picked up two farm boys from Georgia. They were huge, good-natured puppies in plaid shirts and crewcuts with a you-all drawl. I was sure the coaches at some football camp were scratching their heads, wondering where their two freshmen offensive linemen had gone. Something in the way they were thumbing rides made me pull over. Besides, you have to pick hitchhikers up at least once on a trip. It's a rule.

You can cut the hair but not the man. These two had decided to tour the U.S. before college and see what it was all about. They found they could get rides easier with their hair cut. They had done the eastern seaboard, New England, Detroit, and Chicago since the beginning of July, and were all for seeing the Wild West and California before heading home. Don took over driving, and I sat in back with the larger guy who turned out to be some sharp old boy for a nineteen year old, a budding Mark Twain. He told us how, in New York City, they were fascinated by the endless supply of people who committed themselves to disappearing underground. "They'd just zip along the sidewalk, run down these stairs, and, that's it, they were gone. And when they were gone, they were gone, they ceased to exist anymore. It was good there was a bunch coming up the stairs, blinking into the light, to replace them."

We were amongst our brethren. In no time, I fashioned a pipe from an empty Player's pack, putting the bowl in the circle where the sailor's head had been, and cutting a slot on the opposite side to draw through. We smoked hash that had a slight hint of Juicy Fruit from its border crossing. It was easily one hundred degrees Fahrenheit, and with one guy driving, the other three lay passively in the blow-dryer heat, swapping stories. The budding philosophers had us laughing all the way through Wyoming and into Montana. We dropped them off in Hardin before turning back to Crow Agency. It was early evening.

We passed half tons, campers, trailers, vans, school buses, and all manner of Detroit iron in mostly four-door configurations. They were piled high with coolers, clothing, sleeping bags, and blankets. Stuff was spilling out of them toward tents and teepees. There were never less than four people around each vehicle, every second or third of which bore a bumper sticker saying: "Custer Had It Coming" or some similar statement. There were licence plates from just about every state and province, and the cars stretched on for what seemed like miles. The aroma of sweetgrass saturated the air.

The population was exclusively Indian, or First Nations, if you prefer. The men were mostly in denim and cowboy boots with all manner of Stetsons: yellow straw ones, black felt, rounded black stovepipes with a flat brim, the deep arc of the real cowboy kind with the brim folded narrow to the crown. Every hat was decorated with feathers, either in a fan at the front of the crown or stuck in at an angle on the side; many had bands of beadwork as well. And of those men who had long hair, they wore it in braids tied off with leather thongs; they had belts and buckles of silver inlaid with turquoise. The women were in denim too, although many wore dresses, plain and fancy. Their hair was long and braided with elaborate ties. They wore bone chokers and necklaces of turquoise around their necks; moccasins with beautiful patterns of beads; beaded vests of moose hide; headbands from simple to elaborate; and charms for their wrists. The dancers were there, walking to and from events. Women glided by in painstakingly crafted dresses and high-top moccasins, accessorized with beautifully crocheted or woven shawls of a kind you could not buy in stores; some would carry eagle feathers in their hands. The men had fantastic topknots and feathered crests, feathered arms, and gigantic feather bustles behind their breech cloths. You could hear the soft ching of bells every step they took. Through it all, the children played, darting and dodging around tables and legs and lawn chairs in which the elders sat. As far as our eyes could see, were Indians. We were surrounded. Lets hope we didn't have it coming, too.

As we drove slowly through this orderly commotion behind a couple of cars also looking for their camp, the ones who had a spot would look up from what they were doing and scan the cars. We got stares, glares, double-takes, blank looks, smiles, frowns, and more than a couple of V-signs flashed at us — about what we could have expected on Yonge St. above St. Clair. As a matter of fact, I felt more comfortable here than in parts of Toronto. We were at a powwow, and while the methods of travel may have differed, this type of gathering has been going on for a long time. You had the sense of that right away, of the timeless quality, of the eagerness to celebrate and accommodate, of joining the circle. I felt welcome.

We found our camp by the little white clapboard building. Arranged around a circle of cottonwood trees, was Wilfred's trailer, Ted's silver Airstream, a few tents, and a group of guys struggling to erect a small teepee. Johnny Yesno, the actor, had placed the poles so that there was a four-foot gap between the canvas and the ground, a feat that would dog him from powwow to powwow in the years to come. Like the others, he was laughing so hard that it took more time for that to settle down than it did to correct the fault. The women, especially, were having a good time. "That used to be our job," one of them shouted. "It was the women who put the skins on the poles." "Now I know why," another shouted. And they all laughed some more. Jeanette Corbiere-Laval was among them. When Jeanette married Dave Laval, a non-Indian, she lost her treaty rights. The same rule did not apply to her brother, Rick, because he was male. Jeanette took it to the Supreme Court; Indian women should have the same rights as Indian men. She won. Also, I recognized filmmaker and singer, Alanis Obomsawain although I didn't know her as I did Jeanette.

The Travelall was, with the back seat down, our tent, so we parked in a gap in the circle. There was a big field next to our camp piled with hay bales and ringed, in the distance, by the Bighorn Mountains. Wilf and Ted were there; hugs all around. It was the end of the day, you could see lightning flashes in the rosy haze that hung above the mountains and faintly hear the thunder. Above, the sky was a deepening blue. Glad you could make it, Old Bean. Thanks, Old Bean, I'm glad I popped in.

I thought of the hundreds of medicine people and healers who had gathered in this camp. Among them were charlatans, pretenders, wannabes, and men and women of considerable power. These might not be the best or most ceremoniously dressed, and they might not advertise their presence. Even in the tales of European culture, the poorest or most simple person could turn out to be a saint. My hearing became attuned to the drums, beating soft and loud from every direction, and snatches of song, and laughter, and the distant rumble in the mountains. Wood smoke mixed with cut hay and burning sweetgrass scented the breeze, to which I would add a fragrance from Lebanon. Magic was in the air.

Besides Holmes, Stan Stevens was the only guy I knew who actually wore the green, one-piece, terrycloth jump suit. I'm almost embarrassed to say that I don't remember where in northern Ontario Stan comes from. It doesn't matter because, in a way, Stan and I will always be close, as brothers. For one thing, he didn't make much of being Indian, or discount it; it was just part of who he was. He was a comfortable guy to be around, and movie-star handsome, but he didn't make much of that either. I saw him go into Rochdale one day in the green suit, looking like a twenty-something pretty boy, and I dismissed him. I had to reassess my opinion when he showed up at the Indian Institute, and Wilf introduced us.

We were sitting up in the hay bales with the Wood sisters from Scarborough: Shirley, who was Stan's girlfriend, and Nancy, who would soon be mine. Dorrie had gotten word to me earlier to call Clint, which I had, from the administration centre. Sylvia is dead, he told me, some kind of overdose. He thought I would want to know. It was not something I was in a hurry to hear, but I thanked him for calling. It was a shock, although not a complete surprise, and I was surprised at the depth of my feelings. I had a cry, facing the wind. Clint could not have known I had just dropped mescaline.

The moon, near full, shone like a searchlight, creating a world of bright silver and black shadows. Nancy's eyes were like the moon, pale, almost grey, and luminous. She was looking thoughtfully at me, the eternal female face registering concern. Her hair, with bangs, darker than her sister's, was cut just above her shoulders. Every now and then the wind would lift a strand and place it across her mouth. She would brush it back behind her ear. Stan and Shirley had moved on to find their own bale.

The skinny chick in the red, velvet flares was Sylvia. She wore a black, long-sleeved lacy thing for a top, and brownish boots that matched neither. For days, in the afternoon she played catch on the Bloor St. patio with a shorter girl dressed plainly in denim and a tie-dyed T-shirt. It was hard to ignore her, a flash of red and black in early spring like some kind of exotic songbird. She had thin, fine, almost white-blonde hair, worn long and straight. I heard a couple of guys speculating as to whether she might pop the buttons on her top today, like there was some kind of pool going on. In truth, she did seem almost over-developed in that area.

Her most striking aspect, however, was her face. She had high cheekbones, and blueish-white skin stretched tautly over her features, giving her a slightly skeletal look in the manner of some Scandinavians. She threw like a girl; that is to say, she looked more like a girl than one of the guys when she hurled the ball (an old, bald tennis thing) with more push than follow-through, but she threw with force and was deadly accurate. She introduced herself as Miss Sylvia Lalonde, actually saying "Miss," from Montréal, and apologized for hitting me in the "privates" with a toss that had gone astray. Shortly thereafter, Miss Lalonde and I partook of a chaste coffee, "but no drugs," in my room.

Weeks later, she confessed to having "sorta" aimed, which was consistent with the girl I had come to know. Sylvia was simple and direct, unscholarly and naïve in a working-class way with which I was very familiar. China figurines from the five and dime were okay with her, nor was her philosophy much advanced from the homilies found in places like *Reader's Digest* — just like in my old neighbourhood. But, also like girls from the darker reaches of the 'hood, Sylvia was streetwise. It had in no way made her bitter that I had evicted her and her friends from Rochdale or, at least, my signature on a piece of paper had. She told me this shortly after I had told her my name. I apologized, but she wouldn't hear of it. "We deserved it," she said. "All of us were on speed and really fucked up. We didn't pay rent, and we really trashed the place. I kept trying to get it together, but even when I'd quit, they'd slip stuff in my drinks. I got away from them when we got kicked out, so it was a good thing for me."

Sylvia was sincere in that she bore me no ill will, but it really got me to wondering: what was I playing at with this general manager thing? I was making decisions, sometimes, that affected people's lives. Who was I to be doing that? If we are all one, wasn't I just kicking myself out? What seemed to be of no concern to Sylvia bothered me for days. She had been so offhanded about being a "speeder chick." Was it more of her naïveté? Probably.

It was not only the quality of her skin that was transparent. She told me once, as an inducement, as an indication that she was a woman of substance, intimating she was of a family that had significant benefits for those close to it, that her father owned a pool hall, and she was his favourite child. She had a faraway look when she divulged this, I suspect she was indulging in a fantasy of sorts. I found it funny, in a heartbreak kind of way. Her death was not funny. It lay upon me with a surprising and considerable weight.

She never discussed the dark stuff. In unguarded moments, she'd talk up to it, and then skirt around to something lighter. Extrapolating, she had run away from home and possibly abuse of some sort, in her early teens, and had kept on going. She struck me as being very loyal; and when she hooked up with a guy who turned out to be, or turned into, a speed freak, she got into speed as well, running with his crowd. When she tried to get out, not really liking the life, they wouldn't let her. They'd wheedle or cajole until she broke down, or spike her food and drink if she didn't. If we can't escape, you can't either. Who knows what trouble she courted by going up to my room that day, because she would not have been able, quite, to hide the fact.

Sylvia shone in the silent moments, throwing a ball, sitting on the bed in a gaudy housecoat with her wet hair wrapped in a towel, her elegant legs drawn up to her body, and her chin resting on her knees. She would catch you looking at her and, not speaking, cock her head inquisitively to the side before smiling and returning to whatever it was she was doing with her toes. She had a talent for silence, an entire vocabulary of arm clutching, shoulder squeezing, neck burrowing, waving from a distance.

She had a talent for listening, too. It was the words, those clever little bastards with the more informative messages in between, that kept giving her up. Yet what I have to remind me of her, what I have kept as a memorial, I guess, is a letter she wrote. Within its envelope I also keep a news clipping of her death and a postcard from PEI, sent to her by me, which always occasions a moment of brief shame when I see those few words that give me up. She deserved better.

The first time Sylvia and I spent the night together — at my place, she didn't have one — there was no sex. She wanted to but couldn't and was a little worried about that, but wouldn't tell me why. I had a flight to Regina the next day to see Tauno before he moved to the interior of BC with Mel and Degen. It was their turn — most of us boast at least one stab at it — to go back to the land. Sylvia had just completed a treatment for gonorrhoea, I found out later and wanted to be sure. It had been a deliberate, parting gift from her "friend." She stayed in my room until I got back. Days later, we were happy to see one another. It was late May.

Holmes, Mitchell, and I decided on a whim to drive to PEI on the July 1st long weekend. David French and Leslie Gray had rented a cottage in St. Peter's Bay, and we were going to surprise him. All I can remember of the drive down there was being stuck in a line of traffic that went on for miles outside of Quebec City and having to piss in an empty milkshake carton and that it seemed a lot further than I had expected. Frenchie was surprised and so was I; Lee Ann had joined them, as beautiful as ever. Sylvia again was staying at my place, as she did so often, and all she had asked was for me to send a postcard — so unhip, so corny and establishment, but I agreed, finally.

We cavorted at the beach for a day; no one wore bathing suits. Lee Ann and Leslie danced on the shore and played in the water, Nubian and Nordic nymphs, sisters from different realms. Holmes became so aroused lying in the warm sand and watching the spritely pair, that he dared not rise, becoming deep red from it instead. He had, to Mitchell's and my amusement, begged for a towel. The next morning we chose to drive back to Toronto via the "Airline Route" through Maine, bits of New Hampshire, Vermont, and New York State to Montréal, and then the 401.

The new route took us through Saint John. I kept my fear to myself — I always think something's going to get me when I go back. As a form of whistling in the dark, I took Holmes and Mitchell on a "working" tour of my old neighbourhood, showing them the various rooftops and networks of alleys over which I held dominion in my burglary days. It was all very lighthearted — I painted myself as a sort of Zorro figure, el Hombre del Noche — and something I had totally forgotten until reminded of it recently by Mitchell. I didn't look up anyone and can only imagine the relief I must have felt upon leaving town. It would have been huge. We bonded further on the trip back, talking guy stuff through the night: Holmes working at the brokerage firm in his youth and planning a big heist, stopwatch and all, to get through the tedium; Mitchell and Annick on a dig in Mexico, surrounded by a pack of wild dogs; and me, having been sobered up at seeing Lee Ann, wondering aloud what to do with Sylvia.

But Sylvia had gone by the time we got back, early on a Tuesday. There was no sign of her anywhere. I had sent her postcard to my address. She appeared a day or two after it had arrived in the mail. I put it beside the letter she had written, intending to show her later that I had sent the damned card. Even then, I realized what a pitiful thing it was. She had a suitcase and a box and, seeing the look on my face, rushed to say, "I'm not staying. I just need you to store these for a few days. Will you?" She could not quite look me in the eye, I asked her what was wrong. She would only say it was okay, and she could handle it. I put her things in the hall storage closet, and she left.

Two weeks later, Sylvia came by around ten in the evening. I was happy to see her. She had come to pick up her stuff, and could she change into a different outfit in the bathroom? Sure, but why don't you stay? "I can't," she said. Why not? She looked me in the eye this time, long and hard. "I really want to, but I won't right now. I can't. I'm getting a place together and when I do, we can be equal, and then I can visit." She changed into fresh jeans and a sweater in the bathroom. I asked if she wanted her postcard, an underhanded attempt, I admit. "Oh, did you send me one?" she asked. And when I said I had, although it wasn't much, she dropped the plastic suitcase and cardboard box tied with twine and gave me a fierce hug. "You are such a great guy," she said, meaning it, to my shame. "Save it for when I come back." And she was gone.

It was not so much a letter as a poem, or an attempt, written in stanzas of a sort. It is written on unlined, pale blue, six-by-ten-inch onionskin from a pad that would have said "Airmail" on the front. The page numbers are noted in the upper right-hand corner with a roman numeral in brackets and, in the lower left-hand corner, each page is also numbered with the arabic number in brackets. There are eleven pages. Her script is clear and careful. She has made circles instead of dots for each period and dotted *i* although this is occasionally forgotten as if it were a recent addition to her calligraphy. Her signature at the end shows no circle above the *i*, just a very faint dot. The letter says:

For Ralph Osborne   (1)
            (composed by Miss
                  Sylvia Lalonde)

Happiness is found in
      another's joy;

It is not the perfect
      but the imperfect
      who have need of
      love.
Love sought is good,
      but given unsought
      is better.
Friendship is the wine
      of life
Real love begins where
      nothing is expected
      in return.
            (feelings I've had
            and I'd like to
            share them
            with you).

(1)

To someone I know. (11)

I'm sitting here thinking
of someone I know.

Someone who's always
got loads of friendly
words and thoughts
to share,

His loneliness is
hidden by his effort
to make other people
as happy and as
full of beautiful
feelings as he
possibly can,

Without a friend like
him to confide in
and listen to I
would find myself
in such a world
of confusion,

I'm writing about
this special person
because he's the first
(2) and only true friend

that I've ever felt (111)
myself and actually
really started to
enjoy being myself
even though this
person doesn't
realize it will his
actually brought me
through two of the
most depressed days
of my entire life,

(and a friend in need)
is a friend indeed.)

This person is one
that I couldn't
possibly forget as
long as I live, even
though I haven't
got much to give
this person in
return for his
gratefulness I hope
he accepts that I
(3) wish to remain a

friend for as long [IV]
as I'll know him.

I'm now going to
refer to this person
as "you" because
it makes my
train of thought
(which is the
true (so help me god)
feelings) I have
and I'd like to
share them with
you upon paper)
because I find
it a lot easier to
express myself.
Excuse me but I've
just had a small
poetic thought.

(4)

(V)

The Role

Life is just a one-act
play.
Play your part and
you will
stay.

Study your role
Till you reach your goal
If lines get confused
Don't feel you've been used
step aside and you will
be

That there's one thing
you must continue
to be,

Just repeat I must be
me,
I must be me,
and when you establish
this goal
You'll be able to con-
tinue in life's one-act
role.

(5)   (written at random),

(VI)

So as you see I really am greatful for tennis balls cause they've worn ced upon a swell guy. To come right down to the facts Ralph I think your great (And I don't give a fuck what other people think because to me your one of the closest and most beautiful (even handsome) [had to get that in] friend I've ever had.

This next bit of writing is just some poetry I've made up I truly hope you enjoy some of it.

(6)

First I'd like to give (VII)
you these words from a
song I know, maybe you
could somehow put some
music with them.

I'd rather be a sparrow
       than a snail
Yes I would, If I could
    I surely would.

I'd rather be a hammer
      than a nail
Yes I would, If I only
     could
    I surely would.
(I forgot one verse) (sorry).
I'd rather be a forest
     than a street
Yes I would, If I could
    I surely would.
I'd rather feel the earth
     beneath my feet
Yes I would, If I could
(7)   Oh I surely would.

(VIII)

Leaves have fallen
      from the
         trees
As tears have fallen
      from our
         eyes.

Laughs have broken
      dead silence
As sobs have broken
      loud laughter

But most of all a
      kind word
      can break out a
      smile from any-
      one.

(8)

(1X)

The wind is whistling
a haunted tune
tonight
I wish I could I wish
I might
Miss our times and
remove the
fright.

Love is a well from
which we can drink
only as much as we
have put in,
and the stars that
shine from it are only
our ups looking in.

(9)

(X)

gentle sleep is all
    around me,
So I say let the
    night be,
I will surely have a
    pleasant sleep.
Cause I lot of this
    I've always wanted
    to tell you, but
    felt so terribly
    shy and I find
    that I can express
    myself so much
    easier on paper.
I haven't thought about
these thoughts in
the way I've put
them down so please
excuse the spelling
and the laces
(10) y'abbee I've put in

I hope you have a (X)
good sleep.

So my good friend
until tomorrow.

Peace
&
lots of love

Sylvia

P.S. I'd enjoy another
game of shuffleboard
if you have time.
I'll probably be in the
restaurant or outside
of Rochdale,

goodbye for
now.

xox

(II)

I would not see the clipping until I got back to Toronto, including an astonishing bit of information in a backup article, written as a critique of the way hospitals were handling drug cases. Even stoned on mescaline I remember the contents of the card — addressed to Sylvia Lalonde, 1825-341 Bloor W., Toronto 181, Ont. It was a picture of a sand dune and people on a beach. On the back half reserved for the message, with no salutation, not so much as a "Dear Sylvia," or "Hey you," or "Hey," totally devoid of a signature or, in fact, any other words, written high up with lots of blank space underneath, I had inscribed sourly, "Here's your postcard."

Nancy asked me how I was doing. I was attempting to move past it and into the light, but Sylvia lay there heavily for the longest time. Finally, one of them took me by the hand and led me home. Sylvia would have loved it here, I thought. Blonde hair and all, she would have fit right in. They would have seen her right away and taken her in. She would have loved being among these people. I know that Nancy did. And I did, too.

My job, and excuse for being there, was to ferry delegates to the conference to and from the airport at Billings. The first time, I drove Wilf's big Ford LTD. There was no daytime speed limit in Montana. I had gone to pick up Ernest Tootoosis who I had gotten to know a bit since seeing him and Clifton walk down Bloor St. the summer before. Ernest, when he was in Toronto, often stayed in the apartment below mine, in 1725. Barrelling back toward Crow Agency I passed an International Travelall with a brown body and a white roof, just like mine, going the other way, toward the airport. Behind the wheel was an Indian kid in sunglasses going almost as fast as I was. I got a big grin and a wave from him as he zoomed past. Sure enough, when I got back, my "tent" was gone. That's how I met Buckley Petawabano, famous Indian actor. We ferried delegates back and forth during the day — I traded him Wilf's LTD to get my truck back — and we visited tents and teepees in the evening.

Buckley had come with a couple of elders from Mistassini, his reserve in northern Québec. Some thoughtful organizers had arranged for the two men, both in their sixties, to share a teepee. We went to visit them one night, crawling through the little hole. They were actually from a smaller reserve, north of Mistassini, and had had little occasion in their lives to speak anything but Cree. Buckley told me I had to bring tobacco as a mark of respect if I wished the old men to speak, so I brought two packs of Lucky Strike. They entered into a conversation in Cree with long silences; Buckley mostly listened. I looked around the teepee, grooving on the sound of the language being spoken, finding it a great comfort. I admired the design of a tent that allowed you to have a fire in the middle, the smoke being directed up through the vent on top. Being a builder of fires myself, I appreciated theirs, and the way they had cut their wood and stacked it around the perimeter of the fire. It was solid, efficient. Their bedrolls were laid down neatly; ropes had been strung between teepee poles to air out and dry their clothing.

The elders spoke, Buckley sometimes responded, and I was thinking that if you were to substitute fur and hides for wool and cotton, this could have been a scene from a thousand years ago. The men's archetypal features were illuminated by the glow from a fire that required very little attention, and when it did it was with a minimum of effort, a poke to make way for the new wood, a rising shower of sparks, and a leaping crackle soon to quiet down. They wore little adornment — no Stetsons, just green cloth caps of the sort woodsmen wear, and green khakis with plaid jackets. I was off in the clouds somewhere, feeling very content, when they started laughing, quietly, but in obvious mirth. At this point, Buckley translated.

"They weren't going to come here, at first," he said. Then he talked to one of them in Cree to confirm a point. "They thought it would be a long way to go, and they have to get ready for trapping season. But they had heard about conferences from the people at Mistassini and thought they'd like to try one. They'd never been in a big jet, just a bush plane. They thought it was a fine thing, all these Indian people getting together, but they were really looking forward to the rooms they had heard about when you go to conferences, big beds and soft chairs, and televisions. They don't have television." One of the men spoke, a big grin on his face. "Now, he says, they came all this way only to sleep on the ground in a strange tent that isn't even set up for cooking, and the beds are so hard. So they're having a big laugh about that. They did try out one of the rooms a friend of theirs had told them about, at Dorval Airport. You go in this room, the doors shut, and then they open and you're in a different place. Their friend had gone up the elevator at Place Ville Marie and still couldn't get over looking down through the window at people walking around, smaller than ants." I found it funny, too, and we all had a good laugh.

These men knew everything they needed to know about survival in their part of the planet. Along the way, they had learned some things that were useful to pass on, just by, as Aunt Grace would say, "putting in the time." The respect they had earned had not puffed them up or given them airs; they were humble. They were human beings, and the biggest thing I got from them was that a way of life was represented here that hadn't been completely obliterated, and it was a viable way to live. "Before the White Man came" was a familiar refrain; before civilization, it was possible for human beings to live in a kind of harmony with the earth. It had been done not all that long ago. Less than a hundred years before, they had been living that way a mile or so from where I stood, where Custer had met his end.

Just as there were similarities in some tribal costumes, so were Don Black and I similar. He was bigger, but we both were bearded, had long hair, wore T-shirts and jeans, were white as Wonderbread, and wore rimless glasses, except I only used mine to drive, and they were tinted blue. Perhaps he could even claim some Indian blood in his genes as I had been told I could. So, I was very concerned about my brother, who appeared to be wrestling with demons. He was taking being a White Man far too seriously. That's a big burden to shoulder. I saw an expression of solidarity when I spotted another white guy — we weren't hard to pick out — who I took to be Jewish since he had fashioned a Star of David out of straw and wore it on his sweater, above his heart. That's all anyone wants, an identity, something to feel good about. There was also a scattering of anthropologists and priests wandering around, not enough to cause a commotion, but too many to shoot.

Listening to the old people talk one hot afternoon was a classic exposition of form and content. The people — and not just the elderly, but all the generations were there, from babies on up — had spread out under whatever shade they could find. Some were in lawn chairs, others on blankets, or leaning back against the trees. A microphone on a stand had been set up where, one by one, and in no discernible order, people would get up and talk. Many of the older men and women spoke in their own language, usually having a younger relative or member of their tribe translate for them. Whether listening to a translation or someone speaking directly in plain, simple English, I was struck by their eloquence. They were making powerful and moving statements, painting vivid pictures in primary colours, without verbal pyrotechnics or complex vocabulary.

It stands to reason that people with a long history of oral tradition would use language so effectively. There are few greater compliments paid to Indian people than: "He speaks his language well." Buckley had told me this. He was pretty famous then, in First Nations communities especially, for starring as Pete Gawa in the TV series, *Rainbow Country* (still aired on cable on APTN). What he was most pleased about, however, wasn't the series but that the elders from his reserve had asked him to translate for them. This was a great honour for Buckley. Respect for one's language — what a concept. At this gathering, I had never heard mine spoken so well.

In the afternoon speeches, the respect element alone would eliminate the Marxists and other varieties of campus radical. Not everybody was old, tuned-in or particularly wise. There were a few evangelical Christians exhorting their people to embrace Jesus; some assimilationists who wanted to give it all up and join society, and maybe once a year, like the Irish, have a Geronimo day; and a band of radicals from the American Indian Movement whose message at least made more sense than the other two. Every speaker was warmly applauded. Nobody got up to challenge the previous speaker or disagree with anything that had just been said. Nothing was right or wrong or to be debated. It was just how whoever was speaking happened to feel about whatever they were saying. You weren't expected to change sides or become adversarial and bend someone to your will. It was, "That's the way he sees it." Or, "That's how she feels about that." And that person's point of view was respected. No one was shamed or belittled or challenged.

Don and I were both impressed by this, but in different ways. You see something you admire and you want to be part of it. He felt excluded, as did a few other white guys (for lack of a better term). Elder after elder rose and said how happy they were to be at such a gathering at last; how they had long dreamed of such an event. Inevitably they would follow with tales of one indignity after another suffered at the hands of the white man. After all, it was an Indian ecumenical conference, whose manner of worship had been suppressed, ridiculed, deemed heretical, and outlawed by religious bullies. Adherents who revered the Great Spirit — surely the most adequate description of God ever — were whipped, tortured, burned at the stake, and driven like errant sheep toward the righteousness of Christianity.

The stories were tragic, of course, but strangely nonmilitant and, if not outright forgiving, were at least suffused with forbearance. As Ernest Tootoosis would have pointed out, the Christians would even do that to their own people. It was not a call to arms so much as an observation of the behaviour of a particularly dominant and brutal culture toward those who were made subordinate. And because the speakers were still there to tell the tales, they were stories of survival and renewal. They were stories of continuance and hope. But Don, I think, every time he heard the pejorative "white man" connected to some atrocity or other, just felt lower and lower. He had a big heart, and guilt by association attached itself to him and wouldn't let go. I told him he couldn't possibly take any of the speeches personally and to substitute the word *establishment* for the term *white man*, but the mood seemed to hover around him and persist.

Somewhere among these elders, I figured there had to be a Lao Tzu; maybe not using the same words, but knowing the same things. There was a feeling, standing next to some of them, of being close to something essential, like standing in certain groves of trees and experiencing a sudden quiet, a passive strength. You'd never know from talking to them, but even Lao Tzu had nothing to say, as the story goes. He wanted nothing to do with teaching or writing anything down for the benefit of mankind, but got caught by the emperor's priests while trying to slip out of town. He was forced to divulge his wisdom before he was allowed to proceed to the tall mountains.

The two men Buckley had taken me to had reminded me of a kind of security I hadn't felt since childhood, and only rarely then. They felt good and true and important in the way Leonard Cohen had meant. There was no need to go to China to get to the heart of things. It's always good to encounter the ones who know the rocks are alive, that there's a powerful energy in the trees. It's an affirmation that we are not quite finished, that our heart beats faintly.

I had gone wandering, and Buckley showed up in time to rescue me. He's a little guy, my size. He had big, early Beatles hair then, smiled often, and looked younger than he was, somewhere early to mid-twenties. When I trip out with a group or even with one other person, a tremendous act of faith, there's a time early on when I need to be alone. We had ingested mescaline. Peyote would have been even better but there was none around — unlike the second gathering in Alberta a year later, but then you would need an invitation to join the ceremony. Passing a feebly waving Stan Stevens, who had melted under one of the big trees, I found some hay bales and burrowed in. The girls, Nancy and Shirley, had gone back east.

It was the singing and the drums that pulled me to the dance competition. I had stumbled through many campsites to get there, past thickets of stony stares, through groves of laughter, down tunnels of apprehensive looks — I might have been a spirit, no telling what kind. The loudspeakers were an intrusion, and the electric words employed those sugared tones that signify, first and foremost, the love of one's own voice. Then the dancers would dance, and the singers sang in voices far removed from civilized tricks. Raw and powerful ululations pierced the night with a sound that has not been stilled yet, with a song that rivals that of Brother Coyote, the drum beat a pulse in the bosom of Mother Earth. The dancers were in rapture, bells sounded like a show-ring harness, feathers rustled like the whisper of trees.

In the darkened perimeter of tents that sold Juneberries and bannock during the day, out of the glare of floodlights and their captive, whirling figures, I saw an old man. He had no hat. His hair was braided, flecked with grey. He stood deep in the shadows, watching the dancers. His features were impassive. I hadn't seen him arrive. Did I imagine I could read his thoughts? *"We still live, my children, barely. Much has happened and we still live. Dance until the bright lights fail, until we have our fires back. Dance for sadness, dance for joy, give thanks to the Creator. We are all His children."*

"Hey, White Man, what the fuck are you looking at?" came a voice from behind me. I turned to face a skinny young guy, black hat, torn jeans, a dirty shirt half-tucked in. He was tall, weaving slightly. There was a scrape on his forehead. We will now see if love conquers hate. I couldn't speak so I stood there looking at him, wondering what he might do next. He was uncertain, but stepped toward me.

"Hello, Brother. He is my friend," said Buckley who had materialized from nothing and stepped in between us. "He is a good man, and I am taking him back to our camp." He led me away. The old man was nowhere in sight.

"I could have handled that," I said to Buckley, as happy as I was to see him.

"Maybe not his two friends hiding in the bushes."

"How did you find me?"

Buckley just laughed.

The fire was never left alone no matter how many excursions were made. As the supply got thin, we'd fan out in ever widening ranges to scavenge any kind of wood, taking turns to do that or to relieve ourselves. Returning to the hearth, someone would be there, or many, each moving to make room. The air was chill. First, you stare inward at the fire and, turning to warm your back, outward to see the myriad of fires in the sky. Clifton had been there, the big Creek from Oklahoma, where his tribe's diaspora had ended. Buckley, Stan, and I made a thing of following his footprints around the fire; it seemed to spook him. On an excursion, I joined Wilfred, looking up. "There's a billion stars up there, see. If I move two paces to the right, I see as many again." Turning around to yet another billion, I became lost for a time in the wonder of plenty.

In the deepest dark of night, sparks rose slowly and disappeared with a cosmic wink at their sisters, the multitude of stars. Dorrie sat in a lawn chair with a blanket over her lap. She raised her hand to speak to me, faltered, and then broke out in laughter. Looking right at me with a familiarity that had become solid, she said, " I know who you are, but I can't remember your name." It was a sweet moment. Of course she knew who I was. She was speaking to me directly, to who I was. The accessory had escaped her, the word that is my name, which had nothing to do with who I was. It was an intimacy Dorrie and I would always share. She had been the skinny kid from rural Ontario, a wiry Scot, who became Wilfred's fire. The commotion surrounding Wilf was hers to handle, too. She had sheltered and fed armies of people. We laughed with her. What seemed like an hour later, she said loudly, "Ralph." And we all laughed again.

The twigs vibrated on top of Wilf's trailer as a result of his considerable snore. How had we missed them in our searches for any-thing combustible? The night had passed. We were down to four: Buckley, Stan, me, and June, a girl from Winnipeg. She was Saulteaux or Cree, and a sophisticated city girl, a dancer. Buckley reckoned he loved her. We had seen the fire through, watching the last of the embers melt into the grey talc circle of ash. The camp awoke slowly, here and there, in ones and twos. Men stood facing the bush, their legs spread apart; women ducked in behind it. Babies fussed; wood was being chopped. The sun was free of the horizon; the still air stirred into random puffs, already warm, predicting a hot and cloudless day.

"Let's go see Ernest," Buckley said. "He'll be at the battle site."

Less than two miles away, we pulled into the gravel lot beside the monument to the Battle of the Little Bighorn, Custer's Last Stand. There was a small interpretation hut overlooking the spot where the battle had been fought, and a path up to the monument standing at the highest point where you could see down to the river, across to the mountains. The signs warned of rattlesnakes and asked you to remain on the path. Inside the hut was a relief map showing what happened and where.

Even at nine in the morning, there was a crowd of thirty to forty people milling around, waiting for some sort of lecture. There was a freckled family of redheads, looking pinched and not well. The rest of the people, from grandpa down to baby, also had a pale, pasty-faced look, only some of which I attributed to the fact I was still tripping and the colours had perhaps begun to fade. They looked as if they were rejects from a Kellog's cereal ad. I couldn't help but note that my Indian friends looked robust, as did Ted when he arrived in his white GMC half-ton with Ernest.

There was a stir when Ernest stepped out of the truck — as compared to them just stepping back and eyeing us suspiciously when we had arrived. He was really geared up, wearing a full eagle-feather war bonnet, a trail of feathers running all the way down his back. He wore a bone choker and breastplate, a fringed jacket and

pants which, along with his moccasins, had beadwork of great intricacy. His cane was brightly painted with Indian designs. His lined
face, with his mouth downturned on one side, and hawkbilled nose,
was thrust forward defiantly. As he slowly scanned the people, mischief glittered in his eyes. You're on my turf now, they seemed to say.
And the performance was only beginning.

Every now and again someone would slide behind grandma in
a surreptitious attempt to take Ernest's photograph. "That'll be five
dollars!" he'd shout. And the photographers would adopt a silly
grin, wondering if Ernest was kidding as they tried to fade back into
the crowd. Ted had fallen back to stand with us; Ernest stood alone
in the midst of the large circle of space accorded him. A buzz from
the crowd announced the arrival of a college senior, perhaps a
drama major but more likely somebody's well-fed nephew; he was
dressed in the blue uniform of a trooper in the 1870s version of the
U.S. Seventh Cavalry. He took command of the situation and
began a practiced and obvious recital, beginning with, "Good
morning, ladies and gentlemen, I'm going to tell you about a very
important battle in the history of these United States."

"Haw!" said Ernest.

The trooper, who was cradling an old breech-loading carbine,
ignored this intrusion and continued on with the script. He no
sooner found his place when Ernest interrupted again. "What are
we doing listening to you anyway? You guys lost. None of your guys
survived. How in hell do you know what happened?"

The man in blue, whose face was getting a bit flushed, again
took the high road and pressed on. A tension had developed, however, and the space between Ernest and the crowd had widened.
Every so often Ernest would correct the official version with a comment like, "The Sioux would never do that, they were the finest
horsemen ever seen." Or, "How could you know that? You don't
know what you're talking about." And, "I told you, five dollars!" as
another attempt at photography was made. Ernest, a number of
times and at regular intervals, corrected the young man who was

trying to be a trooper, but it was getting to him. Nevertheless, he soldiered on. At least half the crowd threw their support behind Ernest, inching back towards him in a show of approval. One reason was that the guy hadn't varied from his script, which was stilted, nor had he engaged Ernest in any way, or even acknowledged that Ernest existed. He just tried to work around him. It was not unlike the mistake Custer had made, he underestimated his enemy.

Finally, rebuttal was at hand. At the end of his talk, in a choreographed sequence, the cavalryman suddenly raised his carbine and, pointing towards the mountains, fired off a shot. He had used a lot of powder; it was loud and startling. People jumped, oohing and ahhing. The dramatic explosion reverberated in wave after wave of snarling sound. It howled over the soldiers' graves, across the hill where Custer had fallen, over the river where even today the Indian kids were laughing and playing, over to where Sheridan had got it, and past where the buffalo roamed, echoing off the surrounding hills. The sound filled everybody's mind. Nobody expected this. It had become too real. And you could feel sympathy among the tourists.

There were furtive looks toward Ernest. There was a sadness that it had to end that way; the old man had been more than holding his own. A little smile began to form on the trooper. That'll fix that Indian. But the moment was not allowed to settle. Ernest Tootoosis, defender of his people, stood tall and defiant, a giant bird of paradise amidst a field of stunted corn. He pointed his cane toward the trooper and spoke immediately in a loud, firm voice.

"I'm still here!" Ernest declared. "You haven't got me yet."

I thought maybe Buckley and Stan were going to die; they were laughing so hard. Ted was doubled over, and so were another group of First Nations people that had come in during the show and figured out in a hurry what was going on. In no time Ernest, like Custer before him, was surrounded. People were slapping him on the back and shaking his hand — and those were the tourists. There had been no doubt as to whom had won the rematch of the great battle. It was, to repeat history, a total rout. And there was no doubt as to where the sentiments of the tourists lay. They had applauded the outcome as vigorously as Ernest's people; they had become Ernest's people. Like a lot of folks there, I wondered why they had a trooper come out to recite its history in the first place.

There were many tourists who buttonholed Ernest after his performance. He let them take his picture and, very gently, he told them he was only kidding about the five dollars. The trooper was back in the hut, trying to explain things to a small contingent of sniffy folk, but he was just going through the motions. He was a beaten man. Someone had brought a chair for Ernest, and he worked the crowd, paying particular attention to a couple of flustered forty-something women, asking them where they were staying and would they be in the area for long, and so on, until they were blushing and squirming in obvious pleasure.

Ernest had a great smile, warm and wise, like a favourite grandfather. He had photos of himself with his address stamped on the back, and would give these to people who were interested in talking to him further. He'd sign the back and write the message that mattered to him most, "Ernest Tootoosis," it would say, and, "Love All Mankind."

We broke camp that afternoon. We had all been invited to Ted's place in Rock Creek, a dot on the map in BC's southern interior. Ernest's victory seemed to revive Don somewhat, but he found another way back to Toronto. Buckley, Stan, June, and I headed further west. You learn a bit about discrimination when you're a hippie travelling with three Indians through cowboy country. It's a feeling, mostly of eyes boring into the back of your skull. But when we stopped at a KOA campground outside Livingston, we got a different reception. The place was operated by Jehovah's Witnesses, according to the pamphlets strewn about. They didn't sell cigarettes. They smiled a lot, though. In fact, they were positively beaming. We had been up for thirty-six hours, were still wide open, and these guys felt good to be around. I mention it because it's the only time I ever met Christians who seemed fully tuned in to the "love" aspect of Christianity. They didn't try to convert us, or preach, they just "loved" us. They were living the word. And we were beaming it back to them. It was a surreal encounter.

This had been the first, or one of the first, psychedelic experiences for Buckley. He had had a good trip. He talked about being taken away to residential school, not bitterly, just in a matter-of-fact way. They're old news now, but these stories were just beginning to surface. You were punished for speaking Cree, but the kids found all sorts of ways around that. He had just made a feature film with the NFB in which his character dies at the end. It was shown on his reserve and, a month or two later, he came home. Some older women saw him and began to cry. They thought they were looking at Buckley's ghost since they had seen him die. "They were really happy that I was still alive," he said.

Ted had bought ten acres, a flat table of seven acres backed up against a hill, and the three acres below it on which stood an old chicken coop and Ted's Airstream nestled in among some Ponderosa pines. A steep trail ran between the two plots. We were the last to arrive. Ted and Marge were there, their son, Wayne, who I had gotten to know from his visits to Toronto, a few local mountain-variety hippies, and a bunch of people from Rochdale. Among the surprises were Dunc Blewett and Norris Eisenbrey, who I hadn't seen in almost a year. Wayne wheeled out a pair of speakers from the chicken coop that he would later convert to his house. Someone passed me a joint and, to the smell of barbecue, Simon and Garfunkel played "Bridge Over Troubled Water."

This was one of those moments, the kind you never forget that, when you hear the song, you are transported back through time, becoming suffused with a contentment that is ever more fleeting. "Sail on, silver girl, sail on by. . . ." I stood off to the side, smelling the air, looking at the colourful rabble of people telling stories and laughing, really digging the peaceful vibe. I was happy then about the previous few years and how, even five or six years before, a gathering like this might not have been possible. There was a strong sense of being connected to everyone there, as if we were a people, even the ones you didn't know. Maybe, just maybe, we could evolve. Ted came up and passed a joint. "This is so great," I said. "Yes, it is," he agreed. Then, looking me right in the eye, white-bearded and all, he said, "Do you have any idea how long I've been waiting for you guys?"

He Who
Feels Belittled

It felt like I had been gone for years and had returned to a place irrevocably changed. Clint had saved two news clippings for me. The first, an inner page filler, said, "OVERDOSE SUSPECTED IN DEATH — Tests are being conducted at the Centre of Forensic Science to ascertain whether Sylvia Lalonde, 20, was killed by an overdose of methamphetamine, commonly known as speed.

"The girl was found semi-conscious by a room-mate in their Dovercourt Road apartment on Tuesday night and was dead on arrival at hospital. An autopsy yesterday indicated the cause of death was asphyxiation; officials said drugs could have caused smothering but that proving it from tests is difficult."

The second clipping, which I have lost, told more of the story. The hospital had turned her away the first time. She had apparently ingested six grams of speed. Is that a lot? I don't know. The hospitals were turning kids away because treating them was affecting their bottom line; hence, the proliferation of street clinics. It's possible she needn't have died. Sylvia was not an immoderate person.

One of her former companions had a habit of putting speed in her beer whenever she announced she was quitting. This was the guy I wanted to talk to, but I didn't ever know his name or who he was. Sylvia had never been all that fussy about drugs, period. So, if she died of a massive overdose, someone other than Sylvia had a hand in it. I am certain of that. The roommate turned out to be her sister. And Sylvia had escaped at least one thing that her parents had saddled her with. Her name wasn't Sylvia Lalonde, as it turned out; she had assumed that appellation. According to the paper, her real name was Gloria Ewing.

David Humphrey, my next-door neighbour, performed a root canal on me one Saturday afternoon at Downsview. He often helped people at Rochdale, for an extremely minimal fee. It had cost me twenty dollars, and that was only to pay for the nitrous oxide. Brynn, at my request, wrote me a ticket for Valium, but I had to go to her office, and I had to tell her I was depressed. Had I told her I was fine and just wanted to have a small quantity around in case someone was having a bad trip, she would not have prescribed anything. She took her job seriously. " I know what you're doing, or trying to do, but I think you really are depressed," she said. I got my prescription (for ten pills, five milligrams each) but at what cost? Was I depressed? I felt the same as ever; well, almost.

About a week after I had returned from the West, I had been stopped by security as I was entering the building. Who was I and did I have any ID? This was too much; especially to be confronted by some low-life scum who I had never seen before demanding I account for myself. So I tore a strip off him as if he still worked for me — did he have any idea as to who I was, who the fuck was he to be holding me up, and so on. Bob Nasmith happened by and apologized. They had some new guys.

"Are you with security now?" I asked.

"Sort of."

"What's with all this bullshit at the door?"

"There were some problems . . . That's right, you were away, weren't you? We're working on a new system."

"Not much of a fucking system."

Security had become much bigger in the few weeks I had been gone. Welcome to the new Rochdale of dealer boutiques and slot machines on the second floor. This was the beginning of the Rochdale they had to drag people out of to evict, kicking and screaming. Still, when I got up to my room, I had pause to reflect. My floor was still an oasis of calm and good vibes.

What had really been bothering me was I suddenly had no power over events occurring in the building. From the beginning, I had had some control. Now, for the first time, I had none, and there was a vacuum I hadn't reckoned on. It had been a relief to get away, but now I was beginning to wonder if I should have resigned from council. What was that all about? All the time I had been stressing equality and being a nice guy about it, and in reality I was dealing from strength. Admit it, now, weren't you just a bit more equal? This required study. It would perhaps be, as Holmes would say — Sherlock, not Robert — a two-pipe problem.

So I thought the whole thing through, and I realized that I had felt pretty swell clomping around those hallways in my clogs. I had fallen victim to a title. There was a school of thought in the early days of acid that the ego was something you had to overcome to see the white light. It was true; you had to relinquish control, which is firmly seated in the ego. Ted had said that the ego is just as important as your elbow or your left foot; you need it and it should be healthy. My ego had swelled; I had become self-important. It can't be true, but there it is. Somehow my identity had become tied up with my job. My Chinese friend confirmed it, "*He who feels punctured must once have been a bubble. . . . He who feels belittled must have been consequential . . .*"

I gave up on the notion of control altogether and went for walks instead. I had a route, which I travelled almost every day: east on Bloor to Yonge, south on Yonge to Sam the Record Man, and back. I was looking at people. I learned two things: if I thought of someone out of the blue, maybe someone I hadn't seen in a while, I would run into that person less than five minutes later (this didn't work for romantic interests or if I tried to push for results; it had to just happen). I also discovered that if I locked eyes with a stranger, any stranger, and smiled, he or she would smile back. I would try to love all mankind.

Wilfred wanted to play a trick on Poole, who was coming to town for a meeting regarding their fledgling publishing company, Neewin. He introduced me to Ron Christianson, a tall, blond, Nordic type from Thunder Bay. Ron had drawn a great cartoon for Neewin in an attempt to hasten payments for outstanding receivables. It showed an Indian in braids in a beat-up tuxedo. The bib had curled up, the lid was half-torn on the top hat, the waist button on the pants, sans cummerbund, had popped, a toe poked through one shoe, and the guy stood there with a mournful look, holding both pants pockets inside out to signify hard times indeed. Below him, the caption read, "Long time, no fee."

Ron had acquired three of those black shirts with built-in white collars familiar to the clergy. The plan was for Wilf, Ron and I to meet Ted's plane dressed as priests for a lark. Ron would go to the baggage area to collect Ted, who hadn't met him yet either. The more improbable you make these kinds of things, and the more intelligent the mark, the better chance they have of succeeding. Ron, tall, white and goateed would speak in an East Indian accent, which made no sense at all, except he would say he had been born in India to missionaries.

I could do black from the waist up. I wore a black, corduroy, three-quarter-length jacket, a black bowler one size too small, the priest garb, and blue jeans over tan work boots. I had to stand up straight with my head back so that my beard didn't obscure the white collar. Ron could have actually passed, wearing his rig with a nicely contrasting light grey suit. But Wilfred was the prize, and early on we learned to defer to him in public. His hat was one of those black, stovepipe Stetsons with a rounded crown and a flat brim; a lone eagle feather stood upright in a beaded hatband. A black V-neck sweater only emphasized his collar, and he had rustled up a pair of black dress pants. He stood in moccasins, again with a wild pattern of beads. Around his neck, Wilf wore a large, garish cross on a cheap, imitation-gold chain. The purple plastic inlays were meant to suggest amethysts.

Wilf was a superb comic mime. It was his eyebrows, I think, although a certain look would come over his face which at once made you want to laugh, and yet the off chance it was serious pathos held you back. Nobody did a straight face like him. Dressed as a priest, he cranked up the tension between these two states. The result was almost a suspension of belief. Even the walk from the parking garage was eventful, but the main event began in the terminal. Our spaceship had touched down in double-take city — big, broad double-takes of the Candid Camera sort. The three of us walked casually toward the arrival area with Wilf in the middle and Ron making motions like he was guiding us. You could see people's brains working, "What in hell is that?"

People would spot us from a distance then pretend not to notice until we were past them. Then they would poke someone in the ribs and point. I turned a few times to see them recover and make like they were pointing at something else entirely. Only a few laughed, the rest were shaking their heads in disbelief. There were a few direct stares from folks whose mouths were slightly open. We waited calmly in a row for an elevator, looking up at the lighted display with our hands clasped in front of our crotches. The door opened up, and two people saw us standing there about to board. They got out, steering a wide berth around us. I had the impression it was not their stop. We had the elevator to ourselves.

At the next stop, there were three or four people waiting. Their jaws dropped at the sight of us. Wilfred bowed slightly, and they all managed to return the bow and take one step backwards at the same time. One of them, an older woman, made the sign of the cross; she was the first of several people to do that. When the door slid shut, we howled, barely managing to regain our composure in time for the next stop. There were more bows and signings of the cross; people just fell away from us. The two old men Buckley had brought to the ecumenical conference would barely rate a second look from the same crowd. That summed up my research as to the powerful niche occupied by costume. I could never again look at a three-piece suit, or a clerical collar, without wondering about the impostor inside.

Poole was completely taken in by the stunt. Well, not completely. He had the sense that something wasn't adding up but he hadn't figured out what. Wilf and I had hidden ourselves where we could see the action while Ron spun the fiction in his preposterous accent. Finally, when he saw us, it still took a beat or two before he began to laugh. "It felt like a trap door had opened beneath me and I found myself suddenly standing in a different room," he said on the drive back. "I saw you first, looking like a Bowery bum in that bowler. Your beard hid the collar, and I thought, 'Great, Ralph's here too.' Then this ridiculous apparition beside you gradually assembled itself into Wilf. You bastards!"

He had seen, on the walk to the car, the amount of fun we were having. People were still bowing and giving way. Partly, he wished he could have been in on the deal and played dress up too. No doubt he was thinking of a hat he could wear. A few months later and somewhat reluctantly, despite a promise it would be replaced, I gave the outfit to Ernest Tootoosis. One can only speculate as to what he had in mind. I wish I could have been there — for whatever it was.

Stan Stevens and I were partners; at least we called ourselves that after our adventures out West. At one point we almost stayed, determined to set up a cabin somewhere. We hung around Rock Creek a few days, camping beside the Kettle River on land that has since been made into the Kettle Valley campground. It wasn't so bad after the campsites were finished, aided by local help and federal manpower grants. There was a long dirt road into it, which tended to discourage the dilettantes. Then the road was paved, and people in bigger rigs arrived. The tent population dwindled. A pit was dug so these great trailers could dump their shit. But before all this developing and improving began, Stan and I thought it would be a fine place to park a while. It was a gem.

Norris had mapped a trail from the highway, with slashes and bits of ribbon, which led to an old prospector's cabin by the river, close by a disused railway bridge from the depression-era Kettle Line. He was living there, mountain-man like, in the shack with no roof but a tarp, and two walls. He kept a white horse nearby and strode about the place like Hawkeye. We drove as close as we dared and walked the rest of the way to set up camp by starlight. Buckley and June were still with us.

The Kettle River is a pristine little beauty studded with sand bars and lined with Ponderosa pine on one side with long stretches of cottonwood and meadow on the other. For two or three weeks you can swim comfortably, meaning it takes five minutes or so before you turn blue. Jumping from the high-nineties heat of the day into the bracing, fast-moving water is a real eye-opener in a joyful sort of way. The fantasy of going back in time to live a truer existence is never far from your thoughts. The smell of the river mixed with the pines drives you there.

There was an actual road leading to the bank opposite Norris's cabin where Dunc and a small entourage had set up. We woke up to a crowd and coffee. Jay Jordan was there, swimming in the nude, and two local farmers had parked themselves on the bridge to watch her. Upriver around a bend, the local hippies had their own "nudie" hole. Jay was just saving these gents a walk. Soon, the rest of us had joined her, naked as jaybirds so to speak, with Dunc, ever the optimist, panning for gold. It was a fine day, Stan and I wandered off later and got to dreaming.

Back in Toronto, Stan Stevens was still with Shirley, but I was no longer seeing Nancy when he knocked at my door one night around two in the morning. It had been several weeks since I had last seen him. The Kettle River was just a memory. I opened the door and he just stood there with a funny look on his face. His pupils were dilated and he was grinding his teeth, contorting his jaw muscles. He was trying to grin.

"Hey, partner, can I come in?"

"Of course you can. Welcome, it's good to see you."

I brought him in, giving him an embrace in the process. He was flying and, by the look of him and the feel of his vibe, he was having a bad time of it.

"How are you doing?" I asked.

"Uh, okay, I guess. Feeling a little strange."

"What makes you say that?"

"Uh, I dunno. I took a pill. Acid. I took acid."

"A pill?"

"Yeah. A little brown pill."

"What's it doing to you?"

"I dunno. I feel strange. Can't seem to relax."

All this time he was standing rigidly and grinding his teeth. That's the problem with pills, there could be anything in them. There was some stuff around that was essentially acid soaked into an amphetamine tablet. So the deal was to try and relax Stan until the shit wore off a bit. I repeated how good it was to see him and got him to take his jacket off. I sat him in my chair beside the desk, making sure he had his back to the window so the reflection off the glass wouldn't play any tricks on him. After he settled in, I gave him five milligrams of Valium, telling him what it was.

He was struggling but at least I couldn't hear his teeth. The muscles in his jaw were still contorting, however. I put some soft music on. You never know if this is a mistake or not, the music can make you trip out even further. If he was having trouble getting off it might help the launch. It made me feel better. After telling him what I was going to do, I smoked some hash. That way I could get a little closer to his space. He had a kind of repressed panic on his face, as if something was really worrying at him. So I talked to him, and got him talking. When the record stopped I didn't put another on. A couple of hours went by. I had to smoke more hash because I had started to fade while Stan was still gripped in some kind of fear. I had done everything right, I thought, but I couldn't seem to help him. All that remained was to ride it out.

Finally, it was daylight, a grey dawn. Stan got up to pee, and I told him to stay away from the mirror in the bathroom. When he came back, he sat in the old basket chair. Once or twice he stared at the window, but he became more relaxed. And then he thanked me and left. He looked a lot better, but it was not from anything I had been able to do. The Valium would have helped some.

The look Stan had had on his face reminded me of an encounter I had had with Joe Palumbo a few days earlier. Joe had come over to introduce me to Maya, his new girlfriend. She was a dark-haired, almond-eyed beauty of what appeared to be eastern European descent. I had spent a bit of time getting to know Joe a little better. We played chess on the seventeenth floor roof deck, swapping stories and ogling some of the more special sunbathers. There was a group of girls from California, half of whom copped rays in the nude and all of whom were intriguing, particularly a short-haired blonde who never took her clothes off at all. On days like this, the traffic planes for the radio stations would practically collide as they circled overhead — like they had never seen people naked.

Joe, like twenty percent of Rochdale, was American, scholarly and, having spent time at the Sorbonne in Paris, spoke fluent French. He tended to be serious so it was fun to crack him up; he had a sweet smile. In short, Joe was a nice guy, and a handsome guy. He had come to Toronto from France with Suzanne, for whom he bore no malice although she had caused him a bit of grief. Behind both their backs, we, the boys, called her "Dynamite Body" and were prone to swoon and clutch one another in adolescent fashion after she had sailed by with a look of what would have been disdain, if she had noticed us at all. She was very French: flashing dark eyes, horizontally striped shirts, passionate speech in excellent English, large gestures and, bien sûr, her eponymous form.

(I am an unreliable narrator when it comes to Suzanne. She

came to my room one night, having been invited on a whim with a proposal of such a cocky nature that it should have been turned down. It had the opposite effect. I had been caught posing, and she called me on it. These things never go well. She had not feigned the slightest interest in anything I had to say, had not wanted to talk, wanted the lights left on, and didn't care for music. The best and worst thing about the entire event was its brevity, for which I received an over-the-shoulder glance — another minute or so might have entitled me to a full-fledged look — of scorn and pity when she left. It was not, apparently, going to be the best two out of three.)

Joe and I smoked some hash; Maya declined. Because it was my latest rant, I started talking about identity. It had been a great relief to realize the idea of becoming something or becoming someone was a false trail. You were already somebody to begin with. There were several readings and sources on this "being" versus "becoming" business. So simple, really. I was showing off, not being able to help but be forceful in front of the girl. And a concept I had gotten very familiar with ended up giving Joe some trouble. *"Your name has nothing to do with your identity, see. It's just something your parents laid on you."* I had been stunned by this remark, and liberated — there is more than a little relief at not being Ralph, it was also my father's name, for starters. Joe, who was not a regular smoker of dope, had been even more affected. Being intelligent and highly imaginative, he got into it to the extent that he forgot his name. In the confusion of trying to reclaim it, rather than hang onto the revelation, a mild exasperation set in, and his name, although on the tip of his tongue, would not come. "This is stupid, but I can't remember my name," he said with such a curious look that Maya grabbed his arm. "Joe, Joe," she said, calling to him gently. "Of course it is," Joe laughed. For a small moment I had the impression that Joe had been in distress, which had a chastening effect on me. I shouldn't be fucking around with this stuff, I thought, like some sort of latter-day sorcerer's apprentice.

A few days after he had come to my room, Stan Stevens was laughing again. I told him I wished I could have been of more help.

"No, you were good. I was glad you were there, Partner. It was that stuff I took. Wasn't like the stuff in Montana."

"You looked pretty uptight, sitting by the window."

"Well, that's what's so funny. You were helping so I didn't say anything. But, I sat in that chair knowing how high up the building is. And I thought the wall was gone behind me. There was nothing there. I was sitting right on the edge of the floor and nothing but empty space behind me. I was scared I was going to fall off. I could feel the air. I didn't dare move. I figured if I sat perfectly still I'd be okay."

"As long as the building didn't tilt."

"Shit, don't even say that."

A couple of times when I had dropped acid with Wilf, we'd sit side by side on Bloor St. in the late afternoon. People would walk by and you could see them react to our vibes as if hit by an invisible but tangible force, like magnetism. Some of them would veer out and away, bewildered. Others would lean into it, in the know, grinning at us. Wilf would bless them with a salute from his wiggling eyebrows and one of his beautiful smiles.

You'd run into people all the time who were tripping. I loved the feeling I got off them. It was like being brushed with a golden wind.

I Know

Around the time of the October Crisis when I had to revise downward my opinion of our prime minister, around the time of my
twenty-seventh birthday, I woke up one morning and realized I
knew everything. Not only had I solved a small piece of the puzzle
as I had set out to do, but I had surpassed myself and cracked the
whole damned thing.

All the teachings had come together. They had attached themselves to my experience and resided within, joining God and the
Devil, who were one and the same. No longer could I place them,
and the resident domains of Heaven and Hell, outside of myself.
No. They were inside and, although it was more convenient for
prayer — a fleeting thought, no kneeling — I would have to take
responsibility for my own actions. Much as I tried to summon
humility to attend this revelation, I was caught up in the exhilara-
tion, and all before my second cigarette. I looked out, in that first
waking hour, at the rosy glow of noon, and was content.

I couldn't speak Italian or fly a plane. But I had nailed the
intangibles down; those things that men more capable than I would
speak of at night when the day's toils were at end, and the approaching night released the doubts and fears of the small and insignificant
beast called man. Is there a god? Not exactly. Is there such a thing
as reincarnation? Sort of, but it's not what you think. What is the
one, true religion? Don't be ridiculous. What is the purpose of life?

I had an answer for each of these questions. It really is my movie; nothing exists outside of it. The universe is one, and I am the universe. You have to make allowances for infinity, of course, in all directions, and allow for a certain elusive wisp of mystery on the periphery of thought. And you might get run over by a truck. Mere trivialities.

I tried very hard to love everyone, and forgive everyone, and to forgive myself if I couldn't love everyone, and to love myself. That, and getting stoned, took up a lot of my day. It's not as easy as it sounds. But bad feelings had become bit players in the cinema of my life. Sure, there were a few down moments when I forgot the message, bouts of ennui, minor tragedies, but nothing that stuck for very long. And when something of a negative nature did happen, I'd just roll with it, slough it off. I could have lost half an arm during that time, and I just would have concluded that it would help me turn circles faster while swimming. A significant body of wisdom had piled up in my head and lay there in a heap of enlightenment for the picking and choosing. You had to believe to make it work. You had to be secure in your faith. *"When you get a good feeling, you should hang onto it for as long as you can. Try and get a few days out of it at least."* Well, I had to laugh. A few days? I felt good all the time, man. But I had failed to heed, or even take note of, Lao Tzu's advice, *Conduct your triumph as you would a funeral.*

All that remained was to carve out some sort of empire and complete the circle by acquiring female companionship to share it with, since the last thing hadn't quite worked out. I had the power of love. On my daily ramble, I spied a familiar, duck-like walk approaching from the distance. It was Miranda and before I had time to check my thoughts, I asked her if she had any new friends I might meet? Alas, she did. The lady was known as Mou. "As in what a cow says?" I asked. "Just shush, Ralphie. It's short for Mary Lou."

Somewhere, nibbling at the extremities of thought, was a cautionary song whose chorus repeated, "It rhymes with be wary, you." After all, did mates just appear for the asking? Why not? Intrigue had beguiled me into forgetting that the only thing that can screw up love is romance.

Little David Wall had taken to visiting in the late afternoons. He was Marty's boy from his first marriage, all of five, Tauno's age. It's the last age that magic is possible, before schools drive it away. He had followed his nose through my open door one day and before Shelley came rushing in to collect him, we had managed to determine that we could be friends. He had been fascinated by a Mickey Mouse night light I had, whose provenance escapes me although it may well have come from Jim Neff. But then I think anything I can't remember having acquired at that time came from Mr. Neff, except, of course, decent smoke.

Children can always spot the good stuff in any room. After we had introduced ourselves, the plastic Mickey head with two prongs sticking out from behind, positively leapt out at him. He looked at it with great interest.

"Do you know who that is?" I asked.

He nodded in the affirmative. "It's Mickey Mouse."

"Watch," I said, and plugged Mickey into the baseboard outlet. Mickey glowed brightly. We both thought that was pretty neat. This is when Shelley came in.

David was back the next day. Would I plug Mickey in again? Yes. And again? Okay.

"Maybe you'd like plug it in yourself." I suggested.

"Could I?"

"Come over here, and we'll try," I said, and we sat on the floor beside the outlet.

I could tell from his approach that he was a bit apprehensive about the whole thing. So I told him it wasn't as easy as it looked, that it might take a while. At first he got the prongs near the hole and let go. Mickey hit the floor. I went through the procedure slowly, and he took it all in. This was one of those things I had forgotten about, one of those fascinating things that you got to do when you grew up some more, when you solved the mystery. He got the prongs into the slots, but not far enough and Mickey took another fall. Then it was time for his supper.

He was a determined little chap and regular in his habits. I had been running late, and I saw him down the hall knocking on my door when I got home. Marty and Shelley were both there, trying to persuade David that I might not be at home today. He hadn't bought into that. Of course I'd be there. I invited them in.

"Could you show me again?" he asked, getting right to it.

So we got down on the floor, and I plugged Mickey in. "You have to press hard," I told him. He nodded affirmatively.

His hands were a bit shaky, and he almost dropped Mickey but caught it himself this time. Then he got the prongs in again and pushed. It really is not so easy when you're five. But he pushed and pushed, and bingo, Mickey lit up. At once, David's arms went up in the air in triumph.

"I did it! I did it!" he said. And it came bursting out of him from where the hope and effort and the wanting so badly to do it had been pent up. For all any of us knew, he might have dreamed about it. He was radiant, beaming. "I did it," he said again in wonder.

It was an impressive moment of simple, uncomplicated joy. I was grateful. Marty may have lost a few buttons on his shirt from swelling up in pride, and Shelley looked suspiciously moist around her eyes. We had been handed a gift. The least I could do was bestow Mickey upon his rightful owner. First, we had to repeat the process a few times. And we had to master unplugging Mickey, taking care to never touch the prongs. When they left, David looked straight ahead, with Mickey clutched tightly in his hand.

Gary Anweiler used to philosophize, when we'd get stoned and talking and someone would go, "Shit, I forgot what I was going to say." "Don't worry," he'd grin. "If it's important enough, somebody else will remember." So, if I missed a moment like this with Tauno, maybe I get to experience it somewhere else.

Mou charmed me right away. At Miranda's suggestion, I went to the house they were all living in for an early afternoon coffee. It was midweek. Mou, who worked nights as a waitress, was still in bed. Miranda took me upstairs anyway and introduced me to a covered-up bundle — on what looked to be a Rochdale mattress — on the floor. Mou poked her head out for the greetings, holding the sheet up around her neck, and then covered up again. Three seconds and I was a goner. The haunting brown eyes of a doe had paralyzed the hunter. By the weekend we were talking about having children and living in a tree. Dogs, too, of course, and perhaps a cat.

She was small, saucy, and vivacious, and you could see the solid features of her French ancestors beneath the permanent flush in her cheeks. Her dark eyes missed nothing and were never still. They glittered and flashed like stones by the water. You could feel the energy surging around her, Tasmanian devil-like, and the power it had to attract. She had a charisma that drew everyone to her, a mental electromagnet, an unseen, irresistible force. And she shone: her hair sparkled, her skin glowed, her eyes were full of mischief.

She knew the power she had, and that she could reverse polarity in a flash. I was only aware of the first part. The rest was contained in a story to which I had only half-paid attention. "I hid myself last winter," she said, as if it were so long ago. "I was in plain sight, and no one could see me. I put on weight and hardly bathed. I kept my eyes down. Even when I talked to someone, they'd see greasy hair and look right through me. I knew how to change but it was my secret. I knew how pretty I could be."

There was a new paradigm of love in room 1825. It had sprung up fully formed overnight, like waking to see a strange pod on your lawn around which butterflies sported in whimsy. People visited just for the vibe. Mou and I sat there in a rosy sort of glow, humming like dynamic little spheres, as the folks edged closer and closer to warm their souls. In this new domestic paradise, I had taken up knitting for a laugh and, with assistance to cast on and cast off, I knitted and purled my way to a scarf for José Garcia. And that was the first three weeks. I remember nothing except the glow and people coming by to watch love in progress, leaving with serene looks on their faces, and perhaps a trace of envy. Had I known that my room, my sanctuary, my retreat would never be mine again, had passed forever, I doubt I would have cared. There were dinner invitations, a social whirl, and everyone would have us.

Every now and again a bell would ring faintly, like somebody stranded in a far-off elevator, but I paid little heed. Her trunk arrived while she was at work. I guessed, starkly for a flash of time, that she was moved in with me now. Oh well, it had to happen some time, didn't it? Her reaction was altogether different. She looked stunned, almost worried.

"Where did this come from?" she demanded, as if I had anything to do with it.

"I don't know. Some guy delivered it this afternoon."

"What did he look like?" She asked this in a panic.

"Fuck, I don't know . . . a delivery guy, I guess. What's the problem?"

"It's from Boo," she said and started to cry softly.

"Boo?" I asked, and then I stood waiting for the punch line, like it was some kind of knock-knock joke.

"The guy I lived with in Montréal."

"And he had your trunk? How long ago was this?"

"A few months. The trunk was at his mother's place." She was snuffling while she talked. "Look, I don't really feel like talking about this now. Okay?"

"Tell me one thing."

"What?" There was a wary look in her eyes.

"Were you really part of a couple called Boo and Mou?"

"Don't be so smart," she laughed, and she seemed to cheer up somewhat when she saw I was going to let it all go. Actually, I wasn't about to, but I needed to think for a while. I couldn't resist another shot.

"So, is it short for something, or is that his real name?"

I was curious. It's not the sort of name one hears every day. Perhaps it was a pet name, and that's why she never told me. Neither did Miranda, although she said Boo was a good guy, and not to worry; it was definitely over. So I didn't. Weird name, though. It became the first little nag in a corral of worrisome ponies. In the meantime, the evening feasts of love continued. We spent hours cataloguing the contents of each other's eyes. Her trunk glowered in a corner.

Early December brought a nice dusting of snow. Our weekend retreat in the country, courtesy, I think, of the U of T Advisory Bureau, would be a cosy affair. There would be over a dozen people there, but we knew most of them. Troyer, Rose Marie, Marty, Shelley, Mou, and I represented the eighteenth floor. José, his friend, Judy, and Wilf and Dorrie were also part of the group. Somehow, John Bradford also received an invitation, but not Miranda. We all went to one of those big houses in the country whose name I forget, Something Blah-Blah Farm.

There's a deceiving conviviality to these weekends where at least half the people there think they know several of the others better than they actually do. For spice, add the odd X factor: someone you've never met, branching into those you'd like to and those you're glad you haven't; a mysterious or intriguing member of the opposite sex; and, someone you know behaving strangely in the presence of the mystery person. A drink or two is standard, possibly harmless, and it always helps to have a toke if you happen to be so inclined. Under no circumstance should you drop acid or open yourself up in any meaningful way to the group dynamic. If you're in the midst of a whirlwind romance, all of a month old, run to the neighbouring farm and call for a taxi to take you home.

Troyer, of course, being the devil, started it all. I knew better. I had brought some hash and a pipe, which I could handle. I was looking forward to snowy walks and perhaps making the acquaintance of some trees. The first day, after lunch, the devil appeared.

He was offering these tiny purple pills, the size of my grandfather's saccharin tablets. His eyes were already glazed and red-rimmed and, beside the pills, he had a powdered substance in a plastic bag that he would offer as a mystery supplement, daring you to try it. He went up and down the three long tables in the dining room with his infernal dessert. The people who didn't know him recoiled almost in horror — Troyer was looking that wild, deranged, in fact. I had a private laugh about that. "Good for you," I thought. I had no trouble turning him down. "Really?" his raised eyebrows queried, before moving on.

In all the time I had known him, I had never taken acid with Troyer. I'd probably had more laughs with him than anyone in Rochdale, but even then he kept you sharp. It's one thing to stroll through the Gates of Perception and down the garden path with a half-mad companion who must be closely watched, and quite another to rely on him to man the oars on a river ride through the rapids of Hell. I had even left Rock Creek a day early with Stan Stevens to avoid a group drop in the mountains. There are too many people, too many heavens, and too many hells. It was one of the basic rules: be very sure of who you're with before committing to a psychedelic adventure.

Bradford, apparently, had no such qualms, and neither did Mou. It was almost a betrayal that she dropped after I had refused. "Almost" nothing, it *was* a betrayal, and it stunned me momentarily. And so, for the very worst of reasons (jealousy, not to put too fine a point on it), I took acid as well. My plan to just stay with the hash, a good one, was abandoned. In less than an hour, I had been too.

The interior of the house, unfamiliar to begin with, had become angular and gloomy, as if Dr. Caligari lived there. There were various souls wandering around: those who hadn't dropped, with oddly phoney expressions, and those who had, in various states of what I can only describe as anguish. A tension had grown between the two groups, now factions. I couldn't find any place private or quiet enough to dump my garbage. I found "home" in some Celtic music, but there was so much activity in the room I had to move on. I was overcome by a sense of dread and moved from room to room, trying to escape it. My teeth were grinding; it hurt behind my eyes. There wasn't one room that was empty except for a sinister bedroom that I would not enter. Troyer kept showing up, leering, and I knew I had to get away from him. Where's Mou?

Finally, I got it together to go outside. It was not yet dark. I felt better immediately in the rush of cool air. What had taken me so long? Oh yeah, I was looking for Mou. A trail led to a grove of cedars, my childhood tree of choice. There were bigger trees there too. I rushed to them along the path. It was snowing in fine grains, and blowing directly at me, so I kept my head down. It was perhaps not too late to achieve the peace of equilibrium. A voice called out and I looked up to see Bradford hidden behind a tree. I had almost made it to safety. He persisted in being company. He was on a cave-man trip, something about killing animals to survive. Fucking A-types always need to kill something. I could kill him and get some space. Oh no, he had me doing it too.

Bradford headed back to the farm — maybe he sensed my vibe — and I had the woods to myself. It was cold, and I began to shiver; walking wasn't helping. Besides, I didn't need to walk. I needed to lie down, shut my eyes, and relax.

How long has it been dark out? I have no watch. It's really cold. My head feels like it's in two or three places and none of the places connect. One is whining about something, one is skin-crawlingly uncomfortable, and one is small and terrified. No, no, please, no. There is a disembodied voice laughing at that. There is more laughter behind me, derisive laughter, coming from the woods. My skin gets goose bumps as I turn to see who it is. There is nothing there except a fearful sense of dread. I try not to run back to the farmhouse. Mou was standing outside, alone. She stared at me. She was not a refuge.

She told me I had abandoned her. She sounded like my mother

did when I had been naughty. She sounded like an old teacher whom I had let down very badly. "But you disappeared," I pleaded. "You went running through the house with Bradford, and you disappeared. I looked all over for you." She smiled faintly in a cruel way. I thought I couldn't be seeing this correctly. It's me, something I'm doing. I had become a little boy, the bad little boy I knew I was. I reached out for her but she didn't move. Mou stood there and looked at me, a direct gaze. Had it been a stare, I would have concluded it was inspired by anger. This wasn't anger. In fact, it wasn't anything; there was no emotion whatsoever in her eyes. They were blank. I was nothing. Because you can see people's thoughts and feelings when you're open like this, much as a child knows the moods of its parents. She would have seen how deflated I was, how empty, how devastated by her look. Still, she looked at me, and I was nothing. All I could do was walk past her into the house.

It never got worse, nothing could have been worse; it only became a different kind of hell. Troyer asked sweetly to see the child one couple had brought, an infant. Being straight or stupid, they handed it over, only to have Troyer hold it aloft by the fireplace, asking them what might they do if he were to dash this child's brains out on the bricks? A horror filled the room; no one knew what to do. His evil laugh broke the spell. It was a lesson, that's all. Why he liked to do this was a mystery; he just had to find ways to bring people down. He'd behave after that, as he did in this case.

The real hell of that room was how unconnected everybody really was to one another. You could see all the hidden areas — hidden to themselves as well as to others — that people glossed over in their communications with one another. "It's all phoney!" I hollered, not being able to stand the hypocrisy a moment longer. "It's fake." And Wilfred came over to quiet me down. Where had he been? But I looked at him and could tell he wasn't having such a shit hot time either.

José was my saviour. Neither he nor Judy had taken anything. He knew something was wrong, you'd have to be catatonic not to, and he didn't understand. He and Judy sat on a wooden bench at one of the tables, and I sat beside him. "Just let me sit here a while, Jéfé, let me sit close." I sat next to José, and I leaned into him, feeling his solidity, and it warmed me. I took strength from José; he had plenty to share. "Everybody seems kind of crazy today, Jéfé," was all he said. They sat with me for a long time, until I could take care of myself again.

The next day, on a grey, sleety afternoon, we all left. No one had slept very much. There were six of us in the car and in almost two hours not more than a few words had been spoken. I couldn't even look at Mou. She was a strange weight pressing against me in the back seat. I was living inside the word *bleak*. At Rochdale, we were like dead batteries, unable to provide even feeble illumination. I had been filled with a terror that I must have known at one time but could not ever remember.

My commune and my room, once rosy and vibrant with life, seemed stark in the lamplight, as if the shades had been removed. What I had felt was terrible, so much so that I was prepared to believe it had all been a false thing, not of my own making at all, some weird effect of the drug. I would survive the first little while through denial. The alternative, of admitting to those feelings, was something I couldn't cope with.

It would take five years for me to get over this trip, five years of nightmares and, whenever it crossed my mind during the day, naked fear. But with the resilience we all seem to have in these things, it only took a week for folks to gather in my room again, shooting loving glances, and pretending none of it had ever happened, not the bad stuff anyway.

Mou and I got a dog and crabs, in that order. I had become privy to the more salient features of her past, as she had with mine. Hers was more complex.

She grew up in the BC Rockies, near the headwaters of the Columbia, where the orientation is more toward Calgary than

Vancouver. Her father was a merchant. She had had a baby, fathered by someone she had loved dearly, more dearly than he perhaps had felt about her. They were teenagers. The baby had been adopted. This, apparently, was not a choice Mou had made, but she had been pressured into it and agreed. She and the boy would get together, break up, and get together again. Giving up that baby stood between them.

She fell in love with Boo, a guy from Montréal. She also grew quite close to Boo's mother. Apparently, she became pregnant again, only this time she had an abortion. This gave her two children with which to torment herself, one living, one dead. It became more than their relationship could bear, and she and Boo split up a few times. A few months after the final break-up, Mou ran into me, a guy who knew everything. What could be better for her? This is the simple version of her story to that point. None of us could ever know how much and how deeply all this had affected her.

Jack Jones, fifty-something, was an absolute hoot when it came to his dog, Millie, a silky, prancy, goofy Irish Setter, who had grown up at Rochdale. Just watching this giant, booming-voiced, red-headed and bushy-bearded Viking of a man baby-talking his darlin' Millie was worth the price of admission. He appeared to have more affection for the dog than the new family he was starting with his teenaged wife. They moved to a ramshackle house on Clinton St. where they grew marijuana in the yard. Millie was to be bred to supplement their income until "the ugliest fucking dog in the world knocked her up." This outraged Jack. He could go on about it for hours, much to the delight of everyone who saw the cosmic humour of it all. For ten dollars, Mou and I reserved a pup, a wire-haired, sandy-red female with the form and grace of a setter to compensate for her lack of breeding. She was highly intelligent, as mixed-breed dogs often are, and possessed the sweetest of natures. We called her Cushy Butterfield; she was a much-loved pup.

About a week before Cushy was ready to pick up, I looked down at a tiny scab on my crotch after a shower, and just before I could pick it — a compulsion of mine — it moved. This is a disgusting discovery to make, nor had Mou been spared. We were covered in them. One treatment — a vile smelling brew — followed another and another. You can have no self-esteem whatsoever when you are hosting pediculus pubis, and failures to eradicate the little crustaceans can put wild thoughts in your mind of gasoline and lighters. I had to tell Stan Bevington. He took it well. Then he said, "That's what I forgot to tell you. I let a friend of mine use the shower a few times, because he had crabs too and was trying to get rid of them." I just looked at him. The upside was that Stan didn't have much of a beef while we were paper training Cushy. It didn't take very long; she much preferred to go out.

Fighting crabs seemed to bring Mou and I together for a while. It was the type of disaster we could face together. It had dimensions; there were procedures. There were a lot more things nagging at me by then, but I was totally sucked into the trip. It had gotten to the point in our death struggle with one another — because that's what it was — a probing for weakness in the emotional judo that often parades about disguised as love, where I blinked, not first, but I had taken the high road. She was more tormented.

Both of us must have needed drama, which we supplied one another in non-stop fashion. In the end, she had better writers. Willingly we suspended belief and entered into a mutual storybook fiction. "Lets have a baby." "Cool." She even had me try to remove her IUD one night by pulling on the plastic string. I kind of eased up on that one. She went to a clinic. And then it was done. She became pregnant. That's when the big waves came.

And what was I doing all this time? Trying to reassemble the pieces of the guy who knew everything. Nothing rings more hollow than philosophy when you're all twisted up in knots over love. It isn't love, really, which is where the confusion lies. It's something more like need, a desperate need, which can seemingly never be satisfied. All the suicides, assaults, kidnappings, drunken binges, and you-done-me-wrong songs aren't about love. They're about possession and why you're so desperate for it. You think it's love, and you wonder what's the matter with you that you can't measure up. But I was trying to measure up, which is where I got lost.

Obviously, 1825 was not going to be large enough. So we rented a place from Henry Tarvainen. Mou had second thoughts and we declined. Henry wanted to sue. When I asked him for what, it seemed to sober him up. On the whole, I felt he wasn't being very sympathetic. Next, we found a place on Davenport, between Bathurst and Christie. This time I had to give a deposit, something Henry hadn't asked for.

I remember how grey the days were. Mou would stay at Miranda's, sometimes until late at night. They even went to the States for a weekend, although Bradford was involved in that one and they hadn't really gone to the States at all. Things had really gotten weird. I had Cushy at least. Mou started talking about an abortion. At one point she moved in with Wilf and Dorrie for a while to make up her mind. All my failures pressed in on me. I had completely lost my confidence. It was embarrassing to admit even to myself that I had become someone small whose entire world revolved around another person's approval. What we call love can do that for you. What sort of identity is that?

Around the end of March, I visited a Salvation Army thrift store. I had ten dollars to spend, and Mou had been making noises about having been a decent seamstress, and she should be sewing some stuff. Or not. Perhaps it was me with the nesting instinct. There was an old fashioned, foot-operated sewing machine, a Singer, and I bought it and carted it home. The choice, which I related to Mou, had been between it and an old woman's bicycle, the kind with no crossbar. She was less than enthused. She had apparently booked her ticket and had hardened totally into leaving. Mou was off to Montréal. "You should have got me the bicycle," she said archly.

Cushy would go with her. She hadn't decided about the baby and would let me know. The only remaining power I had was the ability to drive. I took her to the airport. We stood by the ticket counter while Cushy was put into a cage. She was shivering when the baggage handlers took her away. To make it two for two, Mou's lower lip quivered when her flight was called. And I looked at her, right in the eye. I looked at her and registered no emotion in my face. I looked at her as she had done that day at the farm, like she was zero. There was nothing for her in my blank stare. Nothing was all I had left. She said, "Please don't look at me like that. Please don't." My eyes bore into her as she walked through the gate, back to Boo. At least that fucking trunk went with her.

Could You
Repeat That?

I sat musing in that bitter, ironic, theatrical way of the scorned, refusing at first, as is the breed's wont, to admit that I had had any part in the drama of my fall from grace. It wouldn't fly. I was drinking a Club Ale on the deck that overlooked the TTC yards that I shared with the lady next door and her basset hound. She was afraid of me, I think, making the deck mine; her basset would have moved in — in a flash. Members of the group, Edward Bear, lived next door. Gina, a pretty Italian girl who had shouted her name up one day, lived across the street. We flashed the "V" or waved at one another, never talking face to face. I couldn't pull the bitter act off for very long, especially with just myself; I knew better. I could do irony, though, it was a staple; theatre too. In fact, I laughed ironically to myself. Mou had at least helped get me out of Rochdale. And it had been time to go.

The young student doing a summer internship in social work had just left my apartment. My unemployment insurance had exhausted itself. She told me, baldly, that all Maritimers were useless and should go back home immediately. Could she not find it in her heart to send me back to Saskatchewan instead? She confessed her dad was from Nova Scotia. We both knew she was not going to do well in this profession. I qualified, only just, for half a month's assistance. I asked if I could call and take her to dinner when the

cheque arrived? She hurried down the stairs. I was just kidding —
she should be picking up the tab.

Beer and cheap wine were helping to get me a few hours sleep
every night. They were not much for providing illumination, but
sometimes it's good to keep your head down. They're great for self-
pity, though, and thoughts of revenge. But even with their help,
another voice inside told me to give it a rest. I just couldn't figure
how everything had fucked up so badly or, in retrospect, given all the
information I had, why I had tied my boat to Mou's wharf. The good
stuff I had learned before running in to her was true, so why couldn't
I access it now? The words would come but not the feelings.

This place was not yet a hovel like the one I had left so long
ago in Saint John. That would take a few months. I saw the big
cockroach on my first day. He was moving slow, like he had a death
wish, so I let him live. Misifus needed company; I was away most of
the time. She was a pretty little kitten, donated and named by José;
a short-haired grey who I found a good home for a week or two later.

Really, now, what the fuck had happened? There's a question I
would become real tired of. I had no desire to even walk past
Rochdale. It *was* becoming a hovel. I recognized all the signs: too
many boys, not enough girls. You could play the slots, buy beer, and
sit back and watch cops and robbers, live and in colour. There was
a card game every night. Bob Nasmith and Jimmy Newell each
became president. Oddly, I felt encouraged when I heard that. But
I never went there again, and I passed by the articles about it in the
paper. I have no quarrel with those who stayed. Obviously, even in
decline, there was a need.

One morning, around eleven, I got a wake-up call from Mou,
literally and figuratively. This was after her note about the abortion.
I couldn't accuse her of not keeping me informed. I was bleary from
a hangover. Who? What? Oh . . . What is it now? She had called to
say that she was pregnant again, she and Boo, but this time she was
really happy. After a moment to digest, I realized it didn't matter
why she felt it necessary to tell me that. So I did what anyone would

have done and wished her all the best. And she really needn't feel
she had to keep me updated; she could be assured of my continuing
good wishes. I meant it . . . all of it.

My new roommate, Michael Hubar, had scored some Mexican
grass. It was full of seeds and lumber and hints of past glory. I gained
some insights. If you're not wide open, you don't get the big ride.
But you have to hang on a little. What was strongest in me had
expanded to a great strength. Weakness had left me temporarily
without a spine. I was thinking I might have to make friends with
each.

The only person I had ever known both Ted and Wilf to be in
awe of was Farrell Toombs, the head of the U of T's Advisory
Bureau. Needing another perspective, I went to see him. Farrell was
a man of enormous intelligence, and a man who truly had compas-
sion. He wasn't about groovy; you went to Farrell's office and you
talked to him while he listened. We had met before. Even as I began
to speak, I saw part of the problem. "I'm a little confused, see. And
what I'm wondering, what I need to know, see, is what is that all
about?"

Farrell did see. I had been so caught up in the power of the message that I was beginning to imitate at least one of the messengers,
probably both. Although I saw the truth in them, it was their words
I was using. I had begun to rely on that and became frustrated when
it no longer worked for me. None of it had helped me with Mou. I
kept asking Ted and Wilf what I should do about Mou, and they had
no answers. I needed my own truths, the ones I had earned, the ones
to which I was entitled. Toeing the party line wasn't doing it for me.

It was odd how it became so clear while I was talking to Farrell.
He said nothing while I talked. When I was finished, he told me
two stories. The first, which I later related to Hubar, who loved it,
was about Lev Isaac, a Jew in Poland, who lived among the rubble
of his home, destroyed in the last pogrom. Everything was gone;
what was he to do? He had a dream one night that under a bridge
in a neighbouring city a great treasure was buried there. The

country was in a state of war so it took Lev Isaac a while to get to that town. When he found the bridge, it was exactly as it had appeared in the dream, however, search as he might, he could find no treasure. He took to wandering, checking under bridges whenever he happened upon one. One day, he came upon a soldier, mortally wounded, and befriended him. He related his dream to the soldier by way of helping him take his mind off the pain. "You know, that's very strange, brother," said the soldier. "I have had the exact same dream as you. Only in my dream the treasure was to be found inside a chimney in a ruined house in a small village not far from here. I was on my way there when I became injured." The soldier died in the night, and Lev Isaac rushed home. It was his village that the soldier had named, his house that he had described and, sure enough, hidden inside the chimney of his own house, Lev found the treasure.

The second story Farrell told me was about Dostoyevsky, the time he had fallen afoul of the Tsar and had been sentenced to death. The night before his execution, he was visited by an angel who wore a long robe, covered with a thousand eyes. The angel gave a pair to Dostoyevsky through which he saw a heavenly paradise. In the morning, he learned he was pardoned and was not going to die. This was good news, of course. Apparently, however, he would be plagued for the remainder of his life with angel vision. He would see the rude, homely, day-to-day existence of things through his angel eyes and was never able to reconcile that reality with his vision of heaven.

That was all Farrell had to say to me, and I thanked him warmly. The first story told me where to look for the treasure. The second gave me pause to think about cosmic matters and their relative worth in the "real" world, and that some sort of balance is required. I have always been grateful for the encounter.

Which means more to you, you or your reknown? Which brings more to you, you or what you own? And which would cost you more if it were gone? . . . The least ashamed of men goes back if he chooses: he knows both ways, he starts again.

Sometimes I think my search for "the answer" is like assembling a giant jigsaw puzzle. It takes an inordinate amount of time, painstakingly scrutinizing each piece before placing it in the proper context. When it's done, you can only admire it for so long before tearing it apart and starting again. After all, it's a puzzle. It's meant to be like that.

Ted came by one evening with some very decent weed. He took one look at me — I had been a little down — and clapped me on the shoulder. "You know," he said, "a few more times around the circle, and it all gets funny." He gave such a wicked laugh as he passed me the joint.

I have managed to accumulate and lose various estates since then, and I have to agree he was right.

It *is* funny.